IF YOU BELIEVED MOSES

VOLUME 2

THE CONVERSION OF THE JEWS AS THE CLOSE OF HISTORY

FR JAMES MAWDSLEY

Cover: Caravaggio (1571-1610), *The Conversion of St Paul.*

Please note that many modern Bibles depart from the Church's traditional chapter and verse numbering, notably for the Psalms. Whereas this book follows the Vulgate and DRB, which, for example, reference Ps 50:11-12, judaised Bibles will reference these same verses as Ps 51:10-11, causing confusion over both chapter and verse. Similarly, the four books traditionally (and below) called 1-4 Kings are in modernised Bibles called 1-2 Samuel and 1-2 Kings.

Published by New Old
© 2023 Fr James Mawdsley
ISBN 978-1-7395816-4-0

For salvation is from the Jews.

John 4:22

FOR THE
CRUCIFIED

Contents

Introduction   **3**

Part I: Why has God Allowed the Delay?   **17**

Heresy Purifies Doctrine   21

Persecution Provokes Growth   47

Enduring Hatred Perfects Charity   58

Witnessing to the Church's Divine Origin   70

The Best Possible Ending to Human History   88

Part II: The Jewish Question   **99**

The Status of the Old and New Covenants   109

Zionism, Globalism and the Jewish Antichrist   137

Judaism's Endgame is Totalitarian Domination   173

Gentiles and Jews cannot Share Sovereignty   193

Weaponisation of the Holocaust Narrative   207

Part III: What Can Catholics Do?   **251**

Good Friday Prayer for the Jews   257

Maintain the Traditional Liturgy   280

Love Abraham, Moses and David   297

The End   **309**

About the Author   318

The New Old series   319

Prologue

In 2018, fifty places in the world were granted permission to do the best thing on Earth. It was to be a three-year experiment. If it went well, the same goods were to be made available to all who sought them. But the experiment was never completed. The 2020 Covid lockdowns derailed it. Then in July 2021, a devotee of Judas issued an illegal instruction aimed at forever depriving the world of the chance to regain these great goods which appear to be all but lost.

Two anomalies stand out. First, the erroneous idea that permission is required to participate in these great goods — that is, in the celebration of the Easter Triduum according to the most venerable rites of the Church. By an insidious deception, the notion has become widely received that it lies in the authority of the Vatican to decide whether or not priests in good standing may celebrate the ancient liturgy. It is falsely claimed that they can be forced to do a newly fabricated rite.

The next anomaly was a condition imposed upon the fifty apostolates 'permitted' to celebrate the pre-1955 Triduum. Participants had to agree to an extra genuflection on Good Friday — to appease the Jews. This was a pinch of incense.

These limitations were not the fault of the *Ecclesia Dei* clerics who proposed the experiment. But when the wolves (who chased Pope Benedict XVI into retreat in 2013) saw Tradition being marvellously recovered, they surged in attack: the Pontifical Commission *Ecclesia Dei* was dissolved in 2019 and the war against Tradition has intensified ever since.

Who is behind this war? The writing of this New Old series was prompted by the author's belief that the godless powers behind the 2020-21 global lockdowns — banefully keeping souls out of churches for the Easter Mysteries — are the same powers which persuaded Jorge Bergoglio as Pope Francis to issue *Traditionis custodes* in July 2021. The spiritual damage inflicted by both measures is incalculable. The instigator of it all is satan. He is cunning and his agents are ruthless.

Thanks be to God, there are souls who are not interested in what the dragon, beast or false prophet have to say. Instead, they are attentive to God, Who lovingly guides our salvation through Scripture and Tradition. He desires our participation in His sacred mysteries. *Fiat*.

Introduction

Apocalypse 13:4 RSVCE

If we look at the ruthless reach of the political Leviathan, we might be paralysed with fear, saying — *"Who is like the beast and who can fight against it?"* (Apoc 13:4). But the Life of Christ gives us the plan for victory: to live simply for God. Our *"faith"* truly *"overcomes the world"* (1 Jn 5:4) and all its obstacles — globalists included.

The highest truths demand the greatest faith, and this is the foundation for the most powerful love. We live this now by worthily receiving the Real Presence of Jesus Christ in the Holy Eucharist — Body, Blood, Soul and Divinity. He offers us a foretaste of heaven. But rebellion against Divine truth summons hell on earth.

The cosmic opposition of good and evil is played out through human history as a combat of two nations struggling in the womb: Judaism and Christianity (Gen 25:23). Despite worldly expectations, the contest will end with the Jews' conversion to Jesus Christ.

If You Believed Moses (Volume 1) posits that the final conversion of the Jews is foretold throughout the Old Testament (OT), provided it be read in the light of the New Testament (NT), that is, in the Light of Christ. The principal theme of this present work, *If You Believed Moses (Volume 2)*, is the world-changing effects of men's opposing reactions to the Crucifixion of the Son of God — faith versus anti-faith, Emmanuel versus Antichrist. If detached from this context, none of the following chapters make sense. Indeed, that is the enemy's aim: that we remove our gaze from the Cross.

Part I of this book asks *Why has God allowed the Delay?* Why do the Jews not convert till the end of history? The key to understanding this lies in the Cross. It is the hinge of history. Adoring Christ Crucified, souls are transformed unto His likeness, freely choosing contradiction, persecution and even martyrdom for His sake. God allows this delay because He works a greater good from the evil of impenitent men who despise the Crucified and His disciples. Such men serve to increase God's external glory and the holiness of the Saints. The delay is optimal for Jews and Gentiles.

Part II concerns *The Jewish Question*. It assesses the relation of the Old Covenant to the New; it enters minefields about Zionism, world domination and the Antichrist; it raises supposedly unspeakable points about sovereignty and the Holocaust. *The Jewish Question* is essentially about the damage wreaked by false messianism. Jesus is God's Anointed, the crucified and risen Messiah, Who brings the tranquility of order. Those who oppose Christ, the Prince of Peace, are deceived by satan, the prince of this world, whose hellish plans, if unopposed, lead to global totalitarianism.

Part III asks *What Can Catholics Do?* Political action is certainly needed, but this must be spiritually rooted. Seeking order in society requires first giving God the respect due Him — no authority is greater.[1] Thus, Catholics must lovingly restore the higher order (things of God) before the lower order (things temporal) can be set aright. To enable political and social improvements, Catholics must restore the ancient liturgy, develop love for the Saints and foster love for the OT. When Catholics give God right worship, a torrent of grace will flood this fallen world and, in God's good time, rescue even our enemies from the snare.

Who are the Jews Truly?

Before proceeding, what is the definition of a Jew? A Chief Rabbi of Israel, Yitzchak Halevi Herzog (d.1959), asserted

> That according to Jewish law only the offspring of a Jewish mother can be considered a Jew... And the only way a person can become Jewish if his mother is not Jewish is to convert. For a female conversion, immersion in a ritual bath (*mikua*) is necessary; for a male, immersion and ritual circumcision are required.[2]

---

[1] St Augustine, *De civitate Dei*, XIX, 21, "Justice is that virtue which gives every one his due... where, then, is the justice of man, when he deserts the true God?"

[2] Rabbi Alfred Kolatch, *The Second Jewish Book of Why* (1985), p.17.

This long-standing religious definition is hardly acceptable to atheist Jews, whose number has been made visible by political emancipation and by the establishment of the State of Israel in 1948. David Ben-Gurion (d.1973), Israel's first Prime Minister, argued for a wider definition, opining,

> Anyone who declares that he is a Jew, lives a Jewish life, and is interested in the welfare of the Jews is to be considered a Jew, regardless of the faith of the mother.[3]

This dispute about a definition, which churns around genetic lineage, religious belief and social identification, is likely irresolvable. God knows who is who. For the purposes of this book, it is necessary to add the view from the Cross.

Our Lord declares: *"Salvation is from the Jews"* (Jn 4:22). That is an unmatched privilege. Yet Scripture warns that before their conversion the Jews *"are adversaries to all men"* (1 Thess 2:15). Are they enemies or saviours? With personal experience of dramatic conversion, St Paul distinguishes:

> *As concerning the Gospel, indeed, they are enemies for your sake: but as touching the election, they are most dear for the sake of the fathers.* (Rom 11:28)

The duality of *"enemies"* who *"are most dear"* can only be resolved in Christ. As long as Jews choose to be *"enemies of the cross of Christ"* (Phil 3:18), then Jesus identifies them as those *"that say they are Jews and are not, but are the synagogue of Satan"* (Apoc 2:9). In the face of this fact, we must remain meek, for all who have sinned are causes of the Crucifixion. We, too, *"were enemies, we were reconciled to*

---

[3] Rabbi Alfred Kolatch, *The Second Jewish Book of Why* (1985), p.17.

God by the death of His Son" (Rom 5:10). Jews who deny Christ's Divinity refuse this reconciliation with God. Yet they remain *"most dear"* as having potential to follow *"the fathers"*, the Patriarchs of old who confessed Christ.

The unity in Christ of believers from both the OT and NT was extolled by St John Chrysostom (✝407), commentating on St Paul's verse *"One body and one Spirit… One Lord, one faith, one baptism"* (Eph 4:4-5).

> Now what is this *one body*? The faithful throughout the whole world, both which are, and which have been, and which shall be. And again, they that before Christ's coming pleased God, are *one body*. How so? Because they also knew Christ. Whence does this appear? *Your father Abraham*, says He, *rejoiced to see My day, and he saw it, and was glad.* (Jn 8:56) And again, *If you had believed Moses*, He says, *ye would have believed Me, for he wrote of Me* (Jn 5:46). And the prophets too would not have written of One, of whom they knew not what they said; whereas they both knew Him and worshipped Him. Thus, then were they also *one body*.[4]

Jesus stands in the midst of His sheep and knows them all (Jn 10:14). He identifies Nathaniel as a *"true Israelite"* — a man *"in whom there is no guile"* (Jn 1:47). Christ's comment regarding Nathaniel shows that the spiritual has priority over the material. Identification with the spotless soul of Christ counts infinitely more than one's biological ancestry, for we are children of God by adoption (Eph 1:5-6). Thus, St Paul explained:

---

[4] St John Chrysostom, *Homily X on Ephesians* (4:4-5).

Who are Israelites... For all are not Israelites that are of Israel. Neither are all they that are the seed of Abraham, children... That is to say, not they that are the children of the flesh, are the children of God; but they, that are the children of the promise. (Rom 9:4-8)

There are Israelites who are not Israelites. That is, there are Jews who are biological descendants of Abraham and Israel (Jacob), but by rejecting Christ, they are not the spiritual descendants promised by God, they are not spiritual Israelites.

This is how to understand the apparent paradox spoken in the Apocalypse of them *"that say they are Jews and are not, but are the synagogue of Satan"* (Apoc 2:9). They are excluded from being children of God because, unlike Nathaniel, they harbour guile, *"who say they are Jews, and are not, but do lie"* (Apoc 3:9). The lie is to contradict God, most destructively in denying Jesus is the divine Messiah.

Raising minds to the spiritual, Jesus did not deny the biological descent of *"children of Abraham"* (Jn 8:37). But He charged them to *"do the works of Abraham"* (Jn 8:39), for *"they who are of faith, the same are the children of Abraham"* (Gal 3:7). Confronted by Jews who sought to kill Him, Jesus exposed their spiritual ancestry was not godly like Abraham, but *"You are of your father the devil"* (Jn 8:44).

To be meaningfully counted among the children of Israel, conversion is clearly required (Lk 1:16). A true Jew is a child of Abraham spiritually, which means to live in Jesus,

In Whom also you are circumcised with circumcision not made by hand in despoiling of the body of the flesh: but in the circumcision of Christ. (Col 2:11)

Therefore, it matters little if we follow a definition based on self-identification or biology and belief. What matters more is acceptance of the Messiah of God — Jesus Christ Crucified. The division for or against Him did not begin on Calvary, but is already seen in the OT. Certain Israelites forsook the covenant, rebelling against God and His prophets (3 Kgs 19:10; 2 Esd 9:26; Rom 11:3). St Stephen identifies the false sons of Abraham:

> *You stiffnecked and uncircumcised in heart and ears, you always resist the Holy Ghost: as your fathers did, so do you also.* (Acts 7:51; cf. Mt 23:30-39)

Daniel the Prophet tells the story of the beautiful Susanna, who, while bathing, was spied upon by two senior judges of Israel. When they could not pervert her by their lust, they told murderous lies to destroy her. Truth prevails and Daniel hails Susanna as a daughter of the house of Judah, while decrying the judges as *"seed of Canaan"* (Dan 13:56) — namely, blood-letting idolaters condemned by God. Seeing their depravity, Daniel states they are *"not of Judah"*. Daniel is not denying their genetic lineage but is teaching that the spiritual is determinative. The temporal is dependent upon it.

Accordingly, Jesus did not come to found a new religion. He came to institute a New Covenant. The religion of the Old and New Covenants is one and the same.[5] The Old is for Hebrews, anticipating the Messiah, Jesus Christ. The New is for the whole world, remembering the same Jesus Christ and

---

[5] Pope Pius IX, *Mortalium animos* (6th Jan 1928), 6, "[T]here can be no true religion other than that which is founded on the revealed word of God: which revelation, begun from the beginning and continued under the Old Law, Christ Jesus Himself under the New Law perfected."

anticipating His return. If we are not accustomed to thinking of how Christ is concealed in the OT, let St Augustine renew our minds with insights into St John the Baptist leaping in his mother's womb at the proximity of the Messiah.

John was a figure of the Old Testament and showed in his own person a typical embodiment of the Law. John heralded beforehand the coming of the Saviour, even as the Law was our schoolmaster to bring us to the grace of Christ (Gal 3:24). That he prophesied while yet in the hidden depths of his mother's womb, and while himself lightless bore testimony to the truth, we are to understand as a figure. Namely, while John was wrapped round with the veil and carnal ordinances of the letter, he by the spirit preached unto the world a Redeemer, and testified that Jesus is our Lord even while for himself, working under the law, the birth of the new dispensation was still in the womb of the future, and not come to day. The Jews were estranged from the womb, that is from the Law, that womb heavy with the Christ that was to be; they went astray from the belly, speaking lies (Ps 57:4), and therefore John came for a witness, to bear witness of the Light, that all men through him might believe (Jn 1:7). [W]hen John had heard in the prison the works of Christ, he sent two of his disciples (Mt 11:2); this is the Law sending to the Gospel. For John in gaol was a figure of the Law, imprisoned in ignorance, lying in the dark, in a hidden place, and fettered through Jewish misunderstanding within the bonds of the letter. But of him Jesus said (as is written by the Blessed Evangelist), *'He was a burning and a shining light'* (Jn 5:35), that is to say, that, when the whole world was wrapt in the night of ignorance, this Saint was kindled by the fire of the Holy Ghost, to show before men the light of salvation, and at the hour of the thickest darkness of sin, appeared like a bright morning star to herald the rising of that Sun so right gloriously radiant, the Son of righteousness, Christ our Lord.[6]

St John's joy before birth over Jesus and his fidelity in prison at the end of his life is a summary of the OT's anticipation of the Son of God. The generations of Jews through the OT have always included two camps — those for Christ and those against. These camps continue after Christ came, being counted respectively as Christianity and Judaism.

The incongruity in those who say they are Jews and are not (Apoc 2:9), count themselves sons of Abraham and are not (Gal 3:29), and imagine themselves true Israelites and are not (Rom 9:6), is not a denial of Jewish physical descent. Rather, it raises our mind (Rom 2:28-29) to spiritual birth in Christ and calls all to acknowledge Him as Messiah and Lord.

Tradition and Scripture assure us that at the end of the age the Jews will convert in great numbers. We will see in Part III how this truth is contained at various levels of our liturgical traditions. As for Scripture, *Volume 1* of this work explored how Jews and Christians are brothers after the manner shown by Cain and Abel, or Ishmael and Isaac, or Esau and Jacob.

---

[6] Feast of the Nativity of St John the Baptist (24th June), Matins, *Lectiones* IV-VI. St Augustine, *Sermon XX on the Saints*.

That is to say in each case, the elder (Jews) persecute the younger (Christians). But at the end of history they are reconciled, which is prefigured in Joseph's moving reunion with his brothers, as told at the close of Genesis — an event we will revisit in Part III.[7] Peace is seen in Aaron and Moses.

Being descended from Abraham biologically is an honour, only it counts for nothing if not animated by the spirit. Considering Christ's rebuke of those who *"say they are Jews and are not"*, we should ask ourselves if we be counted as they who 'say they are Catholics and are not'. St Paul gives the single principle determining the answer. It is life in Christ which determines the full brotherhood of the Church:

There is neither Jew nor Greek: there is neither bond nor free: there is neither male nor female. For you are all one in Christ Jesus. (Gal 3:28)

St Paul is not denying there are Jews and Gentiles in the Church (St Matthew and St Luke), nor denying there are men and women in the Church (St Joseph and the Virgin Mary).

---

[7] A detail woven into Genesis' account of the twelve sons of Israel (Jacob) hints that there will be a slight switch at the close of history, with the Jews who enter the Church counting as the younger brother to Gentile Christians, who are elder. The first ten of Israel's sons had various mothers. The last two sons, Joseph and Benjamin, were born to his beloved wife Rachel. Hence the sons of Israel were Joseph's half-brothers, except Benjamin, who was a full-brother. Now Joseph is a figure for Jesus Christ, while Benjamin, as the last generation of Israel, stands for the last generation of Jews. This signifies that this final generation will be full brothers of Christ, that is by biology and grace, not biology alone. Former generations of Christians and Jews are like half-brothers, as Joseph in relation to his elder brothers. But with the final conversion of the Jews, when we share the same mother — Mary, the Church — then we will be full-brothers, true brothers, not because of biology alone, but because of spiritual descent. And as Joseph favoured Benjamin exceptionally, so Christians should favour converting Jews (Gen 43:29-34; 45:14-22).

Only it is not biology that is determinative of Christian unity but souls belonging spiritually to Christ. When the last Jews come in, *"all Israel will be saved"* (Rom 11:26). The Church is the New Israel. Spiritually.

The Chief Target of Evil is the Highest Good

The most important events in history — Christ's Crucifixion and Resurrection — accomplished the work of the New Creation. In that first Holy Week, the New Adam rose from the tomb in the very place where God first appointed the first Adam after forming him from the earth. Consequently, nothing is more important than the memorial of Our Lord's Passion, for it carries the power to redeem the world. It brings supernatural graces and provides spiritual lessons to inform every political, social and personal step we take. It teaches us incontestably that no effort to oppose evil can succeed except it be based on self-sacrifice and include love of one's enemy. It cannot involve deceit, injustice or cruelty, for all these serve satan. Through celebration of the Sacred Triduum, the Crucified forms our hearts in benevolent love for all — Jew and Gentile.

In our Christian approach to the Jews, we find a lesson from the OT. King Saul, who was jealous of David, sought his death. Yet, when David had chances to kill Saul, he spared God's anointed (1 Kgs [1 Sam] 24; 26). David's respectful treatment of Saul is a profound allegory for the New Covenant taking the place of the Old Covenant, the throne, without acting vengefully or unjustly.

All David's behaviour toward Saul [shows] Christians ought never seek vengeance or harm against the Jews. Rather, as Pope Callixtus II commanded in his twelfth-century Bull *Sicut Judæis*, when the Church was ascending to the height of political influence, Christians should grant protection to the Jews, who should suffer no prejudice, no violence against person or property, no extortion by the hands of Christians, no damage to their graveyards, no pressure to be baptised. Numerous popes before and after him decreed similarly.[8]

Long before this, Pope St Gregory the Great (✝604) enjoined upon Christians, in multiple epistles to bishops and monarchs, not to mistreat Jews, but also to set at liberty Christians enslaved to them, lest these Christians be corrupted in faith.[9] These policies were reiterated by various popes leading up to Pope Callixtus II's (✝1124) Bull *Sicut Judæis*, and renewed by more than a dozen popes in the following three centuries, notably by Popes Alexander III (✝1181) and Innocent III (✝1216).[10]

David's benevolent attitude towards Saul, coupled with his robust self-defence, informed the Church's approach toward Jews. Protecting them came as part of a package which also safeguarded Catholics from Judaism.[11] Vitally, Jews were

---

[8] Fr James Mawdsley, *Adam's Deep Sleep* (2022), p.112.

[9] As examples, Pope St Gregory I, *Epistles*, III, 38 to Libertinus, Prefect of Sicily; *Epistles*, IX, 6 to Januarius, Bishop of Cagliari.

[10] Pope Alexander III *Sicut Judeis*. Pope Innocent III, *Etsi Judæos*.

[11] Pope Clement VI *Quamvis Perfidiam* (1348). Pope Eugene IV, *Dundum ad nostram audientiam* (1442). Pope Paul IV, *Cum nimis absurdum* (1555).

heavily restricted in municipal rights across Christendom, for they were opposed to its very foundation, Christ.

If we are rooted and grounded in Christ, we must show justice to all. But the wise social arrangement limiting Jewish political influence has, over centuries, been undone, therefore weakening Christendom, as outlined in the chapters below.

The conclusion of this book reflects on the most far-reaching conspiracy there has ever been. But it is not needful to expose evil in every detail in order to come to the truth. Instead, we can observe what evil attacks most vigorously, and realise that the target of satanists must be the highest good. The most pressing problem for the Church today is not about priestly celibacy, or women priests, or Holy Communion for adulterers or active homosexuals. That these disasters are even discussed is a consequence of a deeper disorder. Without addressing the root, we will have more and more chaotic consequences to press us.

A more foundational problem is liturgical corruption.[12] The answer to this disease is to return to Tradition. The Church's crisis is liturgical; we have forgotten our means to pray for what is otherwise impossible, including the conversion of the Jews. And this is a good so high, and a problem so deep, that we have been terrorised into burying it.

We might be awakened to the goods of Tradition by learning how determinedly they have been under attack by the enemies of the Cross (both inside and outside the

---

[12] Joseph Cardinal Ratzinger, *Milestones: Memoirs 1927-1977* (1988), p.149, "I am convinced that the crisis in the Church that we are experiencing today is to a large extent due to the disintegration of the liturgy, which at times has even come to be conceived of *etsi Deus non daretur*, in that it is a matter of indifference whether or not God exists and whether or not He speaks to us and hears us."

Church). Here Holy Week comes to the fore. The wording of the traditional Good Friday intercession for the conversion of the Jews is possibly 1,700 years old.[13] But in recent decades it has been weakened again and again and again. If we rescue that prayer, we can begin to rescue our whole liturgy, and thereby doctrine and morals, and thereby Christendom.

Starting with the public prayer of the Church, Christ reigns on earth. The very struggle to adhere to our traditional liturgy, the courage and sacrifice this calls for, makes us the Catholics we are supposed to be. We have to know why we are doing it or we will give up. But if we persevere for love of God and neighbour, then this very charity ruling in our hearts, ordering our lives aright, makes our prayers irresistible to God. Then what can possibly stop the conversion of the Jews? Our win will be their win, and their win will be ours.

---

[13] Josef Jungmann *The Mass of the Roman Rite* (1955), Vol I, p.481-82, "It is a well-grounded hypothesis that in these Good Friday prayers, whose echo goes back to the first century, we have the general prayer of the Roman Church in the exact wording in which it was performed… since the third century."

For the text of the prayer in Latin and English, see Part III below, *What Can Catholics Do? Good Friday Prayer for the Jews.*

PART I: WHY HAS GOD ALLOWED THE DELAY?

Behold, I will bring of the synagogue of Satan, who say they are Jews, and are not, but do lie. Behold, I will make them to come and adore before thy feet. And they shall know that I have loved thee.

Apocalypse 3:9

What was done to Jesus Christ by the Sanhedrin (Caiaphas) in collaboration with corrupt churchmen (Judas) and a weak state (Pilate), has continued to happen ever since to the Bride of Christ. While it is clear that the State has often been hostile to the Church, and more obvious than ever that churchmen betray her, what is not so conspicuous is the historical role of Judaism's hostility to the Church. Uncovering this could provoke anger, for naturally "the presence of evil gives rise to the passion of anger".[14] Yet *the anger of man works not the justice of God* (Jas 1:20). Instead, let wrath be tempered by understanding. Perceiving God's patience bids us to imitate Him.

God chose the Hebrew people to receive the Old Covenant as preparation for the New. By God's Providence, Hebrews produced the greatest saints the Church has known and can know: the Apostles, the Precursor, St Joseph and the Mother of God. Why, then, has God permitted other Jews to oppose the promised Messiah and the New Covenant?

While men oft abuse their God-given freewill, the Lord has not retracted His gift. Man's opposition to God never threatens His plan, because, as the Bible shows, evil backfires and sows the seeds of its own destruction. Evil corrupts good like a parasite, threatening to consume its host. In its 'success', evil destroys its own basis. Except the Church cannot be destroyed. She rises anew — purified by suffering. Those who oppose God actually serve His purpose, inducing fruitful sacrifices by the saints. Like the Crucifixion, these sacrifices always bestow more life on the Church than is lost. Martyrs lose their earthly lives, but inherit eternal life, and from Heaven they vivify the Church Militant on earth.

Going against God is an act of futility. Pharaoh learned this long after the order had gone out to kill Hebrew infants. In time, this positioned Moses to bring Pharaoh down.

Moses triumphed over the murderous law, being saved
at first by his parents and then by the very persons who

---

14 St Thomas, *S.Th.* II-I, Q.25 a.3.

laid down the law [and even provided] his highly esteemed education.[15]

After the same pattern, satan instigated the Crucifixion, which brought Jesus into satan's ambit — death. The Lord of Life trampled upon the gates of hell and the devil was forever denuded of his spoil — godly souls — who now enjoy eternal life. Essentially, darkness is a backdrop enhancing the glory of light.

History, philosophy and divine revelation all concur that there are two ways to serve God: by willingly following His commands or by wilfully rejecting them. Both paths serve His purpose and each one of us is free to choose our path. Love of God is rewarded with salvation but hatred of God brings damnation. It is always better we obey God than not. But the NT shows, as does every century since, multiple paradoxical ways by which Jews rejecting Jesus and opposing the Church have actually served God's plan and the greater good.

As God knew that His enemies would falsify history to lead souls astray, He gave us the veracity of the NT to guide those who seek truth. It seems God has delayed the Jews' conversion for several reasons. The following chapters explore these in detail.

In brief, first, attempts at Judaizing serve the purification of Church doctrine. Second, Jews engineering persecutions has served the spread of the Church worldwide. Third, withstanding hatred perfects charity. Fourth, attempts to maintain the Old Covenant actually testify to the divine origins of the Church.

---

[15] St Gregory of Nyssa, *Life of Moses*, II, 308.

We can add a fifth reason. God is never cruel. He excludes no one who seeks Him. The long delay of the conversion of the Jews *en masse* — some two thousand years, and counting — will serve the depth of that conversion, the profundity of their contrition, the ardour of their zeal for Jesus, and the glory of the witness they give in overcoming the Antichrist. All of these qualities will produce an ending to human history better than anyone can imagine. It will be enjoyed for eternity.

HERESY PURIFIES DOCTRINE

They went out from us, but they were not of us; for if they had been of us, they would have continued with us; but they went out, that it might be plain that they all are not of us.

1 John 2:19 RSVCE

The radiance of a light is accentuated by the depth of darkness which surrounds it. The splendour of truth is made more brilliant as error fails to overcome it. Church doctrine shines with ever more clarity as waves of pernicious heresy fail to extinguish it. We must not be unnerved by darkness.

When Jesus taught the Jews of His eternity, being the Son of God His Father, *"many believed in Him"* (Jn 8:21-30). Despite this initial belief, a little later Jesus says to these, *"Now you seek to kill Me, a man Who have spoken the truth to you"* (Jn 8:40). He gave the reason: *"You are of your father the devil"* (Jn 8:44). In short, they turned against Christ when He revealed their slavery to sin. He had stated:

And you shall know the truth, and the truth shall make you free. They answered Him: We are the seed of Abraham, and we have never been slaves to any man: how sayest Thou: you shall be free? (Jn 8:32-33)

From this passage, St Thomas Aquinas identifies three errors of those Jews who had been listening to Jesus.[16]

First, they boasted of their Abrahamic ancestry, as if a noble birth suffices for godliness. Second, they lied, saying they had *"never been slaves to any man"*, forgetting how God saved the Hebrews from Pharaoh (Ps 105:21) or how they paid tribute now to Caesar (Lk 20:22; Jn 19:15). Third, they failed to see *"freedom"* as spiritual and did not perceive they needed liberation from *"sin"* (Jn 8:34). Due to their pride, dishonesty and carnality, they spurned the Saviour.

To think oneself chosen by God *to the exclusion of others* causes the most vaunting pride. To use God's Revelation for one's own agenda, not His, nurtures the most shameless dishonesty. To reduce God's promises to temporal things, forgetting Heaven, results in the most barren carnality. From these three evils, all rooted in a failure to understand the OT, germinated Judaism. Inverting the highest truths makes Judaism inordinately dangerous — *corruptio optimi pessima.*

Those who preferred *"darkness [to] light"* (Jn 3:19) feared the truths Jesus taught. God allowed them to kill His Son, resulting, through the Resurrection, in the propagation of the Gospel to the whole world (Mk 16:15). Just as the *"light of the world"* (Jn 8:12) was not extinguished but increased in radiance, so too the Bride of Christ must rise ever anew to illumine the darkness.

The worst crisis in Church history has been metastasising today under Francis. Such evil is not easily understood, as by nature darkness cannot be seen. But it becomes apparent

---

[16] St Thomas, *Commentary on St John* 8, Lecture 4.

when we take in a wider sweep of history — the present is largely explained by what happened before it. To understand what is now causing the disintegration of the institutional Church, look to Vatican II. A fruitful perspective on this is given by an appraisal of the Reformation, which in its turn is clarified by an understanding of the Arian and Gnostic crises. On the surface, these disasters differ. In reality, much is the same, stretching back to Calvary. In short, the NT provides us a true measure of all history: the Church is built up by those who love the Crucified and torn down by the crucifiers. That has not changed.

The Beginning of Judaizing in the Church

Jesus told the believing Jews: *"If you continue in My word, you shall be My disciples indeed"* (Jn 8:31). But the allure of sin leads souls astray. We must not prefer anything to Christ, lest it separate us from His Body.

Rejection of Christ opposes life and truth (Jn 14:6). Heresy and obstinate doctrinal error are not matters of innocent confusion, but are weapons wielded by the *"father of lies"* to murder souls (Jn 8:44). Because we would avoid obvious traps and snares, the devil's lies are presented to us dressed up as truth, and, at times, even coming from members of the Church hierarchy.

The NT shows that the early Church understood Judaizing to be a mortal threat, an attempt to superimpose Jewish categories onto the Church. Left unchallenged, attempts to align Christianity with Judaism, rather than with the OT, would destroy the Church. Christianity is fully divine and fully human, coming from Jesus Christ, true God and true man. Therefore, Christianity is apt for all men. Contrary to this, Judaism is for an elite among nations, people who count themselves a superior race.

Without the revelation of the God-Man-Messiah, a false ceiling is imposed on reality, closing us off to the height of God's design for all men. Judaism's denial of the Incarnation inevitably cramps cognate concepts embodied by Jesus — of divine revelation utterly transcending mortal expectations; of the eternal informing the temporal; of the immunity of royal service from prideful domination; of freedom in charity as liberation from the yoke of the law. Judaism refuses to recognise a Messiah unless his success be visible now, unless he bring perceptible peace to the world today, unless he reward his followers with exterior goods, unless he be seen to dominate all. A crucified Messiah is unthinkable. The heavenly Jerusalem counts for nothing without the earthly Jerusalem. In a word, without Jesus Christ, circumcision of the heart is forsaken for circumcision of the flesh.

The *"circumcision party"* (Gal 2:12; Tit 1:10 RSVCE) seemed strong enough to subvert the first papacy, except that St Paul withstood them, going on to resist also St Peter, loyally, *"to the face"* (Gal 2:11). St Paul warns there are many *"vain talkers, seducers... of the circumcision... who subvert whole houses, teaching [wrongly] for filthy lucre's sake"* (Tit 1:10-11). These prefer mammon to God. The Jesuits are an example of a *"whole house"* subverted. St Paul uses language so direct it is unthinkable in the Church today ("βλέπετε τοὺς κύνας" — *"Beware of the dogs"* Phil 3:2). But if, being lukewarm, we shy from his clarity, we are vulnerable to becoming prey.

Rabbinic-Judaism is a man-made religion, formulated in expectation of another messiah by those who rejected Jesus as Messiah, though it began establishing its power base before His Advent. Influenced by diabolical narcissism, it prefers *"the work of human hands"* to God's tabernacle which is *"not of this creation"* (Heb 9:11; cf. Mk 14:58; Acts 7:48; 17:25; 2 Cor 5:1). Even if it had not lost Temple, altar and priests, the Old Covenant is no longer of use, because it puts false hope in atonement through animal blood (Heb 10:4), instead of the Most Precious Blood poured out by the Lamb.

With antecedents in those who murdered the prophets, Judaism began as the rejection of Christianity and therefore is logically subsequent to it. Any reader with faith can verify this by consulting Acts 11:1-18; 13:6-12; 15:1-29; 18:24-28; 19:11-20; 26:20-23; Gal 2:3-21; Col 2:8,11,16-17,20-23; Apoc 2:8-10; 3:8-13. If we disregard these Scriptures, we could be misled into believing that Judaism is a continuation of the Old Covenant. It is not. Christianity is. Meanwhile, these same biblical passages prove that each assault on truth yields the opposite of its intended effect on those who persevere in faith: *"So the word of the Lord grew and prevailed mightily"* (Acts 19:20 RSVCE).

Gnosticism, Arianism and Early Church Councils
The enemies of Christ never cease seeking to have the Church adopt their errors. Those who follow them fall. Many have heard that Gnosticism and Arianism were virulent heresies. But one has to do a bit of digging to discover the impetus given to them by Jews. This aspect is key to understanding the targets and potency of their errors.

Before the Church had any political presence, rabbis drove Christians away from synagogues because unconverted Jews could not withstand the Christians' apologetic arguments. The divisions which arose between Judaism and Christianity are not due to antisemitism from the Church, but hardness of heart in the Synagogue, in clinging to anyone but Christ. To deny Jesus is the Christ, some rabbis claimed during this early period that the promised Messiah was King Hezekiah, or even Abraham, or other impossible figures, though only Jesus fits the prophecies.

Trying to enter the spiritual world without following Jesus, some have turned to demons for 'help'. The ambitious Simon Magus, likely a Samaritan, is called by St Irenæus "the father of all heresies".[17] His spiritual ancestors in dark magic include the sorcerers of Pharaoh's court who were confounded by Moses (Ex 7:11-9:11), as Simon, in his turn, was roundly rebuked by St Peter (Acts 8:9-24). For Jews hungry for gain but averse to Jesus, these pagan and Samaritan exponents of magic were models to emulate.[18]

An early example of this corrupt spirit, *"a Jewish false prophet... Elymas the magician"* (Acts 13:6), was struck blind by the Apostle Paul, who filled with the Holy Spirit denounced him, saying with every word measured:

---

[17] St Irenæus, *Adversus Hæreses*, I, 23, 2.

[18] Guy Strousma, *Jewish Thought and Philosophy*, Vol. 2 (1992), p.58, Jacques Matter's "own conclusion as to the sources of Gnosticism insists on Judaism in general ('Jewish metaphysics') and on Kabbalah in particular."

Moshe Idel, *Kabbalah: New Perspectives* (1988), p.6 & 156*ff*, argues that both Gnosticism and Kabbalah have roots in ancient Jewish theurgy — "operations intended to influence the Divinity".

O full of all guile, and of all deceit, child of the devil, enemy of all justice, thou ceasest not to pervert the right ways of the Lord. (Acts 13:10)

Elymas portrays a prototype Gnostic, one who wilfully deals in *"knowledge falsely so called"* (1 Tim 6:20 ψευδωνυμου γνωσεως).

Not long after Elymas and Simon Magus, Gnosticism proliferated.[19] In his day, Valentinus of Alexandria (d.180) was the best known 'Christian' Gnostic. This term is oxymoronic. Valentinus' teaching is not Christian. His so-called *Gospel of Truth* is at war with truth, filled with confusion over the Father and Son, having disdain for creation and matter, involving satanic fancies about demons. Valentinus' Gnosticism is easily discoverable but few know he was "presumably of Jewish descent".[20]

Valentinus is obscure in comparison to Arius (d.336) — the most famous heresiarch of the first millennium. With demonic guile, the priest Arius adamantly denied Jesus' Divinity, supporting his arguments with misunderstood

---

[19] Though not holding all the conclusions of those cited, Stephen Haar, *Simon Magus: The First Gnostic?* (2003), p.28, writes, "Pearson supported the thesis of Moritz Friedländer that 'Gnosticism is not, in its origins, a Christian heresy, but in fact a Jewish heresy;' and, nominated apostate Jews in Egypt and Syria-Palestine as possible sources. Quispel likewise argued for the roots of Gnosticism to be found in Jewish heresy, attributing its development to heterodox Jews living in Palestine or Egypt during the first century CE. Robert Grant claimed instead that disillusionment and despair among Palestinian Jews, after the military defeats of 70CE and 135CE, provided the background for the Gnostic movement. The publications of Rudolph, Böhlig, and Pokorny, also have emphasised the role of heterodox Judaism in the formation of Gnosticism."

[20] Johann Neander, *Genetische Entwickelung der vornehmsten gnostischen Systeme* (1818), p.92.

William Thomas Walsh, *Philip II* (1987), p.241.

citations from the OT.[21] His unbending determination to degrade Jesus never made sense to me, until I read Arius, like Valentinus, was of Jewish heritage.[22]

A historian in search of truth, St John Henry Newman, found Judaism to be a direct and indirect cause of multiple heresies which battered the early Church.[23] This explains the vigorous preaching of St John Chrysostom (✝407), as also of St Bernard of Clairvaux (✝1153) and much else in Church history falsely labelled antisemitic.

St John Chrysostom is supposedly antisemitic for robustly defending his flock against Judaizing, that is, from embracing errors which would lead his spiritual children to hell. In truth, he was inflamed with love for souls. Therefore, he was right to forbid Christians from participating in Jewish feasts, for by attending them they would imply Jesus was not the Messiah.

As Judaizers provoked the imperishable homilies of the golden-mouthed St John, so Gnosticism and Arianism occasioned early Church Councils which produced the Nicene-Constantinopolitan Creed. This is the most masterly symbol of our Faith, securing souls ever since in truth, while stripping the heretics of credibility among Christians. The attacks on the Faith resulted in glorious, enduring and precise expressions of the Faith.

The enemies of Christ would have to find other ways to assault truth. They did, yet with similar results.

---

[21] Philo of Alexandria (d.50) is a key Jewish link between Platonism and Arianism.

[22] William Thomas Walsh, *Philip II* (1987), p.240.

[23] St John Henry Newman, *Arianism of the Fourth Century* (1833), p.18-25.

The Reformation and Trent

The Renaissance is not what we are told. Born from it, the anti-doctrinal programme of the Reformation shares its dark roots in Jewish magic, Kabbalah.[24] The Jewish writer Josué Jéhouda pertinently recounts how scholars in the fifteenth century would meet at the princely house of the nobleman and philosopher, Pico de Mirandola.

> The discovery of the Jewish Kabbalah, which [Pico then] imparted to various enlightened Christians contributed far more than the return to Greek sources to the extraordinary spiritual blossoming which is known as the Renaissance. About half a century later, the rehabilitation of the Talmud was to lead to the Reformation... Pico de Mirandola had understood that the indispensable purification *[that is, corruption]* of Christian dogma could only be effected after a profound study of the authentic Jewish Kabbalah.[25]

Worldly Christians took their lead not from Christ but from His enemies. Clerics infatuated with fashion and nobility were seduced. Kabbalah, aimed at tapping divinity for a universal transformation of mankind, promises power through occult arts of divination, not holiness; or of dominating the divine, not surrendering to it. Similarly, the esoteric art of gematria imposes numerical codes on the

---

[24] Michael Hoffman, *The Occult Renaissance Church of Rome* (2017).

Francis Yates, *The Rosicrucian Enlightenment* (1986); *Giordano Bruno and The Hermetic Tradition* (1964).

[25] Josué Jéhouda, *L'Antisémitisme Miroir du Monde* (1958), p.164. He adds: "if the Renaissance had not been deflected from its original course... the world would have doubtless been unified by the creative thought and doctrine of the Kabbalah."

Hebrew text of the Torah to draw out secrets, effectively ceding a power of free interpretation to the reader. In contrast, traditional Christian hermeneutics allow biblical numerology only in so far as it is subordinate to doctrine established by rational study and inspiration. Rabbinic gematria, assigning false powers to the letter, fathered the Protestant error of *sola scriptura*. In like vein today, increasing computing power is inflaming fascination with the absurd 'Bible Code' among certain Protestants. This is not how to study the Scriptures.

Martin Luther is famous for the bile he poured forth against Jews. But he did not start this way.[26] At the beginning of his rebellion, studying the Talmud and gaining kabbalistic teachings from Johann Reuchlin, he was enamoured of the Hebrews and hoped to find allies among them against Rome. His rebellion could never have succeeded on the merits of his theological raft (Lutheranism makes no sense). But he carved out a massive space thanks to the sponsorship of ambitious German princes, political actors willing to collaborate in order to repeal the old order and assert themselves as regional rulers. Who financed their forces? Jews had long been involved in running the finances of the mighty Teutonic Order and, until its suppression, the Knights Templar. Would these Jews now support the anti-Catholic Reformation?

> [I]t is beyond question, as a Jewish historian says, that the first leaders of the Protestant sects were called semi-Judaei, or half-Jews, in all parts of Europe, and that

---

[26] William Thomas Walsh, *Philip II* (1987), p.246, "The so-called Reformation, adds Abrahams, 'drew its life blood from a rational Hebraism.' Luther naturally employed Jews in preparing his German Bible. Jews were the most successful agents in the printing and distributing of Protestant Bibles and tracts in all parts of Europe."

men of Jewish descent were as conspicuous among them as they had been among the Gnostics and would later be among the Communists.[27]

The respected Jewish historian Cecil Roth recounts that certain Marrano Jews (reluctant or insincere converts to Christianity), kept their judaic religious identity hidden over generations, for they were weary of the disadvantages it incurred in Christendom.

> Marranism's… essential characteristic is that it was a clandestine faith passed down from father to son. One of the reasons put forward to justify the expulsion of the Jews from England in 1290 was that they seduced newly-made converts and made them return to the 'vomit of Judaism'. Jewish chroniclers add that many children were seized and sent to the north of the land, where they continued for a long time to practise their former religion. It is owing to this fact, reports one of them, that the English accepted the Reformation so easily; it also explains their preference for Biblical names and certain dietetic peculiarities which are preserved in Scotland. This version is not so improbable as would seem at first sight, and constitutes an interesting example of how… crypto-Jewry can appear in places which seem obviously so little suited to it.[28]

It is no antisemitic conspiracy theory but the diligent work of contemporary Jewish scholars which traces an unbroken

---

[27] William Thomas Walsh, *Philip II* (1987), p.248.

[28] Cecil Roth, *History of the Marranos* (1946), p.185. Note that despite the official expulsion of the Jews from England in 1290, not all of the richest actually left.

hereditary of Jewish influence in Scotland from pre-Reformation crypto-Jewry to today, whose

> 'craft' was a mixture of technology and magic, as developed in the esoteric teachings of the architects and builders of the Temple in Jerusalem and preserved by the kings of Scotland [through to] the international emergence of 'higher degrees' of Cabalistic mysticism in the Écossais Masonic lodges that wielded such a mysterious and powerful influence on the culture of the 'enlightened' eighteenth and 'progressive' nineteenth-centuries.[29]

Schuchard quotes documents which "span seven centuries" to illustrate increasing kabbalistic influence on European society. Jewish academics take pride that the Reformation in Scotland could not have happened without the Jews, claiming Presbyterianism itself has Jewish roots. A strong case for this is made by Hirschman and Yates.[30] Referring to Jews expelled from Spain in 1492, they conclude:

> The displaced Jews, like so many tiny floating seeds… landed on fertile ground in Holland, France, Scotland, Germany, Switzerland, and England, where they grew into the Protestant Reformation.

Many Sephardic Jews expelled from Spain ended up in Holland or England, harbouring a deep hatred of Catholicism.

---

[29] Marsha Keith Schuchard, *Judaized Scots, Jacobite Jews, and the Development of Cabalistic Freemasonry* (2000), Introduction.

[30] Elizabeth Hirschman, Donald Yates, *When Scotland was Jewish* (2007), p.200-204. The authors speculate, though admit they fall short of demonstrating, that both John Knox and John Calvin were aware of being of Jewish descent.

If one hears of the horrors that these Jews expelled from Spain experienced at the hands of Barbary pirates, then, on a human level, one might understand the inter-generational, pan-Catholic hatred. This factor helps explain the otherwise inexplicable: how Catholic England was tipped into the night.

The English Reformation was a close-run thing. No one who attempts to defend it theologically can stay the course, because when investigated in any detail, it is so evidently evil that any Anglican researcher must desist or convert. Most desist. So, it prevailed, and so it has been maintained, thanks to ruthless coercion.

After Elizabeth I took the throne in Catholic England, her Protestant advisors had her make war on Catholics at home and abroad. Mary Queen of Scots and her supporters were murdered. England thieved from Philip I's Spanish ships with a relentless violence that were not acts of war but pure piracy, absolutely lawless. Until today England is proud of this, just as the tyrannical monster Henry VIII is still held in esteem. The Elizabethan court launched a terror campaign, but on this mainstream historians prefer to stay silent. Putting down the Western Rising, the government used, for the first time in England's history, foreign mercenaries to kill Englishmen. This is not natural law but early globalism surging forth.

The enemy hysterically accused Catholics of their own misdeeds. Jesuit priests, sent as missionaries to provide the Gospel and Sacraments for starving English faithful, were falsely accused of being spies, political agents of overthrow. Most historians admit that the maintenance of early Anglicanism could not have been achieved without the international spy and finance channels of Francis Walsingham and William Cecil. How did these networks grow so readily?

Jewish merchants provided a ready-made web across much of continental Europe. Some, remembering the influence their families used to have, saw an opportunity to regain it and to take revenge on the Church. Supported by these, and with demonic cunning, Walsingham made innovative use of codes, ciphers, bribery, kidnappings (targets abducted from abroad and brought to England for interrogation), torture, show-trials and murder, to deepen the crown's political stranglehold. England, so quick today to accuse others of tyranny, still shies away from facing her own past.

Englishmen, not Jews, are responsible for Anglicanism. Germans, not Jews, are to blame for Lutheranism. The Scots, not Jews, will have to answer to God for Presbyterianism. It is by satan and sin working through all men, all nations, that such things come about. Indeed, it is necessary that those with a heart for heresy be separated from the Church (1 Jn 2:19), for this serves clarity. But the fact that opposing God invariably serves His purpose does not justify that opposition.

How many heretical-political movements have arisen and survived thanks to Jewish ignition and support? Gnosticism, Arianism, Protestantism's anti-sacramental, anti-ecclesial, anti-sanctoral, anti-Marian theology, and their faux OT basis, all demonstrate a succumbing to Judaizing. We will answer for our sins; they for theirs. But we will not have peace or stability if we pretend that the Jews are one nation like any other. They have a deeper role.

Meanwhile, as in former scourgings, the Church survived the Reformation and grew more secure thanks to the Council of Trent. That holy convocation produced some of the richest theological documents ever penned: on the Holy Sacrifice of the Mass; on the seven Sacraments — notably the Holy Eucharist; and on original sin and grace.

We are experiencing today another Reformation, only this time it is Rome in rebellion. The Vatican's new hatred of traditional morals, doctrine and liturgy is nothing new at all. Seeing Arianism and Gnosticism were led by Jews, and that Jews were decisive contributors to the Reformation, we can inquire what influence they had on Vatican II.

The Catholic City Overrun

In 1907, Pope St Pius X condemned "modernism" as the "synthesis of all heresies".[31] Modernism is not a rejection of particular truths but a denial that truth itself is real and knowable by man. As such, it is a wholesale rejection of Jesus Christ (Jn 14:6). It is an evil which has been growing in the world ever since the misnamed Enlightenment. After a long incubation, it gained traction in the Church with Vatican II.

In 1961, the American Jewish Committee (AJC) requested that Pope John XXIII direct the Vatican to

> cleanse all Catholic educational and liturgical publications of inaccurate, distorted, slanderous or prejudiced statements about Jews as a group.[32]

The aim was that catechisms, breviaries and missals be expurgated of whatever Judaism found objectionable. The

---

[31] Pope St Pius X, *Pascendi Dominici Gregis* (1907), 39.

[32] AJC, *The Image of the Jews in Catholic Teaching* (1961), I.

request was courteous but deadly. More shameful than the AJC asking for this was that the Church hierarchy fell for it.

That said, it is no coincidence that that for which the AJC was asking was precisely that which the Church perceived she needed to do in order to adapt herself to the modern world, using Vatican II to achieve it. It is not that the Vatican took direct orders from the AJC. Rather, the Jewish spirit of modernity had successfully shaped the context wherein the Church discerned that if she did not strive to conform to the world, then she would suffer relentless calumny. Members of the ecclesial hierarchy were tired of withstanding the waves.

Jewish influence upon the thinking of the Church hierarchy had already been waxing for decades (see Part III below). Especially after WWII, the bishops, like many men, were terrified of being labelled antisemitic. The fall out from Vatican II demonstrates that the bishops took their eyes off Christ and followed the spirit of this world instead.

Fruits of Judaizing are obvious in the *novus ordo missæ* (the New Mass). The Offertory prayers of the traditional Mass are twelfth century Gallican masterpieces concerning the salvation worked by Jesus Christ, in Communion with all His Saints, through the acceptance of our present sacrifice by the Blessed Trinity. In the New Mass, these various prayers have been drastically curtailed or completely replaced with what resemble Judaic table prayers. The old offertory prayers are replete with majestic acts of God. The new delight instead in "the work of human hands", an echo of idolatry.[33] The old prayers strike us with the priest's admission of unworthiness,

---

[33] 2 Chron 32:19; Ps 113:12; 134:15-18; Is 2:8.

his "innumerable sins, offences, and negligences". The new prayers skip lightly over contrition, conforming to Judaism, which takes a superficial view of sin.[34] The *novus ordo's* Judaic offertory prayers are for a meal, not a sacrifice — typically spoken by a family father, not a priest. As prayers focused on the temporal, they are mediocre, not duly proportioned for a memorial of the Crucifixion.

This faux imitation of Judaism by Catholics is more likely to win contempt from Jews rather than conversions, as they mark our lack of trust in our own tradition. Why should they convert if they are the determinative party?

Moreover, the degrading of a sacrifice to a meal has resulted in confusion among many Catholics, who think they can participate in seder meals as a form of liturgy or worship. But this attempt to persist in the Mosaic Covenant is a rejection of Jesus. With St Augustine, St Thomas teaches:

> Now, though our faith in Christ is the same as that of the fathers of old; yet, since they came before Christ, whereas we come after Him, the same faith is expressed in different words, by us and by them. For by them was it said: 'Behold a virgin shall conceive and bear a son,' where the verbs are in the future tense: whereas we express the same by means of verbs in the past tense, and say that she 'conceived and bore'. In like manner the ceremonies of the Old Law betokened Christ as having yet to be born and to suffer: whereas our

---

[34] Alfred Kolatch, *The Jewish Book of Why* (1985), p.64 "The doctrine of original sin is totally unacceptable to Jews… Jews believe that man enters the world free of sin, with a soul that is pure and innocent and untainted." Denying that the price paid for sin is Christ's Most Precious Blood, sin's seriousness cannot be perceived.

sacraments signify Him as already born and having suffered. Consequently, just as it would be a mortal sin now for anyone, in making a profession of faith, to say that Christ is yet to be born, which the fathers of old said devoutly and truthfully; so too it would be a mortal sin now to observe those ceremonies which the fathers of old fulfilled with devotion and fidelity.[35]

That which the Angelic Doctor identifies as a mortal sin, the US Conference of Catholics Bishops actually encouraged Catholics to do in Holy Week, to celebrate the ceremonies of those who reject Jesus: "Seders arranged at or in cooperation with local synagogues are encouraged."[36] The Bishops' Committee on the Liturgy insisted that Catholics engaging in Judaism's rites may not introduce Christian elements:

> When Christians celebrate this sacred feast among themselves, the rites of the *haggadah* for the seder should be respected in all their integrity.[37]

This is the blind leading the blind.

The turning of our liturgy upside down has its counterpart in the crippling of exegesis. Judaism determinedly rejects the allegorical and anagogical senses of Scripture because the Apostles and Church Fathers demonstrate that all Scripture points to Jesus Christ. To hide this, it is declared illegitimate to read more into the Scriptures than was intended by the author. This principle is exalted in order to exclude Christ. It

---

[35] St Thomas, *S.Th.* II-I, Q.103 a.4. St Augustine, *Contra Faustum* XIX, 16-18.

[36] USCCB, *God's Mercy Endures Forever: Guidelines on the Presentation of Jews and Judaism in Catholic Preaching* (Sep 1988), 28.

[37] USCCB, *Bishops' Committee on the Liturgy Newsletter* (March 1980), p.1.

ignores the fact that God is the ultimate Author. Modern Catholic exegesis, embracing Judaism's pitiful reductionism, seemingly scorns to rise above the literal sense of Scripture. Of course, the literal sense is fundamental, but we are not meant to remain there, rather to ascend to the spiritual.

Instead of this, for decades, academic exegesis has been thoroughly dominated by the historical-critical method. Its advocates carry great weight in the Vatican, apparently enough to veto traditional theology in documents regarding Judaism. But the Church confining herself to textual criticism and archeology, to arguments about historicity, is like a plane which taxis but never takes off — useless for salvation.[38]

With some blessed exceptions among modern exegetes, spiritual senses of Scripture are ignored, seemingly so that Christian differences with Judaism are not exposed. At the same time, on historical and textual criticism, we are meant to defer to Jews as experts and thereafter remain silent. Gaslit Catholics have taken on board anti-Christian criticism and mope under an inferiority complex.

An example of this false humility, allowing Judaizers to mesmerise the Church, is the recent re-numbering of the Psalms. The learned Jews who penned the Septuagint generations before the coming of Christ, knew full well how to divide the 150 Psalms. Their system was adopted by the early Church and used in the Vulgate, and passed on through all generations, until the Church lost confidence at Vatican II.

---

[38] The Servant of God, Fr Dolindo Ruotolo (✝1970) wrote in his 1941 pamphlet *Un gravissimo pericolo per la Chiesa e per le anime*, that the historical-critical method arose from an "accursed spirit of pride, presumption, and superficiality, disguised under minute investigations and hypocritical literal exactness."

Judaism numbers the Psalms differently. About one thousand years *after* Christ, the rabbis added Psalm numbers to the Masoretic text, differently from other traditions.[39] Protestants copied Judaism's numbering, pleased to slight the Catholic Church and pose as if they understood the Scriptures better. In our age, infatuated with heretics like Harnack and beguiled by modernists like Rahner, insecure, faithless, whoring Catholic exegetes decided like Protestants to follow the Jews. On this point, almost the whole Church has since gone after them.

Does re-numbering the Psalms matter? Yes. One reason is the unnecessary difficulties caused for study.[40] Worse is detaching the Church from the authority of the Vulgate and Septuagint. Who can think that Jews one thousand years after Christ understood the Psalm divisions better than the Jewish scholars who translated the Bible into Greek some two hundred years before Christ and whom the Church had followed for millennia? The false signal sent by re-numbering the Psalms is that the Church, inferior in understanding, has to catch up with Judaism and Protestantism. Thankfully, the Orthodox retain the traditional numbering.

---

[39] Psalms 9, 24, 34, 37 and 144 are acrostic (whereby initial letters form an alphabetic pattern). The compilers of the Masoretic version split Psalm 9 into two. They also split Psalm 113 into two, although the original forms a marvellous unity. To cover these tracks, Psalms 114 and 115 were merged as were 146 and 147.

[40] The New Advent website, for example, is a helpful resource but it numbers the Psalms differently in its biblical section compared to its patristic section. The impressive Nestle-Aland Greek Bible annotates the *"bread of heaven"* (Jn 6:31) as being a quote from Ps 78:24. But turn back to the OT in the same volume and you find Psalm 78 has only 13 verses. It is the wrong Psalm. The solution is that according to the divisions in the Septuagint and the Vulgate it is from Psalm 77. Within one volume there is needless disparity between OT and NT references.

None of this is to dispute Jewish expertise, obviously, with Hebrew. Nor is it, obviously, to deny that Jews can understand the Bible — along with St Luke, a Gentile, they wrote it! The point is that Judaism is in no condition to give lessons to the Church on hearing the Word of God.

Jewish influence on the Church's Magisterium is made obvious by *Nostra ætate* (1965), the drafting of which was dominated by Jewish converts.[41] Originally, it was meant to focus solely on the Jewish Question. In fact, it was to be a Cultural-Revolution-style self-accusation by the Church for her history of hating Jews.[42] The German Jesuit, Augustin Cardinal Bea, made multiple trips to New York where, in his weak eagerness to please, his mind was formed by Jewish lobbyists, including of B'nai Brith — "Sons of the Covenant" (founded as a secret society lodge in 1843 by twelve Jewish freemasons). Bea transmitted their agenda to the Vatican.

As a mercy, faithful bishops were able to broaden the scope of *Nostra ætate*'s final text to cover all religions and to limit its undermining of the Faith. With equivocation, the truth about religious freedom can just about be read into this document, but it is much obscured. To be clear: error has no rights. It is tolerated for the greater good, for it is impossible to eradicate error by force. True worship generates freedom and is the purpose of freedom. There is no other god beside God (4 Kgs 19:19; Is 45:5). All other religious systems will be crushed by or tend toward satanism.

---

[41] Working under Cardinal Bea, the small drafting committee included the Jewish converts, Fr John Osterreicher, Fr Bruno Hussar and Fr Gregory Baum.

[42] E Michael Jones, *The Jewish Revolutionary Spirit and its Impact on World History* (2015), p.893*ff.*

Although Catholic resistance spared *Nostra ætate* from being much worse, its spirit is abroad — invoked as ammunition for heretical claimants that all religions are equal or that various religions can be pleasing to God.[43]

Many devout Catholics suppose Vatican II was designed to please the world and the New Mass was compiled to please Protestants, for example by removing references to sacrifice and priesthood. But behind worldly atheism, behind Protestant errors, are Judaism's jealous rejection of the Blessed Virgin Mary, the Holy Sacrifice of the Mass, the sacramental priesthood and the papacy. To claim Catholic teaching and liturgy is being undermined by Protestantism is true, but this does not get to the source of the contamination.

Could Protestants have gained their platform or defining ideas without Judaism? I do not believe so. Rather, the two-thousand-year course of indefatigable Judaizing includes the birth of Protestantism.[44] The collaboration of Jews with Puritans in England, and with WASPs (white Anglo-Saxon Protestants) in America, draws from the same malevolent roots. Judaizing deforms Christian society to be carnal, legalistic, materialistic, money-led. The growing acceptance of divorce (and therefore contraception, abortion and transgenderism), and the growing domination of global finance, are two sides of one materialistic coin. The marxist revolution in economics, inflaming antagonism between

---

43 *Nostra ætate*, 3 claims that Muslims "adore the one God, living and subsisting in Himself", which is impossible to reconcile with Islam's active and persistent denial of the Holy Trinity. Islam does not serve God but denies His Revelation.

44 E Michael Jones, *The Jewish Revolutionary Spirit and its Impact on World History* (2015), p.160-161 & 232.

classes, is mirrored in the cultural revolution fracturing families, neighbours and nations — an agenda which has been deliberately pursued by the predominantly Jewish Frankfurt School (Horkheimer, Adorno, Marcuse, Grossman). Catholic countries have followed Protestant countries in submitting themselves to this Christless worldview.

Infected with this spirit, now Francis and his hierarchy are promoting a worldly messianism: social justice, mass immigration, environmental alarmism, religious syncretism. The Church is becoming dangerously legalistic: producing verbose documents which bury truth with wordiness; promoting worldly prelates who replace the family of God with bureaucracy, one which cares not about prosecuting clerical abuse. Law is weaponised to eradicate the worship of God (*Traditionis custodes*), amounting to spiritual genocide.

How deep is the disorientation? The USCCB advises:

> Pope John Paul II's visit to the Chief Rabbi of Rome on Good Friday, 1987, gives a lead for pastoral activities during Holy Week in local churches. Some dioceses and parishes... have begun traditions such as holding a 'Service of Reconciliation' with Jews on Palm Sunday, or inviting Holocaust survivors to address their congregations during Lent.[45]

It is important to listen to Holocaust survivors. But why in the context of Lent, of Holy Week? Priests have internalised the obscene accusation that remembrance of the Passion causes antisemitism (see below). There is a like insinuation in

---

[45] USCCB, *God's Mercy Endures Forever: Guidelines on the Presentation of Jews and Judaism in Catholic Preaching* (Sep 1988), 27.

having Holocaust survivors come to address Catholics preparing for Holy Week. Such events could never occur without tacit agreement that all keep silence on Judaism's total opposition to the central mysteries of Catholic Faith. The holocaust survivor we should be hearing from in Lent and Holy Week is the Victim of the worst crime in history: Jesus Christ. One can see that Jews do not yet accept this, but how have bishops lost sight of it? Have they, too, *"loved the glory of men more than the glory of God"* (Jn 12:43)?

A Pattern throughout Church History

The early Church's vigilant self-defence against Judaizers is recorded in the NT not as an historical curiosity but for the constant exhortation of Christians (cf. Acts 15:10).[46] Woe to the Church when she neglects this vigilance.

> It is out of place (ατοπον) to profess Christ Jesus, and to Judaize. For Christianity did not embrace Judaism, but Judaism Christianity, so that every believing tongue be gathered into God.[47]

---

[46] *Dominica X Post Pentecosten*, Matins, *Lectiones* IV-V. St Ambrose, *Treatise on Psalm 18,* "The Jews have a truly fervent zeal for God, but since they have not knowledge, their very zeal and fear do cause them to do things contrary to God's will. That they circumcise their children, that they keep holy the Sabbath-Day, shows how they fear the Lord, but knowing not the spiritual meaning of the Law, they circumcise the body and not the heart. But wherefore should I speak of Jews? There are those among ourselves who have the fear of God, but not according to knowledge, and set up hard ordinances which the weakness of man is not able to bear… [T]hey feel not for the weakness of nature, nor consider whether a thing can or cannot be done. Let not then the fear of God be unreasonable. True wisdom begins with the fear of God: neither is it spiritual wisdom without the fear of God, but neither ought the fear of God be without wisdom."

[47] St Ignatius of Antioch (consecrated the third Bishop of Antioch by St John the Apostle), *Letter to the Magnesians*, X, 3.

Today, we see a fearful corruption of Catholicism. It is difficult to uncover its roots, for the devil begins his operations in darkness. But a deplorable influence of Judaism on the Church's liturgy, Scriptures and Magisterium has now become unmistakable.

It is not love of Jews which accepts all this influence but fear of them. This fear is well grounded in temporal terms but supernaturally it makes no sense at all. Our Lord told us:

And fear ye not them that kill the body, and are not able to kill the soul: but rather fear Him that can destroy both soul and body in hell. (Mt 10:28)

Until we learn this, one redeeming advantage of widespread gloom is that the darkness of falsehood accentuates the splendour of truth. The whole is set for a dramatic correction. The longer the delay, the deeper the descent, then the more glorious the correction will be.

Meanwhile, nurturing indignation toward Protestants, atheists or Jews is no remedy. Making regular examinations of conscience, questioning our own fidelity and repenting of our infidelity is the beginning of the remedy. A little bit of grit results in a pearl, even one of great price. As the circumcision party provoked St Paul's *Letter to the Galatians* to the eternal benefit of the Church; as Arianism prompted the Council of Nicæa to the eternal benefit of the Church; as the Reformation motivated Trent to the eternal benefit of the Church; so, modernism, the "synthesis of all heresies", is inducing a restoration of Tradition which, we may be sure, will be to the eternal benefit of the Church.

To maintain a serene courage, we may meditate on the Crucifixion as a pre-condition for the Resurrection. Analogously, the global strangulation by modernism, denying the existence of truth, may be a precondition for the Triumph of Mary's Immaculate Heart, the establishment of global Christendom — morally strong, unshakeable in faith and unmovable from liturgical Tradition.

God allows men to pronounce untruths, including Judaism, so that other men may cleave even more closely to the one truth. Heresy purifies doctrine.

PERSECUTION PROVOKES GROWTH

When they persecute you in one town, flee to the next; for truly, I say to you, you will not have gone through all the towns of Israel, before the Son of man comes.

Matthew 10:23 RSVCE

Ever since Cain, God's enemies have been confounded, because persecuting the good actually increases the strength and presence of godliness. Abel's glory is eternal, Cain has none. Abel's legacy is still working good; Cain's legacy is increasing his final punishment, which, like Abel's reward, will not be finally reckoned until the Last Day when all its consequences are manifest. The paradox has become axiomatic: the blood of the martyrs is the seed of the Church. This is completely coherent, for the Church takes her very life from Christ Crucified, from His Heart pierced on the Cross.

By God's grace, those who persecute Christians may themselves be converted, profoundly strengthening the Mystical Body by their faith (Acts 7:60-8:3; 9:1-19).

Because first-century Jews rejected Christ, the Apostles turned their attention to the Gentiles, bringing *"salvation unto the utmost part of the earth"* (Acts 13:45-47; 18:5-6). Those *"dispersed by the persecution that arose on occasion of*

Stephen" brought the Good News to *"Phenice and Cyprus and Antioch... also to the Greeks"* and *"a great number believing were converted to the Lord"* (Acts 11:19-21).

Opposition to the Church is insidious, but works a wider transmission of the Gospel, thanks to the patience of those who endure.

> *And it came to pass in Iconium that they entered together into the synagogue of the Jews and so spoke that a very great multitude both of the Jews and of the Greeks did believe. But the unbelieving Jews stirred up and incensed the minds of the Gentiles against the brethren... And when there was an assault made by the Gentiles and the Jews with their rulers, to use them contumeliously and to stone them: they, understanding it, fled to Lystra and Derbe, cities of Lycaonia, and to the whole country round about: and were there preaching the gospel.* (Acts 14:1-7)

Similarly, the Jews of Thessalonica, filled with envy, covertly organised riots to drive out Saints Paul and Silas. This inadvertently spread the faith to nearby Berea. When the Thessalonians came and persecuted St Paul there too, it prompted him to take the Gospel to Athens. He summoned *"Silas and Timothy"* to join him (Acts 17:10-15). At the Areopagus, St Paul sowed spiritual seeds which have benefitted the world ever since (Acts 17:34).

God's Word cannot be chained (2 Tim 2:9). After being chased out of Ephesus by lunatic pagans, St Paul set his sights on Syria. A plot of the Jews to capture him saw the Spirit send him to Macedonia instead. He took with him men from Berea,

Thessalonica and other parts of his travels (Acts 20:1-4). Thus, persecutions had the cumulative effect of building up a formidable, international team destined to reach all nations.

In God's time, St Paul and St Peter were executed. This achieved in Heaven an eternal reward, and on earth, the establishment of the Roman firmament of the universal Church which has never been overcome. Marvellously, it was the enemies of God who helped dig the foundations. Were these enemies pagans or Jews? Both; but their roles were different. In Jerusalem, Jews had no state powers to crucify Christ, but pushed pagan Pilate into permitting it, exploiting his fear of displeasing Caesar. One generation later in Rome, it was the Gentile Emperor Nero who launched the persecution of Christians.[48] Behind the scenes, it seems Jewish manipulation was at work again, enticing the Emperor to scapegoat the followers of Christ.[49]

Over the next 250 years, ten major persecutions of Christians broke out across the Roman Empire. In their midst, Tertullian testified: "The synagogues of the Jews [are the] fountains of persecution".[50] He explained how the scorpion delivers poison not from the head but its tail, so from beneath was delivered heresy into Christian minds to kill spiritually,

---

[48] Tacitus, *Annals* XV, 38-44.

[49] Jesuit Fathers Llorca, Garcia-Villoslada, Montalban, *Historia de la Iglesia Catolica* (1976), Tome 1, p.178 [translation]: "The Jews were the most active elements in fostering an atmosphere of hatred against the Christians, whom they regarded as supplanters of the Mosaic law… [I]n the context of the martyrdom of SS Peter and Paul, some insinuated that they had been killed due to jealousy from the Jews. With this atmosphere thus established, fuelled by the Jews' hatred, the persecution under Nero is easily comprehensible. As being capable of all sorts of crimes, it was easy to accuse the Christians of causing the Rome fire."

[50] Tertullian, *Scorpiase*, 10.

and persecutions stirred up to kill physically. Tertullian hammers home that the antidote is not violence but readiness for martyrdom. The imitation of Christ arrests the crowds.

'See', they say, 'how Christians love one another', for [the pagans] themselves are animated by mutual hatred; 'how they are ready even to die for one another', for [the pagans] themselves will sooner put to death.[51]

Charity shines more brilliantly when tested amid murderous trials. Love attracts men into the Church as an enticing spiritual sweetness, while the way of the world is bitter. *"Behold I have refined thee, but not as silver, I have chosen thee in the furnace of affliction"* (Is 48:10).

With the eventual conversion of the Roman Empire, the Christian population was relieved of state persecution. Yet it continued elsewhere. The most ferocious persecution of Persian Christians within the Sasanian Empire lasted for forty years under Shapur II (d.379). Hagiographical traditions of Saints Simeon and (his sister) Tarbo report that the Babylonian Jews instigated the persecutions. Modern historians concur.[52]

Judaism set out with a hatred of Jesus which endured even as the Church flourished and expanded.

[T]he most significant text of anti-Christian polemics, the *Toledot Yeshu...* or 'The Jewish Counter-Gospel'... was a virulently defamatory biography of Jesus dating

---

[51] Tertullian, *Apologeticus* 39.

[52] Jacob Neusner, *Babylonian Jewry and Shapur II's persecution of Christianity from 339 to 379 AD*, Hebrew Union College Annual (1972), 43, p.77-102.

back to between the 4th and 8th centuries, disseminated first in Aramaic and later in Hebrew, in slightly different, or grossly divergent versions of the same text, written with the obvious intention of distorting the Christian religious identity by demolishing and ridiculing its memory. Systematic contempt for the figure of Christ and the Virgin Mary… formed the basis of a satirical and mocking tale, presented as a sort of side-show rivalling the Gospels themselves.[53]

The same currents still flow today. Although innumerable Jews bear goodwill to Christians, yet there persists a uniquely Jewish hatred of the Son of God. Its intensity is honestly described by the Jewish writer Albert Memmi, eloquently set out in his 1960s *Portrait of a Jew*:

To the Jew who still believes and professes his own religion, Christianity is the greatest theological and metaphysical usurpation in history; it is a spiritual scandal, a subversion and blasphemy. To all Jews, even if they are atheists, the name of Jesus is the symbol of a threat, of that great threat that has hung over their heads for centuries and which may, any moment, burst forth in catastrophes of which they know neither the cause nor the prevention. That name is part of the accusation,

---

[53] Ariel Toaff, *Blood Passover* (2008), Ch.11, p.187 [translation], continues "It is not surprising that this classic of anti-Christian polemical writing found an attentive and highly satisfied readership among Jews all over the world, from the Islamic countries to Spain and Italy. It is even less surprising that the Jews of Germany adopted this text both enthusiastically and devoutly, as attested by the fact that almost all manuscripts of the *Toledot Yeshu* appear to have been written by Ashkenazi copyists, and that all of the translations of this text into Judeo-Hebraic dialect are in Yiddish."

absurd and frenzied, but so efficiently cruel, that makes social life barely liveable. That name has, in fact, come to be one of the signs, one of the names of the immense apparatus that surrounds the Jew, condemns him and excludes him. I hope my Christian friends will forgive me. That they may better understand, let me say that to the Jews, their God is, in a way, the Devil, if, as they say, the Devil is the symbol and essence of all evil on earth, iniquitous and all-powerful, incomprehensible and bent on crushing helpless human beings.[54]

Memmi is a gifted writer. His tone is fair-minded, mentioning his Christian "friends", asking their forgiveness. We might even like him. Except he is telling us that God is the devil. This most subversive sentiment inexorably disorders societies satanically.

Continuing his thread, Memmi subtly uses madness to justify stamping on images of our crucified Saviour.

One day in Tunis, an idiot Jew (we always had a certain number of them who haunted cemeteries and community gatherings) seeing a Christian funeral pass, was suddenly seized with an uncontrollable rage. Knife in hand, he flung himself on the funeral procession which scattered terror-stricken in all directions. But the idiot, paying no attention to the crowd screaming in terror, rushed straight at the acolyte… grabbed the cross out of his hands, flung it on the ground and trampled it furiously. I did not understand his action until later. Anxiety expresses itself as best it can; the idiot reacted

---

[54] Albert Memmi, *Portrait of a Jew* (1962), p.188-9.

in his own way to our common malaise before that world of crosses, priests and churches, those concentrated symbols of hostility, the strangeness of the world that surrounds us the moment we leave the narrow confines of the ghetto.

It is a miserable state, to reject God's call.

But Memmi does not want us to think assaulting the Cross is madness: rather it is supposed to be insight, righteous. We are supposed to sympathise. It is a voice basically beckoning us to hell. *Abrenuntio!*

However pathetic their appeal, those who insult Jesus must have a change in heart. There is nothing in Jesus to justify rejecting Him. Jews and Gentiles crucified Him. That is too much. We should never excuse the Crucifixion. We have to change, not Jesus, not the Crucified, not the Gospel, not the liturgy, not the Church established by Jesus. Yet before our eyes, the Vatican is surrendering her liturgy, teaching and authority, to please people who hate Jesus Christ.

As it began in Jerusalem, Rome and Persia, there persists an effort to eradicate Christianity from the public space and from people's hearts and minds. With both the Church and her enemies now operating worldwide, there is nowhere for believers to move to, except to be marginalised. Why are crucifixes gone from classrooms? Who hates the Cross so much as to demand its removal?

Whosoever cuts down the Cross, whatever their motives, inevitably exposes society to satan.[55] They might not love

---

[55] *Suffragium paschale*: Say among the heathen, Alleluia. That the Lord reigns from the tree, Alleluia. Let us pray. O God, Who did send Thy Son to suffer death for us upon the Cross, that Thou might deliver us from the power of the enemy...

satan, but aversion to Jesus leaves no other lord. Or why are teachers prosecuted and even imprisoned for refusing to use fake pronouns? That does not happen without planning. It requires a determined demonic force. If the Church does not uphold Christ and the natural law, nobody will. If the Church denies Christ to please the Jews, then the devil will rule, for where Christ is driven out, the devil enters in.

Is Jewish influence amid world powers so great as to be a concern for Christians? In his work *Radici ebraiche del moderno* (*The Hebraic Roots of Modernity*), Italian academic Sergio Quinzio writes:

> If we consider the present reality, one cannot consider the concept of the 'Judaization of the World' to be an exaggeration. Even though the influence of this small race [the Jews] has always been profound throughout the entire history of the Occident... its thinkers and writers never had as much influence previously as they have had in the century in which its complete annihilation was planned... The Judaization of the world which culminates in our century, consists in the implementation of Jewish categories.

Antichrist 'Jewish categories' select Jesus Christ as the ultimate target of cancel culture. Gender ideology, the dismantling of borders, fake democratisation, globalisation, the unification of capital and its unrestricted flow are all expressions of the mercurial Jewish spirit of modernity, becoming instruments to eradicate personality and culture in today's bleak and atomised world. As a Jewish observer succinctly put it, "Modernization, in other words, is about everyone becoming Jewish."[56]

Who is the true light of the world? If anyone denies it is Christ, that is his own tragic choice, leading to eternal darkness. We do not help these to escape that trajectory if we consent to switching off the light. Rather we end up following them to fall into a pit. In this context, St Paul admonishes Christians:

See then the goodness and the severity of God: towards them indeed that are fallen, the severity; but towards thee, the goodness of God, if thou abide in goodness. Otherwise thou also shalt be cut off. (Rom 11:22)

If the Church can now scarcely extend her boundaries geographically, we must grow deeper spiritually — in faith, hope and charity. Being made in the image of God, there is plenty of potential for such growth, for each soul is bigger than the material universe.

The Apostle Paul, evidently, had a total change of heart. He could tell Memmi of his Jewish credentials (Acts 26:5-7) and how he used to *"think that I ought to do many things contrary to the name of Jesus of Nazareth"* (Acts 26:9). Caught then in madness, with all the authority of the chief priests behind him, he projected onto the Church the evil tyrannising his own soul:

Many of the saints did I shut up in prison, having received authority of the chief priests. And when they were put to death, I brought the sentence.

---

[56] Yuri Slezkine, *The Jewish Century* (2019), p.1.

And oftentimes punishing them, in every synagogue, I compelled them to blaspheme: and being yet more mad against them, I persecuted them even unto foreign cities. Whereupon, when I was going to Damascus with authority and permission of the chief priest, at midday, O king, I saw in the way a light from heaven, above the brightness of the sun. (Acts 26:10-13)

The very ferociousness of Saul's persecuting later became within him a motor of contrition, increasing his gratitude and love for God, committing him to the salvation of any and all who would receive it. He understood that we are commanded, not requested or invited, but commanded to love our enemies. St Ephraim describes how it happened.

For when He to whom all things are possible manifested Himself to him, giving up all things else, He spoke to him in humility alone, that He might teach us that a soft tongue is more effectual than everything else against hard thoughts. For neither threats nor words of terror were heard by Paul, but weak words not able to avenge themselves: *'Saul, Saul, why do you persecute Me?'* (Acts 9:4).

But the words which were thought not even capable of avenging themselves, were found to be taking vengeance by drawing him away from the Jews and making him a goodly vessel. He who was full of the bitter will of the Jews, was then filled with the sweet preaching of the Cross. When he was filled with the bitterness of the crucifiers, in his bitterness he made havoc of the churches. But when he was filled with the sweetness of the Crucified, he embittered the synagogues of the crucifiers.[57]

If we Catholics dilute our faith, we are abandoning our enemies instead of helping them. We cannot keep the Faith except by growing in it. Therefore, thank God that opposition, or persecution, provokes both geographical growth and interior growth.

---

[57] St Ephraim the Syrian, *Homily on Our Lord*, 25.

Enduring Hatred Perfects Charity

Blessed are ye when they shall revile you, and persecute you, and speak all that is evil against you, untruly, for My sake. Be glad and rejoice, for your reward is very great in heaven.

Matthew 5:11-12

The geographical expansion of the Church is bounded by the ends of the earth. The overall number of souls saved will not increase beyond the last generation. Such are the limits imposed by space and time. But the spirit cannot be confined, for interior growth has no limit.

Just as persecution provokes a visible growth of the Kingdom of God, so there is an invisible sanctification of souls enjoyed by those who with love endure loathing. *"As silver is tried by fire, and gold in the furnace: so the Lord trieth the hearts"* (Prov 17:3). Hatred sanctifies those who suffer it in imitation of Christ. The good always abounds, for God permits no evil to occur which would be fruitless.

God's ways are not our ways (Is 55:8). Human love is not enough for salvation, not enough for God.

For if you love them that love you, what reward shall you have? Do not even the publicans this? And if you salute your brethren only, what do you more? Do not also the heathens this? (Mt 5:46-47)

To become a son of God, it turns out that the enemy provides the launchpad.

I say to you: Love your enemies. Do good to those who hate you. And pray for those who persecute and slander you. In this way, you shall be sons of your Father, Who is in heaven. (Mt 5:44-45 SB)

How this works in practice is demonstrated by St Stephen. The protomartyr chose the better part and it will not be taken away from him. His killers chose this world and promptly lost their *"place"* (AD 70) and their land (AD 135). Their hatred worked to St Stephen's eternal benefit and for the illumination of the whole Church. And there is no injustice in God's system, for all had the chance to repent, as did one of the witnesses, St Paul.

There is an internal logic as to why even persecutors convert. Anybody reading Acts 6-7 can see how Christlike are the life, final speech and unjust death of St Stephen. Hence God, watching His disciples from Heaven, is reminded, if we may so speak, of the life and crucifixion of His Son. Therefore, it pleases God to hear His martyr's prayers, who being so deeply Christlike, prays for the forgiveness of his enemies.

And they stoned Stephen, invoking and saying: Lord Jesus, receive my spirit. And falling on his knees, he cried with a loud voice, saying: Lord, lay not this sin to their charge. (Acts 7:58-59)

The summation of St Stephen's holiness, the meaning of his life, is identified in the Collects of both his feasts.

> Grant us, we beseech thee, O Lord, so to imitate what we revere, that we may learn to love even our enemies; for we celebrate the finding of the holy body of him who knew how to pray for his very persecutors to our Lord Jesus Christ.[58]

As fallen men, we cannot think or act like this unless the Holy Spirit works it in us. Twice Scripture tells us St Stephen was *"full of the Holy Spirit"* (Acts 6:5; 7:55). The presence of the Spirit means we hate sins, beginning with our own, rather than sinners. It means we recognise any goodness in us is God's gift, and our concurrence is a grace too, rather than a cause for boasting. Being hated does not change this but makes one wonder all the more at how ineffable is the gift.

Not long after St Stephen entered Heaven, the scythe of persecution reaped a Son of Thunder, St James the Apostle, like a ripe fruit. The haters' delight in this spurred the arrest of St Peter.

> *Herod the king stretched forth his hands, to afflict some of the church. And he killed James, the brother of John, with the sword. And seeing that it pleased the Jews, he proceeded to take up Peter also... And Peter coming to himself, said: Now I know in very deed that the Lord hath sent His angel and hath delivered me out of the hand of Herod and from all the expectation of the people of the Jews.* (Acts 12:1-3,11)

---

[58] *In Inventione S Stephani* (3rd August, see also 26th Dec), *Oratio.*

The mildness of the first Fisherman under threat of death allowed for a deepening of his faith, the basis of charity, to the benefit of the whole Church.

Murderous opposition provides the occasion for supreme virtue. Whereas friends of St Paul wept because Jews sought to put him in binds, the Apostle himself was confused by their tears, declaring himself ready to die for the Name of Jesus:

A certain prophet, named Agabus... took Paul's girdle: and binding his own feet and hands, he said: Thus saith the Holy Ghost: The man whose girdle this is, the Jews shall bind in this manner in Jerusalem and shall deliver him into the hands of the Gentiles... Then Paul answered and said: What do you mean, weeping and afflicting my heart? For I am ready not only to be bound, but to die also in Jerusalem, for the name of the Lord Jesus. (Acts 21:10-13)

In a world without sin, without evil seeking to dominate, it would be difficult to see how this level of love could be realised or showcased for our imitation.

Jesus told His disciples to *"pray for those who... calumniate you"* (Mt 5:44). Some of those who listened to the Lord were later victims of life-threatening lies — Christians being accused of idolatry, incest, infanticide and cannibalism. Systematically perpetuating such vile defamation is driven by hatred, not simple misunderstanding. Tertullian identifies, again, the Jews as the most vigorous source of these slanders: "For what other set of men is the seed-plot of all the calumny against us?"[59] Is Tertullian guilty of hatred for this, or is he

---

[59] Tertullian, *Ad Nationes*, I, 14.

telling the truth? We are to face the truth and pray for our enemies.

God loves those who patiently endure even the enmity of satanists. The following verses advert to the inviolability of freewill, of those who, with little worldly power, patiently await the new Jerusalem from above.

Behold, I have given before thee a door opened, which no man can shut: because thou hast a little strength and hast kept My word and hast not denied My Name. Behold, I will bring of the synagogue of Satan, who say they are Jews and are not, but do lie. Behold, I will make them to come and adore before thy feet. And they shall know that I have loved thee. Because thou hast kept the word of My patience, I will also keep thee from the hour of temptation, which shall come upon the whole world to try them that dwell upon the earth. (Apoc 3:8-10)

The *"synagogue of Satan"* will finally adore before the feet of those who, for the sake of Christ, endure their persecutions without losing faith. The last verse tells us this struggle will go global. Reward for victory is eternal.

It is dangerous to pretend that the *"synagogue of Satan"* is weak or the points raised by the Apocalypse are passed. Those *"who say they are Jews and are not"* (Apoc 2:9; 3:9) maintain a spiritual opposition to truth. With validity for today, St John illustrates the paralysing control exercised through *"fear of the Jews"* (Jn 7:13; 9:22; 19:38; 20:19): over society at large; over their own; and, periodically, even over the Church hierarchy.

Regarding the general population, Scripture says many saw Jesus' goodness, *"Yet no man spoke openly of Him, for fear of the Jews"* (Jn 7:13). Are people afraid today that they will be marginalised if they confess their Christian faith? Even bishops are afraid to preach plainly.

Jesus came to defeat the devil's darkness, to restore spiritual sight. To demonstrate this, He healed the man born blind, who, now seeing, confessed Him to be a *"prophet"* and *"Lord"* (Jn 9:17,38). But his parents prevaricated.

> *These things his parents said, because they feared the Jews: for the Jews had already agreed among themselves that if any man should confess Him to be Christ, he should be put out of the synagogue.* (Jn 9:22)

The higher up one is, the harder it is to give witness. Among the members of the Sanhedrin, Nicodemus had been too afraid to visit Jesus openly, so *"at first came to Jesus by night"* (Jn 19:39). Joseph of Arimathea was also *"a disciple of Jesus, but secretly for fear of the Jews"* (Jn 19:38).

What is more powerful than controlling fear? It paralysed good men in Jesus' time and it paralyses good men today. Fearlessness is more powerful. The fearlessness of the few dissolves the bonds of timidity imposed on the many.

God the Holy Ghost gifts us with fearless fortitude. Then the fear-mongers become fearful. While Christ was preaching and working miracles, the Jews had been afraid to contradict Him, because they were *"afraid of the multitude"* (Mt 21:26). In time, after intimidating and manipulating the people, eventually they seized Him and had Him killed. Although the Mother of God never faltered, it seemed that the little flock of followers would be finished. But their fear was suddenly banished when

> *the doors were shut, where the disciples were gathered together, for fear of the Jews, Jesus came and stood in the midst and said to them: Peace be to you.* (Jn 20:19)

Perfect love, which *"casts out fear"* (1 Jn 4:18), then advanced as an avalanche at the Day of Pentecost. Although the would-be-controllers charged St Peter and St John *"not to speak at all, nor teach in the name of Jesus"* (Acts 4:18), the Apostles effectively laughed at them. Flailing,

> *they threatening, sent them away, not finding how they might punish them, because of the people; for all men glorified what had been done.* (Acts 4:21)

The *"people"* have power when they glorify God. Our liturgy is our best defence. Time and again, the wicked authorities sought to cow the people with fear (Acts 5:13). But arresting the Apostles once more, they *"brought them without violence; for they feared the people, lest they should be stoned"* (Acts 5:26).

Today's Church features the same dynamic. Francis' team would gladly do more to weaken the traditional liturgy, even forbidding it altogether. But they fear the faithful's response. Good priests, bishops and cardinals would gladly speak out against this godless infidelity, but are afraid of those men of violence who seem to have born away the kingdom of heaven. The wreckers of tradition call themselves Catholic *"and are not"* (see Apoc 3:9).

Normally, one should fear to cross the hierarchy of the Church (Acts 5:1-11). But *"fear of the Lord"* compels us to do so, as escalating numbers of prelates oppose God, like members of the Sanhedrin toward Jesus. The same forces are at work.

Pointedly and repeatedly, Scripture says *"the Jews"* failed to understand or outright refused Jesus' teaching. They denied that the Temple is His Body (Jn 2:19-22); rejected the doctrine of the Real Presence (Jn 6:41,53); preferred worldly interpretations (Jn 7:35; 8:22); contested His pre-existence (Jn 8:58-59); rejected His Divinity (Jn 10:30-33); and accused Jesus of serving satan (Mt 12:24). This contrary spirit is still strong in the world, intimidating Catholic prelates. Once again, the disciples are afraid of the Jews.

Is it fair to take the constricting *"fear"* of NT times as a model for what is happening at present? Yes. That is part of the reason God has given us the NT. Nothing essential has changed since then but propaganda seeks to turn the facts on their head. Modern man has been programmed to believe that the Catholic Church is historically an association of antisemites, a clique of authoritarian controllers who loathe freedom almost as much as they hate the Jews. Even bishops have accepted this rot. But it is a lie so grotesque as to be blasphemous. The Church is of Jesus, Jesus is Jewish and Jesus is God.

The great lie of Christian antisemitism is impossibly incoherent.[60] Obviously, antisemitism could not have existed in the early Church. The Holy Family are Jewish. The Apostles are Jewish. The disciples on Pentecost are Jewish.

---

[60] The term antisemite, invariably used to mean anti-Jewish, is itself outrageous, discounting other Semitic peoples as if they do not even exist, such as Arabs, Amharas and Aramæans. It is a further contradiction to label these as antisemitic.

Following Jesus, they fulfilled and upheld in Christian fullness the promises and law of the Old Covenant.

For centuries after, the Church remained politically weak and persecuted. She suffered molestation and murder from the Jews with the meekness of lambs to the slaughter. St Stephen set the model for all in the imitation of Christ: lift not a finger against those who hate and persecute you, but pray for their forgiveness. This does not mean one has no right to justice or self-defence, but that these too should be sought with charity. This is the eternal nature of the Church. This is why she grows. If she were to hate, if she were antisemitic, she would disappear.

In modern times, false ideologies fuelled on Judaism, including messianic nationalism, so weakened the Christian order, that doors were opened to ~~demons~~* like Hitler.[61] Some leading Jews have decently acknowledged that brave Christians took risks to help them during WWII.[62] But with passing years, other Jews have vociferously complained that the socially weakened Church failed to protect them from the very forces for which they had paved the way by the dismantling of Christendom and their incessant revolutions.

[61] Yuri Slezkine, *The Jewish Century* (2019), p.44-45, "Nationalism meant that every nation was to become Jewish. Every single one of them had been *'wounded for our transgressions'* and *'bruised for our iniquities'* (Is 53:5). Every people was chosen, every land promised, every capital Jerusalem. Christians could give up trying to love their neighbors as themselves — because they had finally discovered who *they* were (French, Flemish, Swedish). They were like Jews in that they loved themselves as a matter of faith and had no use for miracles."

[62] AJC, *The Image of the Jews in Catholic Teaching* (1961), I, "When Hitlerism — an essentially pagan movement generated chiefly by social and economic forces unrelated to religion — unleashed the most terrible of all persecutions, some devout and valiant Christians courageously saved Jewish lives; but the majority of Christendom stood indifferently by."

* Author's note, Sep 2025. I regret using this unjust term to describe Hitler, who was likely a better man than Churchill, Roosevelt or Stalin, who sold out their nations to the Jews, thereby costing millions of lives. Being over-cautious, Part II of this book still lends too much credence to holocaust propaganda.

When *The Deputy* was disgracefully staged (1963) and *Hitler's Pope* was libellously published (1999), these enemies of mankind over-played their hand. Contrary to the malicious inventions of this theatre piece and book, anyone who cares for truth knows that Pope Pius XII saved thousands of Jewish lives and that he and countless Catholics took great risks to do so. To accuse them of being complicit executioners is breathtaking. It goes beyond personality disorder. Some young Jews even accused the generation of Jews who suffered in WWII of being blameworthy because they did not defeat their enemies! The young Sadducees never faced tyranny but excoriate everyone else sooner than recognise their own fragility.

The hysterical accusations against Pius XII, which Yad Vashem sustains, have helped to expose the boldness of those rewriting history. Wikipedia platforms these lies. But the revisionists cannot falsify the NT. Here we find a pattern of truth which God wants us to know. St Stephen, at his brutal martyrdom, forgives. Tradition tells that St James the Just, thrown from the pinnacle of the Temple then clubbed to death, also forgives.[63] In Scripture again, we read that St Paul,

---

[63] St James, Apostle and Bishop of Jerusalem, is said to have resembled his cousin Jesus in physiognomy and physical features more than did any other man. The devil had wanted to throw Jesus from the Temple; instead his agents did it to a brother of the Lord. Lying broken in body at the bottom and being clubbed to death, St James prayed for his persecutors, as recorded by Eusebius, *Ecclesiastical History*, II, 23 and in the Office of his Feast (1st May), Matins, *Lectio* VI: "His legs were broken by the fall, and he was well-nigh dead, but he lifted up his hands towards heaven, and prayed to God for the salvation of his murderers, saying: 'Lord, forgive them, for they know not what they do.' As he said this, one that stood by smote him grievously upon the head with a fuller's club, and he resigned his spirit to God." Evidently his soul and his charity were consummately intact, resembling Jesus more than his body did (Ps 90:11-12).

whom the Jews had whipped with some two hundred strokes (2 Cor 11:24), was willing to delay his final union with Christ if he could win the salvation of brother Jews: *"Optabam enim ipse ego anathema esse a Christo pro fratribus meis qui sunt cognati mei secundum carnem"* (Rom 9:3). When else has such an expression of love ever been written?

By grace, odium polishes love, adding lustre. The evident truth about St Stephen and Pius XII, who were falsely accused by the Jews, are bookends to two thousand years of historical reality running in between. Like their Master, they overcame calumny by self-sacrifice, exhibiting the unchanging nature of the Church. Not all her members have lived up to this. Catholics have sinned in their treatment of Jews. For her part, the Church preaches against this, teaches against it, legislates against it. She is the Bride of Christ: betrothed to the most famous Jew ever.

To call the Church hateful is a projection. It is an accusation made by those who hate the Church because they hate Christ because they hate themselves for not loving Him. This is how they appraise the world and judge others, as if everyone else also has hearts like flint.

To rescue those who can be rescued, the Church must be herself. She does not need to change; her teaching does not need to change; her liturgy does not need to change; her Sacraments do not need to change. In carrying out the works of salvation, the Church has nothing for which to apologise, as Jesus Christ has nothing for which to apologise.

Enemies find fault with the essence of the Church although sin belongs entirely with men. They try to make Catholics ashamed, but no one ought to apologise for being Catholic. If a public apology is owed, it is for failure to be Catholic. To apologise for anything in the name of the Church is to shift the blame where it does not belong — onto Christ's Holy Bride. Rather, Catholics must repent for lukewarmness, for not being Catholic to the core.

> *For he that shall be ashamed of Me and of My words, in this adulterous and sinful generation: the Son of man also will be ashamed of him, when He shall come in the glory of His Father with the holy angels.* (Mk 8:38)

Let nothing extinguish Catholic witness. If we look to the saints — both those who have been and those around us — then our enemies cannot make us bitter. None will contest that love kindles love; it turns out that enduring hatred does too, to the eternal frustration of the devil (Prov 25:21-22; Rom 12:20-21).

WITNESSING TO THE CHURCH'S DIVINE ORIGIN

God shall let me see over my enemies: slay them not, lest at any time my people forget.

Psalm 58:12

Disordered intellects provoke clarifications of the splendour of truth — heresy purifies doctrine. Disordered wills result in an increase of love — hatred perfects charity. So, a disordered response to God's Self-Revelation serves only to reinforce it — Judaism witnesses to the divine origin of the Catholic Church by affirming that the whole OT is of God. Moreover, Judaism's rejection of Jesus' Divinity has had consequences which have made it impossible for Judaism to keep even the externals of the Old Covenant.

The invincible divine economy, whereby God's enemies become His *"footstool"* (Ps 109:1), proves that the Bible is from God. Only God can disclose the distant future, which He does with innumerable scriptural prophecies. It further exhibits omnipotent wisdom that He underscores the veracity of Scripture through the exertions of His enemies and, simultaneously, their own efforts guarantee the failure of their plans. Hence God can afford to *"sit"* (Ps 109:1) in sovereign leisure while all inexorably proceeds toward His triumph.

The Lord reveals layers of truth through parables; a simple situation is presented which carries an infinitely greater meaning. As the great composer, Jesus teaches their meaning to His closest disciples and this is passed on through Apostolic tradition and the Fathers of the Church. Whether or not we embrace the teaching depends on our good will. As cases accumulate of words, events and traditions, which are truest in Jesus Christ, only men of ill will can deny that the whole is of God.

St Augustine explains how Adam's *"deep sleep"* points to the Passion of Christ. St Jerome tells us how the inebriation of naked Noah foretells Jesus' Sacrifice on Calvary. St Justin argues that the ladder of which Jacob dreamt signifies the Cross. St Gregory of Nyssa identifies the weary outstretched arms of Moses with Christ Crucified. St Ambrose sees Jonah's volunteering to be thrown in the sea as the Lamb of God going meekly to His execution. St Gregory the Great correlates Samson's surprise victory in Gaza with Jesus' defeat of death. The honest must admit that the OT is all about Jesus Christ.

God searches our hearts further by inviting us to honour the Mother of His Son. Protestants boast about biblical knowledge. They might admit the prefigurations of Jesus, but their hearts are too hard to be amazed with St Irenæus that Eve's fall in Eden has been reversed by the Mother of God. Will Evangelicals confess that the Virgin Mary's victory over the Antichrist is prefigured by Judith beheading Holofernes? And by Queen Esther saving her people from genocide? And by Jael cracking open Sisera's skull? There are plenty of other examples. It is perverse to dismiss these, to refuse to acknowledge the unending honours which God has poured upon the Woman He created to be the true *"mother of all the living"* (cf. Gen 3:20). Protestants will have to answer to God as to why they claim to know the Bible yet deny the superlative role assigned to the Virgin Mary.

What of Judaism's role? Open minds cannot deny these divine prefigurations, but skeptics might object that geniuses of old had conspired after the Crucifixion to create all the stories together. Neither Protestants, nor honest atheists, nor even Jews can do this, because Judaism itself insists on the age and integrity of the OT. The very followers of those who called for Jesus' death are the ones who defend the antiquity of written and ritual sources, which testify in numerous ways that the entire Old Covenant was always God's preparation for the New. No sane person can accuse these Jews of conniving to uphold the Church. Yet this they achieve! It is a work of God, He Who separates sides in order to fill the opening with life, and with a plan to bring the sides together.

The Excellence of Separation and Reunion
To maintain unity is good. But somehow God sees a better option in allowing separation, followed by reunion, so that the final result is greater than the initial whole.

In the first three days of Creation, God separates day from night, heavens from earth, land from sea. Then on days four, five and six, God fills these spaces with sun and moon, with birds and sea beasts, with animals and man. Separation makes distinct forms which are to be filled with grades of meaning. In fact, the Hebrew words for *"create"* (בָּרָא) might have origins in the splicing of a reed to make a pen. That is certainly a separation used for expressing meaning — words.

To express the highest meanings, God uses man. The separation of Cain and Abel is followed through the Torah by the theme of brothers reuniting, reaching its high point with Moses and Aaron. Before this even began, we see in Adam and Eve the necessity of a certain separation before union. Adam is created; Eve came out of Adam, a separation; then Adam goes into Eve and new life is conceived, achieving a higher union — three from one is better than two from one.

This inter-personal picture paints a cosmic one. Creation came out of God — not as a pantheistic emanation but out of His understanding (Logos) and His efficacious love (Will), that is, His Son and His Spirit. God goes into His creation in the Incarnation, planting His Seed in the New Eden. And creation brings forth new life for eternity: the Church. The unity increases as more persons are drawn in, more life both by numbers and growth in holiness.

Gratuitously, God wants to do this and gratefully the Church wants Him to do it. So is the love of Bridegroom and Bride. Eve had to come from Adam as creation necessarily had to come from God. Adam and Eve could not suitably have been made separately, as this would symbolise Creation arising independently of God, which is a foul dualism. All this is instructive for the relationship of Jews and Gentiles.

In male-female complementarity, the male represents the divine, the female the created. The male represents form, which is simple and universal. The female represents matter, which is composed and particular. In the Incarnation, there is

One Jesus in relation to billions of human beings; He is the One form, Who informs all the others (Jn 1:9).

Drawing an analogy, with Christ as the New Adam, the Jews are the *"rib"* taken from God's side, around which is built up Christ's Mystical Body, His Bride. The first bone of the Church is Jewish — formed by the Patriarchs and Prophets, Our Lady and the Apostles. Then the Body is fleshed out by people *"of all nations, and tribes, and peoples, and tongues"* (Apoc 7:9). This whole Body is of God: *"Bone of my bones, and flesh of my flesh"* (Gen 2:23).[64]

The Jewish people are smaller than other nations but are called by their history to carry the love of God to inform the world. With the gain of separation and reunion in mind, although the Jews have been broken off *"because of unbelief"* (Rom 11:20), St Paul, recalling their origins, esteems them the natural branch, so God can easily *"graft them in again"* (Rom 11:23).

---

[64] By no means is this reflection meant to support the catastrophic kabbalist view, with a claimed foundation in the Talmud and Torah, that Jewish souls are divine, even part of God, while Gentile souls are animalistic, even evil. Rabbi Avraham Grodzinski (d.1944), *Torat Avraham, Am Segulah*, 1 & 5; cited by Hanan Balk, *Ḥakirah 16, The Soul of a Jew and the Soul of a Non-Jew* (2013) p.54-55, summarised this teaching of the Zohar, saying that the Jewish soul is "a different being, a new creation, of which nothing compares in the entire human species... The most praiseworthy and chosen of the class of men does not approach even the most worthless of the class of Israel."

There are endless similar sources along these lines. Although I would need another chapter to demonstrate it, I believe that what is commonly called 'racism' today does not compare to this theological chauvinism; further, that 'antisemitism' is suspected by some to be everywhere, is largely a projection by those people who look down on non-Jews as animalistic, even evil. Also, the notion that human beings have two different, opposing origins, the Jews from God and the Gentiles from evil, is the cause of a similar notion among Freemasons whereby they bond together while have no compunction about exploiting non-members as if they were sub-human (which I have picked up in conversations with Freemasons).

Each soul has the chance to choose. Samuel exhorted the Hebrews,

Fear the Lord, and serve him in truth and from your whole heart. For you have seen the great works that he has done among you. But if you persevere in wickedness, both you and your king will perish together. (1 Kgs 12:24-25)

We recall that Jesus' great *"works"* were seen by the Jews, yet many chose to reject Him (Jn 5:36; 9:4; 10:25-39; 15:24). Christ the King did not perish but ascended to Heaven. The *"king"* who *"will perish"* is the Antichrist.

Whom shall we serve? Those who choose to serve the Lord testify to His perfection. Those who choose to rebel testify differently but also to His perfection — that His Justice cannot be mocked and His Mercy cannot be exploited.

Psalm 58 *"slay them not"*

Man's beginnings in Eden speak of God's design, while present divisions tell the same story. That God-With-Us, Jesus, is promised by the whole OT is testified today by the very people who rejected Him. St Augustine explains the predictions of God's Incarnation and work of Redemption,

These predictions, I say, have been published by all the promises given to that nation, by all the prophecies, the institution of the priesthood, the sacrifices, the temple, and, in short, by all their sacred mysteries... The sacrifice of Him in Whom the truth, long veiled under mystic promises, is revealed, having been offered, those sacrifices by which it was prefigured are finally abolished by the utter destruction of the Jewish temple. The Jewish nation, itself rejected because of unbelief, being now rooted out from its own land, is dispersed to every region of the world, in order that it may carry everywhere the Holy Scriptures, and that in this way our adversaries themselves may bring before mankind the testimony furnished by the prophecies concerning Christ and His Church, thus precluding the possibility of the supposition that these predictions were forged by us to suit the time; in which prophecies, also, the unbelief of these very Jews is foretold.[65]

Judaism's attempt to cling to the Old Covenant proves it was not invented by the Church after Christ. When the Doctor of Grace writes that the very unbelief of the Jews is foretold, he cites Psalm 58.

God shall let me see over my enemies: slay them not, lest at any time my people forget. Scatter them by thy power; and bring them down, O Lord, my protector: For the sin of their mouth, and the word of their lips: and let them be taken in their pride. (Ps 58:12-13)[66]

St Augustine explains how Jewish disbelief helps to serve the conversions to Christ of disbelieving heathens.

Scatter them by thy power (Ps 58:12). Now this thing has been done: throughout all nations there have been scattered abroad the Jews, witnesses of their own

---

[65] St Augustine, *Epistle 137*, 15-16.

[66] Amid the sins *"of their mouth, and the word of their lips"*, champions of Masoretic supremacy have lead Protestants and Catholics into mis-numbering this Psalm (often called Psalm 59). But it is much harder to hide the meaning.

iniquity and our truth. They have themselves writings, out of which has been prophesied Christ, and we hold Christ. And if sometime perchance any heathen man shall have doubted, when we have told him the prophecies of Christ, at the clearness whereof he is amazed, and wondering has supposed that they were written by ourselves, then out of the copies of the Jews we prove, how this thing so long time before had been foretold. See after what sort, by means of our enemies, we confound other enemies.[67]

The separation of Jews and Christians is fruitful. That the Jews maintain almost the same OT text as Christians is proof that Christians have not forged it. In any case, it is impossible to remove the prophecies of Jesus from the OT without rejecting the whole of it and every part, as He is present throughout at multiple levels.

Is the rabbinic failure to see Jesus Christ in the OT wilful, culpable? Certain messianic Jews allege that it is because Jesus is so clearly prophesied in Isaiah 53 that this chapter has been removed from the reading schema in synagogues.[68]

A more ancient indicator of ill-will, still studied today, appears in a Midrash on the words of Genesis: *"Then Esau ran to meet his brother, and embraced him: and clasping him fast about the neck, and kissing him, wept"* (Gen 33:4). Christians, following St Paul, reckon Jacob and Esau to

---

[67] St Augustine, *Enarration on Psalm 58*, I, 22.

[68] Eitan Bar, One for Israel, *Isaiah 53: The Forbidden Chapter* (article Oct 2017), "Long ago the rabbis used to read Isaiah 53 in synagogues, but after the chapter caused arguments and great confusion the rabbis decided that the simplest thing would be to just take that prophecy out of the Haftarah readings in synagogues."

symbolise Church and Synagogue, whereby this scene speaks of a final reconciliation. Jews reverse the roles, claiming Jacob represents Jews and Esau represents Gentiles, and instead of seeing the scene as a happy reunion, Rabbi Yannai poisons it, claiming an insertion of Masoretic dots here indicates a hidden teaching,

> That [Esau] came not to kiss [Jacob] but to bite him, but our ancestor Yaakov's neck became like marble and that wicked man's teeth were blunted. Hence, *'and they wept'* teaches that [Jacob] wept because of his neck and [Esau] wept because of his teeth.[69]

This unhappy interpretation hangs on a Hebrew pun, the word *nishkek* (kiss) being reread as *nashakh* (bite). Ominously, this latter term is also used for usury, for taking a bite out of your brother — a pound of flesh, as it were. The rabbi's reinterpretation showcases the longstanding contempt Jewish leaders have for Gentiles.

Commenting further on Psalm 58, St Augustine writes:

> *Slay not them, lest sometime they forget Your law* (Ps 58:12); in order that the nation of Jews might remain and by it remaining, the number of Christians might increase. Certainly Jews remain throughout the nations… they hold the law, hold the Prophets; read all things, sing all things: the light of the Prophets they see not therein, which is Christ Jesus. Not only do they not see Him now, when He is sitting in Heaven: but not even at that time… when humble among them He was walking, and

---

[69] *Midrash Bereshit Rabbah,* 78.

they were made guilty by shedding the Blood of the Same; but not all.[70]

This Psalm was first written about Saul trying to murder the loyal hero David. David had just slain Goliath, signifying Jesus' victory over death. David's refusal to wear armour for this shows Jesus overcame sin in His immaculate Humanity. Further, David married Saul's daughter Michol, signifying the care of God's people passing from Saul to David, that is, from the Old to the New Covenant. She who was once daughter of the king rises to become bride of the new king. The Daughter of Sion becomes the Bride of Christ.

In this context, whatever way Saul tried to kill David, he failed. So the Sanhedrin's attempts to do away with Jesus all failed, above all in His Passion and Resurrection. In every generation, Jews have converted to Christ. Thus Saul's own children loved and protected David. No matter how many officers Saul sent to apprehend David, these ended up prophesying the truth, until finally, in the strangest circumstances, the same happened with Saul himself: *"This gave occasion to a proverb: What! is Saul too among the prophets?"* (1 Kgs 19:24). So through the generations and centuries, Israel testifies to Christ and His Church, even when they seek to destroy her.

Vitally, St Augustine never lets us overlook love. The passage quoted above ended with "but not all…". Our *Doctor gratiæ* goes on to write:

This even today we commend to the notice of your Love. Not all: because many of them were turned to

---

[70] St Augustine, *Enarration on Psalm 58*, II, 1.

Him whom they slew, and by believing on Him, they obtained pardon even for the shedding of His Blood: and they have given an example for men; how they ought not to despair that sin of whatsoever kind would be remitted to them, since even the killing of Christ was remitted to them confessing.

We have all sinned. We all need the mercy of God. We cannot expect mercy for ourselves if we deny it to others. The separation of Jews from Christians is bearing fruit. The unity of the Church is growing in the harvest rendered for Heaven. When God is satisfied with the increase, then an indelible seal will be bestowed on the whole by the conversion of the Jews themselves.[71] The separation will be over and all will know that the whole course of history has been a work of God and that it was told long in advance by the creation of the first family in Eden, just as the Torah relates.

To summarise: it is precisely because of Judaism's long-standing opposition to the Church that Orthodox Jews are such credible witnesses against the false suspicion of pagans, heathens and modern atheists that the OT Scriptures were composed post-Crucifixion. Likewise, Judaism's yearning to rebuild the altar and Holy Place in Jerusalem testifies that God desires a perpetual sacrifice. This ongoing divine desire is satisfied only by Holy Mass. That this arrangement originates from divine Wisdom is confirmed by the otherwise surprising fact that the most ardent witnesses to OT

---

[71] Ps 58:14-16 might even suggest the Church's enemies will end up coming to her in search of the Holy Eucharist, the heavenly bread for which they are starving.

prefigurations include both the lovers and the opponents of Him Who fulfils them, Jesus.[72]

Adding a further touch of God's transcendent artistry, it is the very denial of Jesus Christ's Divinity which has prevented the deniers, until today, from fulfilling their alternative dream — the rebuilding of the Temple in Jerusalem.

Judaism Indirectly Caused Islam

The rationale given for executing Jesus was that otherwise the Romans would take away the Temple and land from the Jews.

> *The chief priests therefore, and the Pharisees, gathered a council, and said: What do we, for this man doth many miracles? If we let Him alone so, all will believe in Him; and the Romans will come, and take away our place and nation.* (Jn 11:47-48)

Caiaphas calculated to have Jesus killed, which obviously backfired. It was because they killed the true Messiah that they went on looking for false messiahs. And these, being godless revolutionaries, brought the wrath of the Romans on the whole nation such that the Temple was lost in AD 70 and soon afterwards the failed insurrection of the messianic pretender Simon bar Kochba was punished with the eviction of the Jews from Jerusalem and from most of the Holy Land

---

[72] St Thomas, *Commentary on Romans* 11:11-16, extends hope from St Paul, explaining "the fall of the Jews is not universal" and "that their fall was neither useless nor irreparable". On the usefulness, St Thomas says, "on account of their impenitence they have been scattered among all the nations. As a result, Christ and the Church had from the books of the Jews testimony to the Christian faith helpful in converting the Gentiles, who might have suspected that the prophecies concerning Christ, which the preachers of the faith brought forward, were fabricated, if they had not been proven by the testimony of the Jews."

— *"From him who has not, even what he has will be taken away"* (Mt 13:12 RSVCE). St Augustine elucidates the theology behind the history.

> That they might not lose their place, they killed the Lord; and they lost it, even because they killed. Therefore that city, being one earthly, did bear the figure of a certain city everlasting in the Heavens: but when that which was signified began more evidently to be preached, the shadow, whereby it was being signified, was thrown down: for this reason in that place now the temple is no more, which had been constructed for the image of the future Body of the Lord.[73]

Following a very different strategy to non-believing Jews, Christians did not rebel against the Romans but by charity, patient suffering and martyrdom, the disciples of Jesus conquered the whole empire and went on to the rest of the world. (This struggle is not over but the victory is sure.)

What happened, meanwhile, to the followers of pharisaical Judaism? Because they preferred the way of the world to the Way of the Lord, they lost the Temple, without which they cannot even make a *prima facie* claim to keep the Law of Moses, for example by offering the sacrifices commanded in the Torah at God's chosen *"place"* (הַמָּקוֹם Dt 12:5-26). And with a touch of divine irony, it did not stop there: by denying the Divinity of Jesus in favour of a messiah yet to come, Judaism accidentally played midwife to the ferocious force that has kept them off the Temple Mount to this day: Islam.

---

[73] St Augustine, *Enarration on Psalm 64,* 1 [also 8].

If Jews could take Temple Mount and rebuild the Temple, the world would end soon after. Otherwise a man could reject Jesus Christ and claim to be fulfilling God's commandments. His claim would be false but he could argue: did God not command Jews to follow Moses? Precluding any attempt at this argument, God has permitted that Muslims have built the Dome on the Rock on the only spot where the Temple can stand.[74] The Muslims are not ready to surrender this site to the Jews. God is not ready to end the world. Not yet.

Yet Islam would not have arisen were it not for Judaism's rejection of Jesus and confining the Torah to a materialistic interpretation. This refusal and reduction, combined with conditions prevailing in seventh century Arabia, set the stage for satan to erect a false prophet and launch Islam.

In one of the most famous verses of the Torah, God promised that He would raise up another like Moses. It came to be understood that this second one, the Messiah, would save the world: *"I will raise them up a prophet out of the midst of their brethren like to thee"* (Dt 18:18). St Peter explicitly taught that this refers to Jesus (Acts 3:22). The failure of many Jews to accept the Gospel left a longing among them for the *"prophet"* of whom Moses spoke. Meanwhile, there was also an ardent longing among some on the Arabian peninsula for pure monotheism, for they lived amidst child-sacrificing polytheistic idolatry.[75]

---

[74] Jeremy Sharon, *The Jerusalem Post* (10th Dec 2018), "Asked if restarting Jewish animal sacrifices on the Temple Mount would cause… conflict with the Muslim world, which views al-Aqsa Mosque at the site as one of the holiest places in Islam, Weiss said emphatically that this should not be a concern and that only Jewish courage to rebuild the Temple would end anti-Jewish sentiment and actions."

[75] Ibn Ishaq [d.761], *Sirat Rasul Allah (Life of Mohammed)* (1989), p.66, 99.

In parallel, bitterly resenting the Arabian tribesmen who got the better of them in conflicts, Jews viscerally condemned these tribes for polytheism, boasting that they alone were God's people of the scriptures, and threatened that, with the aid of the prophet who was soon to come, they would kill the tribesmen who opposed them. All this wrong-headedness fed into Islam which adopted the selfsame high claims for itself: people of the Book set for world rule.[76]

Mohammed thought the "religion of Abraham" (*Hanif*, pure monotheism) was nowhere to be found in the Middle East.[77] He overlooked Christianity, falsely supposing it to be at odds with Abraham. To fill the perceived void, he styled himself Moses' promised prophet of Abraham's simple monotheism.[78] He took the differences between Christians and Jews on Deuteronomy 18:18 as his own opening. Shamelessly, Mohammed claimed that he fulfilled the Torah, that he was the "brother of Moses who confirms what Moses brought".[79] But why was Mohammed's outrageous claim of being the promised prophet accepted by anyone at all?[80]

Firstly, without Christ to give the interpretation of love, to translate the priesthood, to raise our understanding from the visible, material and carnal to the invisible, spiritual and

---

[76] Ibn Ishaq, *Sirat Rasul Allah (Life of Mohammed)* (1989), p.93, 254.

[77] Ibn Ishaq, *Sirat Rasul Allah (Life of Mohammed)* (1989), p.103.

[78] Ibn Ishaq, *Sirat Rasul Allah (Life of Mohammed)* (1989), p.252, 261, 269. Abu Amir told Mohammed that he did not have the religion of Abraham, but the objection was not sustained (p.278).

[79] Ibn Ishaq, *Sirat Rasul Allah (Life of Mohammed)* (1989), p.255-56.

[80] Anne Barbeau Gardiner, *Culture Wars Magazine, The Jewish Origins of Islam* (1st Feb 2018), referencing Edouard-Marie Gallez, *Le messie et son prophète: Aux origines de l'Islam* (2005).

eternal, the OT could be twisted to justify lawless violence. Mohammed's violence derives in part from a poor grasp of the OT. It is the sword, not truth, that persuades Islam's adherents.

Then besides reasons of intimidation and bribery, Mohammed's claim was supported by a rabbi who supposedly converted to Islam while identifying Mohammed as 'the one who is to come' as promised by the Torah. It was asserted, contrary to everything verifiable by literacy, that the Torah is Allah's book which speaks of God's covenant with the Muslims through Mohammed.[81]

Then as now, Islam acknowledged that the Torah speaks of Jesus and that the Gospel confirms the Torah, but used this fact to claim irrationally that Christians and Jews cancel each other out.[82] Muslims accuse Jews and Christians of having doctored the Scriptures. But if the Jews did this before Jesus Christ, how is it that all of Scripture points to Him? And if it were done after Christ, how is it that Jews and Christians largely agree on the text of the OT?

With sacrilegious audacity, Mohammed claims, "Abraham was neither a Jew nor a Christian but a Muslim".[83] Though we have no reason to think Abraham ever visited Arabia, Mohammed taught that Abraham not only worshipped at the *Ka'ba* (their temple) in Mecca, but that Abraham and Ishmael actually built it.[84] Islam decisively rejects God's Revelation

---

[81] Ibn Ishaq, *Sirat Rasul Allah (Life of Mohammed)* (1989), p.240-41, 250.

[82] Ibn Ishaq, *Sirat Rasul Allah (Life of Mohammed)* (1989), p.258.

[83] Quran 3:67.

[84] Ibn Ishaq, *Sirat Rasul Allah (Life of Mohammed)* (1989), p.102, 239.

by confounding the descent of the promised prophet. It asserts he came through Ishmael (a child of carnality) rather than through Isaac (a child miraculously conceived). This obscures our spiritual adoption in Christ. Many Muslims erroneously claim it was Ishmael rather than Isaac whom Abraham bound for sacrifice on Mount Moriah. But Jesus confirms that the OT does not rest on Ishmael but on Isaac, the father of Jacob, from whom the twelve tribes of Israel stem.[85] Without Isaac the OT would have stalled halfway through Genesis. That is the logic of Islam.

In summary: while Christian evangelisation is fruitful for the whole world, Judaizing causes misery for many, including themselves. The revenge the Jews threatened to unleash against the oppressive tribesmen came back on their own heads one thousandfold. Denying Jesus' Divinity, they insisted that the monotheistic God was yet to send a prophet who would achieve world domination for the People of the Book, interpreting the OT promises in a carnal and political way. So, Mohammed, urged on relentlessly by his wife, uncle and demons, said that Allah and no other was God, and that he, Mohammed, was his prophet, and that Islam had the mission to subdue the entire world. For Muslims the 'Book' is not the Torah or Bible, but the Quran.[86]

There is a final turn remaining to consider in God's 'plot'. Israelis cannot clear the Muslims off Temple Mount by force.

---

[85] Quran 4:163 nonsensically swaps out Isaac for Ishmael: "We revealed unto Abraham and Ishmael and Jacob and the tribes and Jesus and Job and Jonah and Aaron and Solomon and we brought to David the Psalms."

[86] Jews rejecting Jesus was not the primary cause of Islam, but set the stage for it. Islamic incandescence over the Trinity, Incarnation and Passion, combined with Mohammad's violent and sexual excesses, reveal satan's input.

There are over a billion Muslims who would not stand for it. If Israelis attempt to do it by sweet-talking and bribes, then it will be by way of a one-world religion. Yet these are the very conditions for bringing about the Antichrist, and, in the wink of an eye, that will result in the final Advent of Jesus Christ. The final rebellion will turn out to be of decisive service.

Obduracy, hardness of heart, serves to build God's footstool (Ps 109:1). If the Jewish leaders had *"believed Moses"* (Jn 5:46), and accepted Jesus as Messiah, Islam would not exist. Then there would be nobody blocking the rebuilding of the Temple in Jerusalem. Then again, no one would want to rebuild it. God's Plan is perfect.

THE BEST POSSIBLE ENDING TO HUMAN HISTORY

Israel is a scattered flock, the lions have driven him away: first the king of Assyria devoured him: and last this Nabuchodonosor king of Babylon hath broken his bones. Therefore thus saith the Lord of hosts the God of Israel: Behold I will visit the king of Babylon and his land, as I have visited the king of Assyria. And I will bring Israel again to his habitation: and he shall feed on Carmel, and Bason, and his soul shall be satisfied in mount Ephraim, and Galaad. In those days, and at that time, saith the Lord, the iniquity of Israel shall be sought for, and there shall be none: and the sin of Juda, and there shall none be found: for I will be merciful to them, whom I shall leave.

Jeremiah 50:17-20

The delay of the wholesale conversion of the Jewish people avails for the best possible ending to human history. Their opposition to the Church before their conversion has stimulated a purification of Church doctrine, the worldwide spread of the Church, the perfection of many souls in charity and it adds testimony to the Church's divine origin. Beyond all these gains for the Church, the delay is also serving the immortal sanctity of that last generation of Jews who will receive Jesus Christ with jubilation when He returns.

The final converts to the Faith will have untold depths of contrition for the way the people with whom they have historically identified, whom they have previously admired and defended, have for so long treated the Body of Christ. They will also have a tender love for the Gentile saints who never ceased praying for their conversion. It makes sense that these Jews will have a penitential spirit and an evangelical ardour not seen since the Apostolic Age. Such holiness will be necessary to overcome the greatest challenges ever to confront man: the persecutions from the Antichrist.

The deceptions, cruelty and demise of the Antichrist are given in more detail by the OT than the NT, but one needs the light of Christ to see it. Why this arrangement? Perhaps because when the last trials fall upon the Church, the faithful may well be stirred by ardent Jewish converts. When these read the OT in the light of the New, they might have a greater penetration than Gentile Christians who seem nowadays to neglect the OT. Jewish faithful, passionately loving the OT already, will read the Scriptures most carefully, and believe, and act accordingly, post-figuring the prefigurations.

Can a Gentile Catholic ever take as much inspiration as a Jewish Catholic from the example of the Machabees, specifically for encouragement in the end times? The following passage has helped countless Christians through the ages but surely it is aimed at the last generation who will be in a like situation:

Machabeus, and they that were with him… prayed to the Lord, sprinkling earth upon their heads, and girding their loins with haircloth, and lying prostrate at the foot of the altar, besought him to be merciful to them, and to be an enemy to their enemies, and an adversary to their adversaries, as the law saith. And so after prayer taking their arms... as soon as the sun was risen both sides joined battle: the one part having, with their valour, the Lord for a surety of victory, and success: but the other side making their rage their leader in battle. But when they were in the heat of the engagement, from heaven there appeared to the enemies five men upon horses, comely, with golden bridles, conducting the Jews: two of them took Machabeus between them, and covered him on every side with their arms, and kept him safe; but cast darts and fireballs against the enemy, so that they fell down, being both confounded with blindness, and filled with trouble. And there were slain twenty thousand five hundred. (2 Mac 10:25-31)

This passage is of little use to those who do not believe it really happened, whether ignorant of the OT or who, like modernists, explain it away. Significantly, it references the eternity of God's Law.

The OT is difficult for Gentiles. Understanding comes easier to Jews. They know the characters. Think of Sisera seeking refuge among those he thinks are friends, the house of Heber the Kenite (Jdg 4:17). Sisera does not suspect any danger from Heber's wife, Jael. She appears gentle and responds with generosity to his request for help (Jdg 4:18-19). Next she crushes his skull with a tent peg. So the Antichrist will not suspect the humble of God will defeat him. The NT helps us understand that Jael prefigures the power of the

Blessed Virgin Mary. Familiarity with the OT delivers a hint this victory is also about the conversion of the Jews. How so?

The Kenites were descendants of Jethro the Midianite, father-in-law of Moses. Jethro was a great man but not a descendant of Abraham. Jethro's descendant, Heber the Kenite, separated his household from their kin who remained in Judah and moved north to Galilee. Significantly, this Heber is not the one from whom the Hebrew's get their name, which Heber was the great-great-great-great-grandfather of Abraham (Gen 10:25). What might this detail mean?

It shows that although Heber's household, who might mistakenly be thought to be 'Hebrews', did live in Israel, they were not true sons of Abraham. They were not Hebrews. Then they separated themselves from God's Chosen (Judah), to move away from Jerusalem to Galilee of the Nations, symbolising moving away from God and into the world, where they started a new line (cf. the Talmud). They were at peace with Canaanite King Jabin, enemy of God's People, a figure of satan. And so Heber's family represent the *"synagogue of Satan, who say they are Jews and are not"* (Apoc 3:9). Sisera, prefiguring the Antichrist, was their friend. He sought refuge with them. And what happened?

Heber's wife, Jael, destroyed the Antichrist. She was a true Israelite. She was on the same side as Barak (representing the pope) and Deborah (representing the Blessed Virgin Mary in Heaven). Maybe Jael stands for those of the false House of Heber who unexpectedly consecrate themselves to Mary, and in the final battle, now friends of God, overcome the enemy — a hidden hint that the last generation of Jews will become those holy saints who overcome the Antichrist?

If all that is hard to follow, it is easier for Jews who are already familiar with the characters involved. In any case, we can think up many scenarios of how human history might end, yet Who but God knows what is best? Only I am sure that if the world were to end without the conversion of the Jews then all history would end on a melancholic note. It would be an eternal embarrassment, as if, *per impossibile,* a single thorn spoiling the joy of Heaven.

Whereas all souls who go to hell deserve it, and none of these will be missed in Heaven, it would add to our wonder at God's Wisdom if all the opposition to Him through the centuries, the compounding lies against the Church, the hardening of hearts and stiffening of necks despite the increasingly obvious worldwide fulfilment of all the OT promises in Christ, it would be — I think — a greater ending to history, if all this were seen to be overcome by the grace of God operating fruitfully in the hearts of those who, until a dramatic conversion, have followed those who have most resolutely rejected God's grace.

How will this happen? Is it all the work of the Lord? It is our work too, and the sons of Jacob. If God illumines a man's heart, he will be illumined. He will change. But if his heart is veiled, if it is stone rather than flesh, he will not turn to be converted. God knows each heart, and when, how and why He touches one.

The heart is perverse above all things, and unsearchable, who can know it? I am the Lord who search the heart, and prove the reins: who give to every one according to his way, and according to the fruit of his devices. (Jer 17:9-10; 20:12)

Where God desists from touching a heart, His decision is always just and is used to serve the salvation of many, as with Pharaoh's hardened heart. For our part, Isaiah shows in a few short lines that love of neighbour is decisive (Is 58:5-10). It makes real our love of God, being crowned with loving worship (Is 58:11-14). God rewards love of our visible neighbour by drawing us to Himself through Christ.

And I will give them one heart, and will put a new spirit in their bowels: and I will take away the stony heart out of their flesh, and will give them a heart of flesh... that they may be my people, and I may be their God. (Ezek 11:19-20)

This conversion calls for admitting sin and doing penance, which is always possible as it is God's constant desire:

Therefore... O house of Israel, saith the Lord God. Be converted, and do penance for all your iniquities: and iniquity shall not be your ruin. Cast away from you all your transgressions, by which you have transgressed, and make to yourselves a new heart, and a new spirit: and why will you die, O house of Israel? For I desire not the death of him that dieth, saith the Lord God, return ye and live. (Ezek 18:30-32)

This is the offer that remains open, that is not revoked — the chance of conforming to God's heart:

The Lord will not turn away the wrath of his indignation, till he have executed and performed the thought of his heart: in the latter days you shall understand these things. At that time, saith the Lord, I will be the God of all the families of Israel, and they shall be my people. (Jer 30:24-31:1)

Here, at the very heart of the longest book in the Bible, is announced that the sons will no longer suffer for the sins of their fathers but will be offered the chance of entering a New Covenant (Jer 31:33). Many entered after St John the Baptist proclaimed it. His voice will not desist until it is completed. His spirit will be working unto the end (Mal 4:5-6).

In a moving call to Jews, it was through suffering that Aaron came to understand a profound consummation of God's sacrifice, going deeper than the ceremonial rites, experienced in human flesh. This was an insight of Aaron, not Moses (figuratively: of Jews, not Gentiles). To see it, one must read Leviticus 10, from the first line to the last.

Aaron's sons, Nadab and Abiu, were suddenly slain by God for ritually offering *"strange fire: which was not commanded them"* (Lev 10:1). With costly restraint and reverence, Aaron did not, in the agony of his loss, rail against Moses or God, but *"held his peace"* (Lev 10:3). The priest's work for God and the assembly could not be interrupted even by mourning the death of his sons.

Moses said to Aaron, and to Eleazar and Ithamar, his sons: Uncover not your heads, and rend not your garments, lest perhaps you die, and indignation come upon all the congregation. Let your brethren, and all the house of Israel, bewail the burning which the Lord has kindled. But you shall not go out of the door of the tabernacle, otherwise you shall perish, for the oil of the holy unction is on you. (Lev 10:6-7)

Before this chapter of Leviticus is finished, we will see that the two dead sons served as the victim for the holocaust, burnt indeed by God. Meanwhile, Moses incorrectly thought a lesser victim was needed too.

And Moses spoke to Aaron, and to Eleazar and Ithamar, his sons that were left: Take the sacrifice that is remaining of the oblation of the Lord, and eat it without leaven beside the altar, because it is holy of holies. And you shall eat it in a holy place: which is given to thee and thy sons of the oblations of the Lord, as it hath been commanded me. (Lev 10:12-13)

We might think that on the very day when your sons or your brothers were killed by God for liturgical disobedience, then the letter of the law would be fearfully followed. But it was not so. Discovering the buck had not been eaten but only burnt, Moses was *"angry with Eleazar and Ithamar"*, because they had failed to complete the commandments regarding the sacrifice for sin. Moses asked them:

Why did you not eat in the holy place the sacrifice for sin, which is most holy, and given to you, that you may bear the iniquity of the people, and may pray for them in the sight of the Lord, especially whereas none of the blood thereof hath been carried within the holy places, and you ought to have eaten it in the sanctuary, as was commanded me? Aaron answered: This day hath been offered the victim for sin, and the holocaust before the Lord: and to me what thou seest has happened: how could I eat it, or please the Lord in the ceremonies, having a sorrowful heart? (Lev 10:17-19)

What a chapter. Two sons of the first High Priest are slain by God for offering *"strange fire"*. Holy Aaron, heartbroken, holds his peace. With his remaining sons he fulfils the essentials of his duties but he has no stomach to eat. He told his brother Moses that it was enough that the holocaust was offered. *"Which when Moses had heard he was satisfied"* (Lev 10:20). What does all this mean? First, it is what it is. Second, it is about the New Covenant in Jesus Christ. Third, it is about the conversion of the Jews.

First, what it is shows us directly the importance of liturgical rectitude. Following the rubrics is life and death for the individual and for the world. Disdaining key rubrics is a mortal sin for a priest, for which he earns hell. Disdaining the traditional Mass is a disaster for the Church Militant, for which all get to see hell on earth.

Second, regarding the New Covenant, if Aaron and his household could not eat the victim goat on the day his sons died as sacrifices taken by God, how can God, or the Church, accept victims of goats or sheep since Jesus died? If Aaron's sorrow meant he had no appetite to eat the beasts, and if the consuming of his sons sufficed as the sacrifice for that day, how much more God grows tired of this imagery once His own Son has died, once the reality has been accomplished, Whose Sacrifice was enough for all days, for the eternal Day. After the Crucifixion, God would nevermore sense a sweet savour over animal sacrifices. Rather, the offering now pleasing to God begins with bread and wine, without the death of an animal, for the separate consecrations of the Body and Blood speak of the death of His very own Son. With the arrival of the reality, the figures thereof pass away. Mass gives us the reality sacramentally. The Old Covenant rituals, shadows, are no longer of interest to God or of use to man.

Thirdly, Moses did not quite understand how God dealt with Aaron, nor how Aaron offered within his heart his dear offspring, by calmly accepting God's Will, even in a time of trauma. Aaron did not argue with God and, at this point, needed no man to advise him on ceremony or on how to approach the Lord. The final generation of Jews will have learnt about the Crucifixion through their unique history and suffering. Gentile Christians would do well not to press Aaron, or the Jews, on this, but to let God guide.

Until then, if looking around us today, this final conversion seems unlikely or impossible, we should recall St Paul. He was the fiercest persecutor, enraged against the Church. Yet by grace he became such an apostle of Christ that his conversion has its own feast every year. St Paul desires the conversion of his brethren. He will not be disappointed, nor anyone who prays with him.[87]

Nobody is created for damnation

God's ways are high, but never exploitative. Each person is made directly for God, not as a means for someone else. Three examples pertain.

First, Jews are not made for Gentiles in the sense that by their falling away they serve our growth, as if to indicate God made people to be damned so that others could benefit.

---

[87] The Preface for the Conversion of St Paul [Ambrosian Rite], 25th Jan, prays: "Eternal God: Who allowest not Thy Church, that standeth fast in the preaching of Thy blessed Apostle Paul, to be injured by any deception. For nothing is deemed to abide in the true religion that agreeth not with his teaching."

Rather all are made for God and all can win eternity with God if they choose to do so. Those who are damned are so by their own choice.

Second, Gentiles are not made for Jews in the sense that we are only to keep the Church going for however many millennia it takes for God to win back His favourite, His 'firstborn son'. Our fidelity serves this purpose, but it is not the reason we exist. God is.

Perhaps the best way to avoid confusion or resentment in either case stated is to think how easy it is to love Mary. We are servants of Mary, and every soul which gets to Heaven increases her (accidental) glory and reward, because she certainly interceded to bring each of the redeemed to salvation through her Son. Yet — this is the third example — we are not made chiefly for Mary, but fundamentally for ourselves to know God. From this knowledge we discover only joy to be servants of Mary. We have no jealousy of her, as no little child is jealous of his mother.

Similarly, whether Jews or Gentiles, we can regard one another as brothers. We serve each other in God's plan, but this can be no cause for envy, only gratitude, for it is part of eternal salvation, raising, never deflating, the whole.

The conversion of the Jews, for which we pray on Good Friday especially, will be the consummate end of history. All will know truth triumphed; freewill was never forced; love conquered beyond every limit. Hell will not have one single boast left. Heaven will not have one honest soul missing. אָמֵן

PART II: THE JEWISH QUESTION

The Jews, who killed both the Lord Jesus and the prophets, and have persecuted us, and please not God, and are adversaries to all men…

1 Thessalonians 2:14-15

The difficult aspects of what is sometimes called the Jewish Question are made vastly more difficult by being surrounded by existential tensions. We are walking on eggshells. Voice an unwelcome opinion and you risk being savaged. But try ignoring the question and you will end up enslaved, in time and possibly for eternity.

With everything at stake, this book does not explore secondary distinctions between Jews who are Orthodox, or

Reformed, or humanist, or atheist, or revolutionary. All this would distract from the most pertinent distinction: acceptance of Jesus as Son of God. This determines our eternal destiny and the temporal order. There are Jews, like the Apostles, who adore Jesus Christ; and there are Jews who most decidedly do not. Theological truths set persons free, who thereby illumine the whole world. Conversely, denial of truth enables enslavement, dragging the whole world into the pit. Thus, one's spiritual alignment is upstream of all philosophies, political programmes and social movements.

Certainly, we can distinguish between Jews who may or may not be Zionists; or between Zionists who may or may not insist political or military means are needful. Certainly, each negative generalisation of Judaism can be qualified by acknowledging the admirable virtues of particular Jews. But our focus must be upon what matters most: Christ gathers souls to Himself in His Church, while Judaism's rejection of the Son of God infernally scatters souls (Lk 11:23).

Accordingly, the categories addressed below include spiritual blindness, the relationship of the Old Covenant to the New, Zionism, globalism and the Antichrist. These themes are put into historical context by Jewish emancipation and by the engineering of multiculturalism (to sink the medieval policy of *Sicut Judæis*), both of which developments weaken nations to clear the way for world domination by an elite. Nor can we attain a coherent worldview without facing the causes of the Holocaust and admitting that this tragedy has been weaponised to bury long-term historical truth and to murder perennial theological truth.

Before trying to map out these minefields, I will give an autobiographical note which might dispel at least some misapprehensions about my attitude towards Jews.

The meditations of Primo Levi, a survivor of Auschwitz, in his book *If This is a Man* (1947), moved my mother profoundly. She read her copy so often that it barely held together. As a child, I was struck by how much thought she gave it. We discussed the contents, trying to make sense of man's inhumanity to man. Who could grasp it? Primo Levi could not, concluding that to understand is to justify. Tragically, in 1987, he committed suicide.

Besides other literature, at home we had VHS documentaries about the Holocaust which were so graphic that as little children we were not permitted to watch them. Once we were teenagers, we saw them, with unforgettable footage of the liberation of Belsen. After reading Primo Levi, I followed my grandmother's recommendation by turning to *Man's Search for Meaning* by Viktor Frankl. A Jew of Vienna, Frankl survived Kaufering III (a subsidiary work camp of Dachau), where he sought to understand the psychology of suffering, or more precisely, of surviving. This set me onto reading my mother's well-worn *Gulag Archipelago* and searching out books by others who had resisted tyranny in the USSR, east Asia and the Americas.

Driven to understand how dictatorship could be possible, three times I deliberately got myself arrested in Burma — in 1997, 1998 and 1999 — to get a closer look at the military regime's cruelty. Reading the Bible in solitary confinement, I learned of God's unsurpassable care for the downtrodden — His absolute thirst for justice. But why does He allow evil?

We encounter it in ourselves and realise the undifferentiated obliteration of evil would be the end of us too. God has given another way. Love must conquer evil. Those who reject His gift bring hell upon themselves. But, by grace, many overcome. On the Last Day, all will behold the victory of charity.

In prison, St Paul introduced me to Jesus Christ and I was overwhelmed. What love! I converted, or reverted to the childhood Catholic faith from which I had drifted away. Is anything on earth so sweet as God's forgiveness? After being released I wrote a book about prison which included the line, "I fell in love with the Jews, with their tradition, their struggle, their wisdom".[88] For this, Moses gets the credit. During the last imprisonment, I fell in love with Jeremiah, and with more and more Jews ever since.

The British Embassy brought me word that a Harvard lawyer had taken up my case *pro bono*. Later my sister came and clarified he was a law student. Still, he did an excellent job with my case at the United Nations (UNWGAD), on Capitol Hill and with the media. On my release, he was with my family at Heathrow Airport to meet me. I shook his hand: "Thanks Jared, you saved my life". Previously, after my 1998 imprisonment, a Jewish friend of my father in London funded and constructed a website to support my work for Burma. In this latest detention (1999-2000), a Washington Jew had helped immensely to multiply the effectiveness of the campaign and — as a bonus, I thought — even helped to get me out of prison.

---

[88] James Mawdsley, *The Heart Must Break* (2001), p.183.

Jared and I became good friends, visiting each year across the Pond, in DC or London. I was a member of his wedding party at a synagogue in Toronto. Jared recommended Elie Wiesel's book, *Night*, which I promptly read. I did not need any convincing about the Holocaust. I accepted the mainstream narrative. Twice I had visited the Holocaust Museum, *Yad Vashem*, in Jerusalem, and once in New York City, and naturally cried each time, speechless, as also in Dachau. In Aspen, I had an amiable conversation with a NYC lawyer, a Jew, who won reparations from Germany. I was impressed with his work. It would be many years before I questioned this.

Regarding the State of Israel, I was politically conservative and accepted it as a necessity. Who had not heard Islamic leaders fuming that they wanted to "drive Israelis into the sea"? It seemed to me, that as a matter of natural law, all peoples need their own land. For formerly landless Jews, I thought Israel made more sense than anywhere else.

I do not remember my parents ever bringing up the question of Israel, but upon asking them I realised we differed. My father had spent a lot of time in the Middle East. He grew to admire particular Arabs and to develop a warm sympathy for them. He could see clearly enough that Israel dismissed non-Jewish Semites with deadly arrogance.

Given her preoccupation with the Holocaust, I thought my mother might be sympathetic to the State of Israel. But she was not. Asked why, she recounted a Jewess in Jaffa telling her fiercely that Palestinians are "cockroaches", fit for extermination.[89] Her vehemence made my mother distrustful, deeply, of the Israeli agenda. Even so, I was not persuaded. Were there not Muslims who thought the same of Jews?

So, regarding Zionism, I did not follow my parents' inclination, but the dominant culture. Through my twenties, I was fully pro-Israel. I liked America. Deep down I was cowardly, aligning myself with what seemed the stronger side. I discounted theological questions, having little understanding of why the Jews had lost the Holy Land. Nor did I take God's punishment of Cain seriously.

But my conscience was pricked by an encounter with a furious knot of Palestinian youths. We met in 2002 in the West Bank. After chatting with two of them, when they noticed I was listening, more and more of their friends hurried over. It was during the Second Intifada (called the al-Aqsa Intifada as it concerned the Temple Mount). These Muslim youths were boiling over with uncontrolled anger. It was scary. They were telling me of what they had been through, several speaking at once. All of them had been arrested and detained by the Israeli Defence Force (IDF).

Finally, the group was quiet enough to let one speak. During his interrogation, Jewish soldiers held his face in the

---

[89] Israel Shahak, *Jewish History, Jewish Religion: The Weight of Three Thousand Years* (1994), p.28, "Nor was [Martin] Buber alone in his attitude, although in my opinion he was by far the worst in the evil he propagated and the influence he has left behind him. There was the very influential sociologist and biblical scholar, Yehezkiel Kaufman, an advocate of genocide on the model of the Book of Joshua, the idealist philosopher Hugo Shmuel Bergman, who as far back as 1914-15 advocated the expulsion of all Palestinians to Iraq, and many others. All were outwardly 'dovish', but employed formulas which could be manipulated in the most extreme anti-Arab sense... and all seemed to be gentle persons who, even when advocating expulsion, racism and genocide, seemed incapable of hurting a fly - and just for this reason the effect of their deceptions was the greater."

prison toilet. Reader, have you seen an Asian prison toilet? It is a hole in the ground and, in a cell shared by dozens of men, unspeakably grotesque. To get close to it, the Israeli soldiers must have been determined. They held this man's face in it. He gestured as he spoke, his expression contorted with the memory, outraged at being so shamed. He had been thoroughly violated and the world did not care; woefully degraded and no one would listen.

The mistreatment was not an act of war. He was a prisoner, defenceless. It was an act of hate, mindless cruelty from one race which counts itself better than another. It anticipated Israeli involvement, during the Iraq War, in the torture of Arab detainees at Abu Ghraib.

This inhumanity is not about defence or nation-building. It is a mistake to label it an 'enhanced interrogation technique'. You do not need to be tortured to know it degrades the humanity of the perpetrators more than that of the victim. It also degrades all who approve it. It delegitimises the supposed authority which uses it. Whatever inadequate 'information' it elicits, it creates visceral divisions of hatred which no politics can surmount, only grace.

If anyone thinks that when it comes to war, when it comes to establishing a homeland for the Jews, then there must be some such demonic price paid — no. If Zionism is of God, then this is not how it can be achieved or defended. God does not put anyone's face in the toilet.

The Palestinian convinced me to face what I did not want to see: that the Jews' return to a 'homeland' is predicated on stealing the land of others. Neither biblical history nor the Holocaust justify this. Understood, both absolutely exclude it.

Zionism left me uneasy. The most influential among Jewish politicians, military and secret services, not only do not care about the Palestinians, but expect that we should support the State of Israel without caring about the Palestinians either. But that is not of God. It is of the devil. And it is not about one face in one toilet. It is about all mankind.

The issue does not turn on isolated incidents of inhumanity to Palestinians. Obviously, Muslims commit atrocities, too. Rather, it is the theological ideology behind it, that Israelis act as if they are a Chosen People, elected for a Land, and sent today to wipe out others from it, and as if their claims are justified by the OT. If tolerated, this mentality will subsume the world into accepting a calumny against God. Christ on the Cross turns such megalomania upside-down.

> *Give: and it shall be given to you... For with the same measure that you shall mete withal, it shall be measured to you again.* (Lk 6:38)

One cannot complain of being crushed, if simultaneously one is crushing. One cannot protest oppressors, while one scorns the humanity of one's enemy, one's neighbour or the Crucified. We are all made in God's image. Hence cruelty toward man is always an offence against God.

There is another glaring contradiction in Zionism. Many atheist, secular and political Zionists jointly aspire to restore Israel according to its 'biblical borders' (*Eretz Yisrael Hashelema*), yet ignore God on everything else. The incongruity strikes reflective Jews as insupportable, as Israel Shahak writes:

My own early political conversion from admirer of Ben-Gurion to his dedicated opponent began exactly with such an issue. In 1956 I eagerly swallowed all of Ben-Gurion's political and military reasons for Israel initiating the Suez War, until he (in spite of being an atheist, proud of his disregard of the commandments of Jewish religion) pronounced in the Knesset on the third day of that war, that the real reason for it is 'the restoration of the kingdom of David and Solomon' to its Biblical borders. At this point in his speech, almost every Knesset member spontaneously rose and sang the Israeli national anthem. To my knowledge, no zionist politician has ever repudiated Ben-Gurion's idea that Israeli policies must be based (within the limits of pragmatic considerations) on the restoration of the Biblical borders as the borders of the Jewish state.[90]

If anyone wants to claim the biblical borders, they need to acknowledge the biblical God. He gave the Hebrews the land for a purpose, and when the Jews rejected that purpose by crucifying His Son, God took them away. If they wish to return, it must be on God's terms, which involves fulfilling their calling in Christ. Nothing else can work.

When Joshua and Caleb led a conquest of the Promised Land it was to eradicate evil and establish true worship. Joshua ('Jesus', 'Saviour') and Caleb ('Whole-hearted') stand for the Divine and Human Natures of Christ. Modern Zionism

---

[90] Israel Shahak, *Jewish History, Jewish Religion: The Weight of Three Thousand Years* (1994), p.8-9.

is the opposite: a godless invasion employing evil until it establishes the seat of the Antichrist.[91]

It becomes obvious that this intense conflict is about much more than Palestine. History and theology help us to see that what happens in the Holy Land, by God's design, concerns the whole world. The Cross is key.

[91] Gerald Kaufman, MP, Hansard, 407-08 (15th Jan 2009), "The Israeli Foreign Minister Tzipi Livni asserts that her Government will have no dealings with Hamas, because they are terrorists. Tzipi Livni's father was Eitan Livni, chief operations officer of the terrorist Irgun Zvai Leumi, who organised the blowing-up of the King David hotel in Jerusalem, in which 91 victims were killed, including four Jews. Israel was born out of Jewish terrorism. Jewish terrorists hanged two British sergeants and booby-trapped their corpses. Irgun, together with the terrorist Stern gang, massacred 254 Palestinians in 1948 in the village of Deir Yassin."

St Robert Bellarmine, *Disputationes de Controversiis Christianæ Fidei adversus hujus temporis Hæreticos*, Tom.I, Lib.3, Cap.13 *De sede antichristi.*

THE STATUS OF THE OLD AND NEW COVENANTS

All the nations are uncircumcised in the flesh, but all the house of Israel are uncircumcised in the heart.

Jeremiah 9:26

What is the Law of Moses worth today? Everything and nothing. Everything in Christ, nothing without Him.

Many say that God cannot annul the Old Covenant, for He does not change His mind. This is to misunderstand His eternal decrees, wherein the whole process of change is foreseen in advance and unfolds in time. Nature frequently involves passing over singularities — sharp and irreversible developments from one state to another. A butterfly does not revert to a crawling caterpillar. A branch burnt to ashes cannot be brought back to life. A man cannot climb back into his mother's womb. The New Covenant cannot revert to the Old.

The two sides of the ineffable singularity by which the Old passed over to the New are marked by the Crucifixion and Resurrection of Christ. The difference between the Old and New Covenants is, in the inerrant allegory of the Letter to the Galatians, that difference between Hagar and Sarah. The former brings forth a life by carnality, the natural not crowned with the supernatural, doomed, due to the Fall, to die. The latter conceives and brings forth new life according to God's promise, by God's operation, set for salvation. This the OT promises and the NT actualises.

To try to restore the Old Covenant is a revolt against God's will. It would be to declare that the New Covenant was never promised, that the Messiah has not come, that Jesus' Body is not the true Temple. But a mustard tree cannot revert to seed. A supernova, an explosion of light, cannot be reversed.

How is it that learned Jews, including those who study the Torah daily, fail to see how the OT anticipates Christ's Passion (Acts 17:2-5,10-13; 28:24)? The Bible answers that as vain-minded Gentiles are separated from God *because of the blindness of their hearts"* (Eph 4:18), similarly *"blindness in part has happened in Israel"* (Rom 11:25). God lifts the veil for those who seek truth, but many prefer the darkness (4 Kgs 6:17-22). The difference is in the decision to lament Christ Crucified or not.

The deepest division in the world can be healed only by God. Its hidden depths cut through hearts, yet the accumulating results — for good or ill — will become a spectacle to all the world: the final futile rejection of the New Covenant by attempting to rebuild Jerusalem's Temple in a hopeless push to practice the Old.

The Deepest Division in the World

Thousands of Jews mourned the Crucifixion of Jesus when or soon after it happened. *"And there followed Him a great multitude of the people, and of women who bewailed and lamented Him"* (Lk 23:27). Some were close enough to contemplate the Blessed Virgin Mary spiritually martyred under the Cross. They might also have noticed and later pondered St Mary Magdalen, St John the Beloved Disciple, St Dismas, St Longinus. A spiritual tsunami was developing.

Immediately after the Crucifixion, a tidal wave of compunction flooded the hearts of the Jews:

And all the multitude of them that were come together to that sight and saw the things that were done returned, striking their breasts. (Lk 23:48)

Did God choose the Jews because they had the biggest hearts or the hardest hearts? Which would better show the gratuity of salvation? The Gospels seem to indicate both: there were those close to the Cross who evidently had the best of hearts, while others climbed up Calvary to mock Jesus and did not repent. Their hearts were not wounded by His.

Addressing both kinds of people, St Peter, after bitter contrition over his absence from Calvary, now fortified with love, preached with great effect at Pentecost:

Now when they had heard these things, they had compunction in their heart and said to Peter and to the rest of the apostles: What shall we do, men and brethren? But Peter said to them: Do penance: and be baptised every one of you in the name of Jesus Christ, for the remission of your sins. And you shall receive the gift of the Holy Ghost. For the promise is to you and to your children and to all that are far off, whomsoever the Lord our God shall call... Save yourselves from this perverse generation. They therefore that received his word, were baptised; and there were added in that day about three thousand souls. (Acts 2:37-41)

Many chose salvation, as also will their children *"that are far off"*. But others perversely chose darkness. Those who refused to lament the Crucifixion missed their calling.

> *O that you had hearkened to my commandments! Then your peace would have been like a river, and your righteousness like the waves of the sea; your offspring would have been like the sand, and your descendants like its grains; their name would never be cut off or destroyed from before me.* (Is 48:18-19 RSVCE)

What is at the heart of human failure? What decides whether we can see or not? St John supplies the answer:

> *If any man say: I love God, and hates his brother; he is a liar. For he that loves not his brother whom he sees, how can he love God whom he sees not? And this commandment we have from God, that he who loves God love also his brother.* (1 Jn 4:20-21)

Now Jesus came as *"brother"* to the Jews, to mankind. Everyone in Jerusalem saw Him crucified, or heard about it (Lk 24:18). All men in the world whom the Gospel has reached, or who have beheld a Crucifix, or have watched Mel Gibson's *The Passion of the Christ*, are confronted with their brother in agony. The question is: do they care?

No one ever had a sorrow quite like Jesus' sorrow. If we have any humanity in us, we will want to know who He was, what happened, why. As we discover the answers, we are bound to be sad. This path leads thence to a lamentation of the state of the world, to an honest contrition for our own sins, then a trust in the Lamb's sinlessness, and conversion to the God of Love Who died for us. Before we behold the Cross with gratitude, with awe, with veneration and worship, we begin with com[-]passion.

If someone refuses to commiserate the crucified or His Mother, then he has no love of God. It is wrong to say one loves God if one does not care about one's brother. It is not possible to love God and simultaneously scorn Jesus. This is Divine Law (Jn 15:17-25) and natural law (1 Jn 4:20-21).

Catholics express their contrition in the Sacrament of Confession. God rewards such with sanctifying grace. There are humanists, like Oscar Wilde, who acknowledging Jesus' innocence and admiring His goodness, admit that He suffered gross injustice and cruelty. Rewarding natural honesty, God grants further actual graces, which, if co-operation continues, lead to conversion and sanctifying grace, salvation. Oscar converted on his deathbed. We may hope he is in Heaven.

But there are those who, while still refusing to acknowledge that Jesus is Divine and that He is the Messiah, refuse even that natural debt of acknowledging He was innocent; nor do they compassionate Him Who suffered such fearful agony. Until today, they blank Him out. Privately, sometimes publicly, He is mocked. This is the most damaging problem in the world, for nothing deepens the darkness more intensely than actively rejecting the Light.

Rejection of divine Light follows from Lucifer's fall to man's Fall and thence through all history, from Cain to the Antichrist. A long descent into diabolic corruption was required for obscurity of souls to reach such a low pitch that Annas and Caiaphas wanted Jesus killed. Aaron's High Priesthood had become disfigured beyond spiritual recognition.

Until recently, the Church was not afraid to preach clearly on this. But since *Nostra ætate* (1965), Church documents avoid clarity on the crucial beginnings of Jewish-Catholic relations. Church authorities fatally gloss over what Jews did over centuries to the early Church, what they did to the Apostles, what they did to Christ, and as Jesus said, what their fathers did in murdering the prophets. If these facts are not faced by both sides, how can there be understanding?

Christians are called to love their enemies after Christ loved those who crucified Him. If we pretend they are not enemies (*contra* Rom 11:28; 1 Thess 2:15), if we are guilt-tripped into thinking it a task of the Church to commend Judaism as good, this will provide cover for Jewish exploitation of Gentiles, leading to widespread resentment which, without a Christian perspective, provokes pogroms and worse. But being clear-eyed that Judaism opposes the Gospel, the saving truth, we beg God's graces to endure their opposition, even as we attempt to treat adherents of Judaism and its offshoots with all justice, charity and openness.

How is honest dialogue sustainable with a follower of Judaism unless he can admit that Jesus Christ suffered; suffered gruesomely; suffered unjustly; was innocent; was betrayed; was a victim of a conspiracy by Jewish leaders? Further, that these leaders lobbied the Roman powers to execute Jesus and stirred up the crowds to call for His crucifixion, crowds who lived in fear of them. Moreover, that the leaders responsible harboured the same murderous hatred toward St Stephen, St James, and St Paul; and over centuries their successors have connived against the Church. If these facts are indefinitely avoided, how can a fruitful dialogue proceed? If someone denies these things, he is ignorant, or heartless, or lying.

No one can truthfully fault Jesus: all His words are accurate and the accusation that making Himself God is blasphemy only holds water if He is not, in fact, God. Evidently His claim strains our imagination. Yet Jesus countered charges of blasphemy by instructing His accusers to consider and believe by His works (Jn 10:36-38). At His trial these were not considered, for the process was not aimed at truth. Jesus demonstrated His Divinity by doing such things as only God can do. He knows this is hard for some to believe, so He is patient, crowning His proofs with raising Himself from the dead.

To admit that Jesus is God requires that the Father grant the grace of revelation from Heaven (Mt 16:17). It is hardly possible to recognise Jesus as Messiah without a supernatural elevation of one's sight (1 Cor 12:3). Are we judged upon this? Can a man be sent to hell because God refused to grant him the grace of understanding? These questions miss the point: we are confronted with our brother, our suffering brother, our innocent suffering brother. That is where souls are won or lost. If we care, if we look into it, if we allow what we find to cause us sorrow and increase love in us, then we are on course to receive sanctifying grace and reach Heaven. But if we deny what we see, if we remain indifferent, if we turn away, then how could we possibly fit into Heaven anyway? How could we gaze upon Love and be happy in Heaven if we do not wish to do it while on earth? Grace perfects us, it does not contradict our choices.

With these reflections we are approaching that singularity where the Old is passed over into the New. The fragility of the Old Covenant is demonstrated by its leaders plotting Deicide. The full power of the New Covenant will be seen in the long-promised conversion of their successors, so that finally they enter it.

Jesus came to bring *"division"* (Lk 12:51). He knows and will demonstrate which hearts love and which not. Everyone has a role in this. Even the serpent unwillingly serves God in this, dividing hearts into their two camps from the beginning. This is the deepest division of men. It is not ephemeral, but is absolute in respect to the Crucifixion, whether before or after.

The Bible draws our attention to Sem, father of all Semites. The sacred text preserves his memory as: *"Sem also the father of all the children of Heber"* (Gen 10:21), who are the Hebrews. Here Torah emphasises division, saying: *"To Heber were born two sons: the name of the one was Phaleg, because in his days was the earth divided"* (Gen 10:25). Even if this describes tectonic plates or political conflicts, ultimately it concerns a spiritual division within hearts.

This same division is symbolised in the arrangement made by Abraham and Lot. Abraham allowed Lot to choose whatever land he wanted (Gen 13:9). Lot looked and chose the place of Sodom and Gomorrha. He raced ahead to grasp the world. Demurring, Abraham calmly proceeds to inherit the Promised Land. He even goes on to rescue Lot, the seed of his deceased elder brother, Aran. So, Christians will be there to rescue the last Jews who turn to choose Jesus when Sodom turns upon them. Until then, connecting Judaism's infidelity to Moses with infidelity to the Christ, Abraham says: *"If they hear not Moses and the prophets, neither will they believe, if one rise again from the dead"* (Lk 16:31).

Within the Jewish people and, following their lead, all people, are two nations. God told Rebekah about the brothers contesting within her: *"Two nations are in thy womb, and two peoples shall be divided out of thy womb"* (Gen 25:23). There is a deep spiritual fight, for or against the Logos, for or against the Word of God, Jesus Christ. This is the division of peoples, which is a division of hearts.

The separation of mankind into children of God and children of satan is perennial. It is the Ur-theme of Genesis 1: separating the light from the darkness; above from below; the dry land from the waters (Gen 1:4,7,9). These motifs continue through human society: Cain killed his younger brother; Lamech killed a youth; Nimrod hunted men. Cain's son built a city, signifying a manmade system alienated from nature, in opposition to Noah, the man of the earth, who obeyed all God's commands. Soon the city of man reveals itself, in the Tower of Babel, to have designs on divinity. This impossible hubris is driven by the devil and erupts on earth.

Darkness has no part in light. God laid the foundations for the Holy City. He calls man to participate in building it. Jesus proved that the City of God is built on self-sacrifice. The City of Man is built on sacrificing others. The first City is heavenly, the second is of hell. We choose sides by our response to the Crucifixion. Precisely here on the Cross occurs the unrepeatable and irrevocable transition from the Old Covenant to the New.

Circumcision of the Heart

God has entered the chasm between the uncreated and the created. He spoke to Adam and the prophets. He filled the Tabernacle and Temple with the glory of His presence. In the Incarnation, the uncreated united with the created — God dwelt among us (Jn 1:14). By His Ascension, the created entered fully into the uncreated; in His Sacred Humanity, Jesus Christ sits at the right hand of His Father.

For bridging the uncreated and created, we marvel at the Incarnation and Ascension. These two events in history both reveal God's love for us. Yet these are not the height of the singularity, for between them stands something greater still. It was at the Passion of Jesus Christ that the fullness of God's love was shown to man.

The Old Covenant prepared for this revelation. The sign of membership was real but hidden, indicating the secrets of men's hearts: *"Be circumcised to the Lord, and take away the foreskins of your hearts, ye men of Juda and ye inhabitants of Jerusalem"* (Jer 4:4). What can this be but a spiritual circumcision? The Old Covenant — exterior, material, carnal, bloody — is insufficient. The New Covenant — interior, essential, spiritual, full of grace — enters into the Old to bestow the fullness of life. If we admit what God did on the Cross, if our heart is opened to His limitless love, then the New Covenant lives within us.

I will give them a heart to know me, that I am the Lord: and they shall be my people, and I will be their God: because they shall return to me with their whole heart. (Jer 24:7)

The Spirit of God vivifies the Soul of Christ, which animates the Flesh of Christ; and the same Spirit lives in us who are the Body of Christ. This is the New Covenant in His Blood, His Passion, wherein God was revealed. We cannot revert from New to Old, just as a man once circumcised cannot be uncircumcised. A person who refuses to be cut to the heart by the Passion is not a member of God's People.

Rejecting Jesus' Incarnation, Judaism misunderstands man's spiritual purity and bodily dignity. Christ loves His Church as Bridegroom to Bride, but there is no sexual activity in or by God. Procreation is a good of this life, not of Heaven (Lk 20:34–35). While Christ explained that angels do not marry (Mt 22:30), and it is philosophically absurd to project sexual behaviour onto angels, the Talmud does just that.

> Rabbi Katina said, 'When the Israelites would ascend [to the Holy Temple] on the festival, [the kohen] would roll up the curtain for them, and display for them the cherubs, who were joined together [in an embrace].' The kohen would then tell them, 'Behold the beloved feelings for you on the part of the Omnipresent are like the beloved feelings of a male for a female'.[92]

How confused this is! None of this can be true, yet it is still taught approvingly today (especially in commentaries on the double Torah portion of Vayakhel-Pekudei, Ex 35-40).

The projection of materiality, even carnality, onto angels, goes even further with bizarre and blasphemous kabbalistic accounts of sexual congress among multiple gods. The *Secret Book of John* is a gnostic blasphemy asserting: that God

---

92 Babylonian Talmud, *Yoma* 54a.

[called Yaldabaoth] is monstrously deformed; lied about being the "one God"; that God, not satan, deceived Adam and Eve into eating from the Tree; and afterward He raped Eve.

For their part, human beings are to engage in sexual excess to bring male and female gods together and to restore original androgyny. Modern gnostics still engage "in sexual rituals designed to unite the divine male and female essences".[93] Gnosticism posits matter as radically evil, something to be hated. Calumniously claiming to trace their teaching back to the Epiphany's Three Wise Men, masonic gnostics arrange blasphemous 'Masses' involving sexual intercourse on the altar in a search for immortality and the rebuilding of Solomon's Temple.[94]

The Talmud perverts Adam's jubilant cry, *"This is now bone of my bones and flesh of my flesh"* (Gen 2:23), noting:

This teaches that Adam had intercourse with each animal and beast in his search for his mate, and his mind was not at ease, in accordance with the verse:

---

[93] Ellen Randolph, *Gnosticism, Transformation, and the Role of the Feminine in the Gnostic Mass of the Ecclesia Gnostica Catholica* (2009), p.2. Further on Randolph writes (p.49) that satanic sex rituals "indicate either a Gnostic or Kabbalistic conception of the origins and structure of the universe".

[94] Hugh Urban, *Magia Sexualis, Sex, Magic, and Liberation in Modern Western Esotericism* (2006), p.98, cites Theodor Reuss, *Von den Geheimnissen der okkulten Hochgrade unseres Orderns: Ein Mannifesto des Gross-Orientes*, in Historische Ausgabe der *Oriflamme* (1904), p.31, "One of the secrets which our Order possesses to its highest degree consists in the fact that it supplies the properly prepared brother with the practical means to erect the true Temple of Solomon in Man and to find again the 'lost Word': namely, that our Order supplies to the initiated and chosen brother the practical means to obtain proof of his immortality even during his earthly existence... This secret is one of the true secrets of Masonry and exclusively the secret of the Occult High Degree of Our Order. It has come down to our Order by word of mouth from the fathers of all true Freemasonry, the 'Wise Men of the East.'"

"And for Adam, there was not found a helpmate for him" (Gen 2:20), until he had intercourse with Eve.[95]

Christianity alone gives the truth about Spirit and flesh — the Triune God lives eternally; He alone created angels, matter, and men; He gave Eve to Adam in marriage and commanded them to multiply, and, in the fulness of time, He came to dwell among us in the Flesh, conceived by the Holy Ghost, and born of the Virgin Mary. How great the dignity of the flesh, that it should be united with immortal spirits, and even with God! How pure the Spirit, how simple and imperishable and clear and full of peace is the Divine life, which is immutable Love.

Rebuilding the Temple

What manifests the most determined denial of the true relation of body to spirit, of man to God, of creature to Creator? What showcases a collective and unbroken negation that God's Spirit came to dwell in Christ's Flesh, the New Temple? And that Christ's Flesh was taken up into Heaven, the final Temple? And that God's Spirit dwells in the baptised so that they can worship Him in this eternal Temple? It is the two-thousand-year-long endeavour to re-build the stone Temple in Jerusalem — a sign contradicting God's perfect Plan.[96] Its architect, satan, demands to know whether we will bow to this enterprise or not.

---

[95] Babylonian Talmud, *Yevamot* 63a.

[96] Pope Pius IX, *Mortalium animos* (6th Jan 1928), 11; citing Lactantius, *Divine Institutes*, IV, 30, 11-12. "The Catholic Church is alone in keeping true worship. This is the fount of truth, this the house of Faith, this the temple of God: if any man enter not here... he is a stranger to the hope of life and salvation."

A sojourner receiving visitors in his tent is a metaphor for a man receiving God into his soul (Gen 18). Such hospitality indicates the beginning of devotion to God. Raising the analogy, God's Presence in the desert Tabernacle points to the Divinity within the Humanity of Christ. God dwelling in Jerusalem's Temple anticipates Him living in the souls of the baptised, the Church. The Temple is a visible parable written in stones and gold, in sacred furniture and cyclic rituals.

The Temple and sacrifices of the Old Covenant prepare us to see in Christ the true Temple and the all-sufficient Sacrifice of the New and Everlasting Covenant (Heb 10:1-14).[97] Judaism, which emerged post-Temple, is not Abrahamic, or Mosaic, or Davidic, for St Augustine and St Thomas teach that Abraham, Moses and David had faith in Jesus Christ. It is impossible now to observe the Old Testament *qua* Old, because even in its own time it meant acceptance of Christ.[98]

The absence of the stone Temple also has great meaning: God has come in the Flesh and dwells among us in the Holy Eucharist. What would a re-built Temple mean but a denial of Jesus' Divinity, as if He is not now with us and within us in the Blessed Sacrament? For what does the Scripture say but that our bodies also become temples of the Holy Spirit when we are baptised in Christ. How holy is the body!

---

[97] St Thomas, *S.Th.* I-II, Q.103 a.3 ad 2, On the Cross "Our Lord said then: *'It is consummated'* (Jn 19:30). Consequently, the prescriptions of the Law must have ceased then altogether through their reality being fulfilled. As a sign of this, we read that at the Passion of Christ *'the veil of the temple was rent'* (Mt 27:51)."

[98] When Jesus arranged that He and St Peter have the half-shekel Temple tax paid by a miracle, Jesus explained *"the sons are free"*, not owing Temple tribute as spiritual foreigners do (Mt 17:23-26). This demonstrates that Jesus' own — Christians — are the true children and heirs of the Temple.

Against this, modernity rails in rebellion, spurning God's natural and supernatural order. What is abortion but the genocidal destruction of temples built by God? Given that the male represents the divine, and the female represents the human, what is transgender surgery but a wild manifestation of prideful man demoting God and usurping His place? It presages transhumanism: the attempt to build with human hands our own kind of temple, either a hybrid of beasts with humans or an engineering of man with machine. Both are grotesque; both are man playing God.

Do these attacks on the body have any spiritual connection with the attempt to rebuild the Temple? Are there not rabbis who study the Torah and teach vigorously against abortion and transgenderism? They are. But it is demons, not men, who coordinate assaults against the true and beautiful Body of Christ: transgenderism against the biological body; rebuilding the Temple against the Mystical Body. Neither the human body nor the true Temple is a "work of human hands". So long as Jews, whether Orthodox or humanist, deny Jesus Christ, they facilitate the devilish damage done by the kabbalists among them.

Each baby killed in the womb, each child manipulated and mutilated by sexologist surgeons, is a depraved rebellion against God.[99] Each sin affords an accumulation of dark capital in the spiritual accounts of those serving satan directly, who lead the lobbies and legislatures for public and even

---

[99] The Torah absolutely forbids child sacrifice. So does the Talmud, though it enjoins hostility to Christians. Meanwhile, Kabbalah is lawless, a way to total corruption. Though many of its practitioners would recoil from sacrificing animals, let alone humans, it does not require many to empower satan.

state-sponsored evil against the innocent. These men satan makes masters of the universe, to strive toward a final insult to God.

The stones of satan's temple are being quarried by lies and murder. Moses said, *"Choose life"* (Dt 30:19), but the ADL tweeted, "Reproductive freedom is a Jewish value".[100] That one sentence is a lie made for murder: abortion is not "reproductive" and killing the defenceless is not "freedom". Deliriously, the US National Council of Jewish Women is ferocious in its advocacy for abortion, with polls claiming over 80 per cent of US Jews are in favour. Regarding babies as disposable follows intrinsically from advocacy for contraception and fosters intrinsically the mindset for homosexual 'marriage'. The first 'legal' gay 'marriage' in the world was performed 1st April 2001 by Amsterdam's Mayor Job Cohen. A decade later, Vice President Joe Biden praised Jewish influencers, saying:

> I bet you 85 percent of those changes [to acceptance of homosexuality], whether in Hollywood or social media, are a consequence of Jewish leaders in the industry.[101]

Though opposed by many Orthodox Jews, the Jewish leaders whom Biden lauds are among some of the most destructive persons ever born. The demonic Dr John Money of John Hopkins University used a 'botched circumcision' in 1966 to have Bruce Reimer raised as a girl, performing transgender surgery on the 22-month-old boy to mutilate his

---

[100] Anti-Defamation League, X (20th Jan 2023).

[101] Haaretz, *Biden: Jewish Leaders Drove Gay Marriage Changes* (May 2013).

genitals completely. Both Bruce and his twin Brian committed suicide in their thirties. Although Dr Money should be punished, he is lauded by society.

Judith Butler, founder of gender theory and one of the most influential voices to approve drag queen story hours for children, is Jewish. Larry Fink, the CEO of BlackRock, who unabashedly uses his unrivalled financial power to "force behaviours" on gender diversity, is Jewish.

The pioneers of sexual perversion as liberation ideology form a network dominated by Jews. Magnus Hirschfield coined the term 'transvestite' in his 1910 work *Transvestites: An Investigation into the Erotic Drive of Cross-Dressing*. In 1913, Felix Aaron Theilhaber, a lifelong Zionist, became founding chairman of the Society of Sexual Reform (*Gesex*) in Berlin. These medical professionals worked to legalise abortion and contraception, and to reform laws on obscenity, homosexuality, exhibitionism and pedophilia. Willhelm Reich regarded premarital chastity and the taboo on masturbation as life-denying and disease-inducing. His book, *The Sexual Revolution* (1935), advocated liberation through sex education, blaming patriarchal society for repressing youth with morals. The collective influence of these refugees from rabbinical Judaism has devastated civilisation.[102]

To be clear, degrading sexuality is a work of all nations. All impure thoughts contribute to it and no nation has a monopoly on those. Alfred Kinsey was a Gentile, not a Jew.

---

[102] Their errors elaborate on Jewish themes: the Zohar speaks of God as androgyne and the messiah as transgender, while there are eight genders in the Talmud, including the false idea that Adam began androgynous. Rachel Scheinerman, My Jewish Learning (Feb 2022), *There Are Eight Genders in the Talmud.*

But examine the worst revolutions: the majority of Bolsheviks were not Jews, and the majority of Jews were not Bolsheviks, yet the Bolshevik leadership was dominated by Jews beyond all demographic proportion.[103]

The hellish gender revolution rolls on. The Jewish Pritzker billionaires are driving a transition "from a dimorphic definition of sex to the broad acceptance and propagation of synthetic sex identities", that is "a new God-like goal: using gender ideology to remake human biology".[104]

Luke Ford once asked why Jews are so markedly over-represented in the pornography industry. Alvin Goldstein, who normalised hardcore porn, explained himself:

> The only reason that Jews are in pornography is that we think that Christ sucks. Catholicism sucks. We don't believe in authoritarianism. Pornography thus becomes a way of defiling Christian culture and, as it penetrates to the very heart of the American mainstream (and is no doubt consumed by those very same WASPs), its subversive character becomes more charged.[105]

Goldstein added, "I believe in me. I'm God... I am the super being. I am your God, admit it".

---

[103] Alexander Solzhenitsyn, *Two Hundred years Together* (2003), Vol II, 15 and elsewhere. In illustration, in the first Bolshevik Politburo, Jews out-numbered non-Jews by four (Trotsky, Zinoviev, Kamanev, Sokolnikov) to three (Lenin, Stalin, Bubnov). [In fact, Lenin's maternal grandfather Sril Moiseyevich (Israel Moses) Blank, was Jewish.] The Central Committee of the Bolshevik Party 'elected' in August 1917 included five Jewish members out of 21. See Seth Frantzman, *The Jerusalem Post, Was the Russian Revolution Jewish?* (15th Nov 2017).

[104] Tabletmag, *The Billionaire Family Pushing Synthetic Sex Identities* (June 2022).

[105] Luke Ford, *XXX-Communicated: A Rebel Without a Shul* (2004).

These people are channelling hell. What have any of them got to do with the Old Covenant, and rebuilding the Temple? The rebuilding seems to be a project of the rabbis who are robust in condemning modernity's demonic ideologies. But therein lies the connection. It is because the position of those who want to hold onto the Old Covenant is patently untenable, even oppressive, that Jews leave Judaism in droves, thinking rebellion is liberation. But without Christ, they do not know where to put their messianic mindset. So they become attached to false messiahs instead.

The height of goodness is God giving His only Son to be crucified, and the height of evil is crucifying Him. It follows inescapably that the greatest ongoing good is the celebration of the re-presentation of His Self-Sacrifice, Holy Mass; and the darkest ongoing evil is the taking of God's children to crucify them. Satanism stipulates that the most valuable victims for its offerings are the most innocent and most intelligent. A human sacrifice is worth more to satan than an animal. And the most innocent victims are children.

The Church once venerated child martyrs believed to have been crucified in satanic rituals: Dominguito del Val of Zaragoza (✝1250), Little St Hugh of Lincoln (✝1255, Holy Thursday); Simon of Trent (✝1475); El Santo Niño de La Guardia (✝1491, Good Friday). Many Jews were detained, tried and executed in each case. A chapel was built to Dominguito in Zaragoza Cathedral, housing his relics. He was beatified in 1807, entering the diocesan calendar. Simon of Trent was listed in the Roman martyrology and an annual procession of his relics persisted in Trent, until suppressed on the day Paul VI signed *Nostra ætate* (1965). A shrine was built to Little Hugh in Lincoln Cathedral, as was one to El Santo Niño in a Dominican monastery in Avila.

Today, these four accounts are dismissed along with scores of others as 'blood libels', the inventions of paranoid, greedy or malicious Christians. The new narrative forbids us from believing that men can crucify children, yet this entails accepting that others fabricate such cases to frame them. For Jews to work evil is impossibly implausible; as for Gentiles, evil flows from their antisemitic nature.

Is it not more balanced to think that though both the Torah and the New Testament forbid the monstrosities of satanism, as well as forbidding bearing false witness, even so, both Jews and Gentiles work both kinds of evil? That is, real instances of child sacrifice have indeed happened, and that following these few cases which are true, more alleged cases, possibly the majority, have been wickedly invented.

Ariel Toaff, Professor of Medieval and Renaissance History at Israel's Bar-Ilan University, bravely published an erudite and objective study, titled *Blood Passover: European Jews and Ritual Murder*.[106] Toaff is the son of a former Chief Rabbi of Rome. Following a furious backlash and death threats, Toaff withdrew the book from circulation. The back cover of an unofficial translation of his book read:

An unprejudiced rereading of the original trial records, however, together with the records of several other trials, viewed within the overall European context and supplemented by an exact knowledge of the relevant Hebrew texts, throws new light on the ritual and

---

[106] Ariel Toaff, *Pasque di sangue. Ebrei d'Europa e omicidi rituali* (2008).

therapeutic significance of blood in Jewish culture, leading the author of the present study to the reluctant conclusion that, particularly where Ashkenazi Jewry was concerned, the 'Blood Libel' accusation was not always an invention.[107]

Before Professor Toaff's book was published, I came to a similar conclusion, having researched specific cases while living in Spain. There is too much corroboratory evidence to dismiss the allegations.

How is child sacrifice unthinkable when the OT is full of it?[108] God commissioned Israel to wipe it out from Canaan and this was partially achieved. But being unfaithful to the Covenant, again and again Israel imitated the surrounding nations in performing child sacrifice, including by their kings.

When today we hear of child sacrifice by Hollywood elites or globalist cabals, why should we dismiss it? We should not be credulous or prejudiced, but given the inherent paucity of evidence, combined with the long history of human sacrifice in various cultures, Judaism's preoccupation with therapeutic and mystical usages of blood, and the grotesque exhibitions of Marina Abramovic's *faux*-cannibilistic parties, let alone the professions of satanists, then the proper response is not to dismiss reports but to reserve judgement and to be vigilant.[109]

---

[107] From a 2011 revised translation of *Blood Passover* by Gian Marco Lucchese and Pietro Gianetti (pseudonyms).

[108] Lev 18:21-30; Dt 12:29-31; 3 Kgs 11:1-8; 16:34; 4 Kgs 3:26-27; 16:1-3; 17:14-18; 2 Chron 33:1-6; Ps 105:37-40; Wis 1:16; 12:3-7; Jer 7:31; 32:31-35.

[109] Hermann Strack's book, subtitled *Human Blood and Jewish Ritual* (translated 1909), which vigorously rejects allegations of human sacrifice by Jews, details the uses of blood from animals, human corpses or menstrual blood *etc*, in Jewish and non-Jewish rituals, oaths, medicines, superstitions, magic and religious deliriums.

The truth is not that child sacrifice does not happen but that it has never stopped. Trafficking in children's blood, child pornography and the demonic lust for abortion make it undeniable that evil seeks to devour God's children. This is spiritual: it is a mocking inversion of the New Covenant, of God giving His Beloved Son in Sacrifice. As Christians adore the Precious Blood of Christ for redeeming the world, so satan lusts after the blood of innocents to corrupt the whole world. The Torah opposes satan; Kabbalah does not.

> Thus, the blood of circumcision, that of the Passover lamb, and that of those killed in defense of their own faith became mixed together and became confounded, hastening the final redemption of Israel and persuading God to wreak His atrocious vengeance on the children of Edom, the Christians, responsible for the tragedies suffered by the Jewish people. The Jews in Germany who, during the first crusade, sacrificed their own children 'as Abraham sacrificed Isaac his son', were perfectly convinced that their own blood, together with that of the two other sacrifices — circumcision and the Passover lamb — all offered to God in abnegation, would not be lost, but would constitute the powerful fluid from which the well-deserved and predicted revenge and the much-desired Redemption would ferment.[110]

Without Christ, dangerous confusion surrounds the religiously minded on the profound meaning of blood.

---

[110] Ariel Toaff, *Blood Passover* (2008), p.146 [translation].

What is New in the New Covenant?

The New Covenant is New because the Incarnation is *"a new thing upon the earth"* (Jer 31:22). It is New because it is cut not in the blood of animals but in the Most Precious Blood of the God-Man. It is New because the uncreated enters the created so that the created can enter the uncreated. It is universal and spiritual instead of particular and material.

In His Sermon on the Mount, Jesus repeatedly said, *"You have heard that it hath been said to them of old…"* The old commandments Jesus elevated beyond all imagining, by directing us to internalise spiritually what had once been more materially understood.

Being eternal, the New even penetrates the past. The biographies of King Saul and King David prefigure the struggle between the Old Covenant and the New — ultimate victory, that is in the spiritual sphere, is achieved by being willing to sacrifice oneself in the temporal. So, the Son of David, not Saul, has the eternal throne.

While the Jews have been made, or bred, to be the first to believe this, to be given grace upon grace and become the greatest lights to the world when they are open to God, so when they refuse grace they become the most dangerous.

For example, the world's idea is to go after money. But an inspired Jew once wrote,

The desire of money is the root of all evils; which some coveting have erred from the faith, and have entangled themselves in many sorrows. (1 Tim 6:10)

Freeing us from mammon's grasp, God wants to enrich us with grace. We are to store up treasure in Heaven through acts of charity and sacrifice. In pursuing grace, Jews excel — look at the Apostles — to the benefit of many. In chasing money, other Jews excel, to the detriment of many.

Great gifts from God will bear great fruits if used faithfully. But if misused, they do great damage. For example: being the Chosen People; receiving the Law from Moses; being led by angels to clear the land of Canaanites.

These three gifts are tectonic. Received well, what do we see? Mary chosen to be Mother of God and through her Son everyone can become a member of His chosen people. A spiritualisation of the Law so that multiplicity is solved in simplicity, the 613 commandments of the Torah being summed up: love God, and like it, love neighbour. Thirdly, the help of angels is offered for driving sin from our souls.

But misunderstood, the material excluding the spiritual, the three gifts become occasions for disasters. A superiority complex which looks down on Goyim with contempt. A suffocating legalism, as witnessed in the Pharisees, which deliberately overburdens men with laws so that they cannot naturally flourish. And a demonic drive to push Palestinians from their land, a plan which, if pursued, threatens to draw down the whole world (if not militarily, then geo-politically).

The Old and the New meet in Christ. To reject Him is to reject also the Old. A worldview which values the material more than the spiritual is necessarily in conflict with the New Covenant, which raises the material, even flesh, through the infinite power of God's Spirit. How, amid orchestrated chaos and deliberate confusion, shall we know what to believe? In the NT, God makes known the inner truth, a mystery which *in other generations was not known to the sons of men, as it is now revealed to His holy apostles and prophets in the Spirit.* (Eph 3:5)

Raising our minds, Jesus taught that His *"kingdom is not of this world"* (Jn 18:36). A fearful Pilate wanted to respect the spiritual unknown, but instead he sold out to the enemy, to those who had been murdering God's prophets for centuries: *"But the Jews cried out, saying: If thou release this man, thou art not Caesar's friend"* (Jn 19:12).

Reckoning that spilling the Blood of Christ was success, they continued by stirring up opposition against the Church:

But the Jews stirred up religious and honourable women and the chief men of the city: and raised persecution against Paul and Barnabas. (Acts 13:50)

After this, in Lystra, the crowds so loved Paul and Barnabas that the two of them had to restrain the people from offering sacrifices to them. But what changed this enthusiasm to worship the Apostles into a mortal hatred?

Now there came thither certain Jews from Antioch and Iconium: and, persuading the multitude and stoning Paul, drew him out of the city, thinking him to be dead. (Acts 14:18)

This multitude represents Christendom, or the world population venerating the saints, yet finally turning against the Church as in today's shrieking, pro-abort, pro-homo, transhumanist persecutors. So, in Thessalonica *the Jews, moved with envy and taking unto them some wicked men of the vulgar sort and making a tumult, set the city in an uproar.* (Acts 17:5)

The State is not always deceived or cowed. Sometimes it upholds justice (Acts 18:12-17). But behind the scenes, deceit is at work. Temptation or pain are set to befall all due to *"the conspiracies of the Jews"* (Acts 20:19).

Because St Paul would not give in to them, *"those Jews that were of Asia... stirred up all the people and laid hands upon him"* (Acts 21:27). They levelled lying accusations, finding ways to bring the powers of the State to work against the Church (Acts 22:30; 28:17-19). So intense is this hatred that some are even willing to starve themselves to death in order to murder, an insanity approved by the Sanhedrin:

Some of the Jews gathered together and bound themselves under a curse, saying that they would neither eat nor drink till they killed Paul. And they were more than forty men that had made this conspiracy. Who came to the chief priests and the ancients and said: We have bound ourselves under a great curse that we will eat nothing till we have slain Paul. Now therefore do you with the council signify to the tribune, that he bring him forth to you, as if you meant to know something more certain touching him. And we, before he come near, are ready to kill him. (Acts 23:12-15)

The High Priest is not ashamed to collaborate with spin doctors and experts in law, to work hypocritical misdirection, to manipulate the powers of the State with outright inventions, hoping to convict under the death penalty those whom they oppose (Acts 24:1-9). They do not relent to have the Church unjustly restrained (Acts 24:27). They want the Apostle *"to be brought to Jerusalem, laying wait to kill him in the way"* (Acts 25:2-3).

The hatred of God runs so deep as to enlist demons, magic, and to try to turn the State from Christ, like the *"magician, a false prophet, a Jew, whose name was Bar-Jesu... seeking to turn away the proconsul from the faith"* (Acts 13:6-8). He is a forerunner of Kabbalah, his efforts making him blind.

And now behold, the hand of the Lord is upon thee: and thou shalt be blind, not seeing the sun for a time. And immediately there fell a mist and darkness upon him: and going about, he sought some one to lead him by the hand. (Acts 13:11)

Others sought to leverage the Name of Jesus for miracles, yet without faith:

Jewish exorcists who went about, attempted to invoke over them that had evil spirits, the name of the Lord Jesus, saying: I conjure you by Jesus, whom Paul preacheth. And there were certain men, seven sons of Sceva, a Jew, a chief priest, that did this. But the wicked spirit... prevailed against them, so that they fled out of that house naked and wounded. (Acts 19:13-16)

More positively, this wrought conversions so that

many of them who had followed curious arts brought together their books and burnt them before all... So mightily grew the word of God, and was confirmed. (Acts 19:19-20)

This fight is not over. It will continue to the Apocalypse, until everyone acknowledges that the Old has given way to the New. The Risen Jesus says to His flock of both the beginning and the end: *"Thou art blasphemed by them that say they are Jews and are not, but are the synagogue of Satan"* (Apoc 2:9). If we are approaching the end, then the conflict between the two sides will be felt by everyone. Each has to choose between everlasting life or death.

What is the Law of Moses worth today? Everything and nothing. Everything in Christ, nothing without Him.

ZIONISM, GLOBALISM AND THE JEWISH ANTICHRIST

The kings of the earth stood up, and the princes met together, against the Lord and against his Christ.

Psalm 2:2

On the day of His Ascension, Jesus commanded His Apostles to take the Gospel from Jerusalem to the ends of the earth (Acts 1:8). From this sowing of the Word, the Church would grow to cover the globe. The Church is by nature universal, meaning the whole is contained in each part — exemplified by the diocesan bishop, actualised in the Holy Eucharist.

This spiritual and apostolic mission, by drawing up men, thereby draws up families and nations. By purifying and elevating souls, Christianity animates everywhere the social and political spheres.

The enemy is watching closely. Yet satan, the prince of privation, cannot build anything. Instead, he infiltrates, corrupts, lies, kills and takes over where he can. His desire is to seat his man on the throne of the world and insult God. Human beings are incapable of foreseeing the historical phases to bring this about, but cooperate with the demonic agenda through their own pride, greed, lust and ongoing resentment of Jesus Christ. It is satan who works out how to

harness the sins of billions to feed his long-term strategy —
except he miscalculated the last act.

Despite the devil's formidable intelligence, determination
and ruthlessness, he is, obviously, no match for God. All the
efforts of those who serve satan, knowingly or not, inexorably
serve the purpose of God: *"He that dwelleth in heaven shall
laugh at them: and the Lord shall deride them"* (Ps 2:4).

Aping the Lord, the devil wants a one-world religion. To
convince most, its palace must be in Jerusalem. For this satan
needs Zionism. Inseparably, he needs globalism. If, for one
moment, he could corrupt the whole world, turn all from
Jesus to himself, then he would be quasi-consoled for
eternity.[111] Obviously, this is not going to happen.

The return of Jews to geographical Israel is permitted by
God but is not willed by Him. Pope St Pius X told Theodore
Herzl, the father of modern Zionism:

> We are unable to favour this movement. We cannot
> prevent the Jews from going to Jerusalem — but we
> could never sanction it. The ground of Jerusalem, if it
> were not always sacred, has been sanctified by the life
> of Jesus Christ. As the head of the Church, I cannot
> answer you otherwise. The Jews have not recognised
> our Lord, therefore we cannot recognise the Jewish
> people… And so if you come to Palestine and settle
> your people there, we will be ready with churches and
> priests to baptise all of you.[112]

---

[111] satan's satisfaction would not be in winning man's admiration, for he despises
us, but rather, in despoiling God.

[112] Raphael Patai, *The Complete Diaries of Theodor Herzl*, translated by Harry
Zohn (1960), Vol IV, p.1601-1605.

The audience took place on the Feast of the Conversion of St Paul. God desires a far greater good for the Jews, a far better Promised Land — the eternal home of Heaven. It is to this that the OT prophecies refer, when they speak of Israel returning to God: it means their conversion to Jesus Christ.

The long and apparently successful campaign by Jews to retake the land of Israel has depended upon a manipulation of great powers, and is sustainable only by weakening the world through globalism. But the manipulators are being manipulated, the deceivers are being deceived, the use of terror will backfire. For it is all leading to the establishment of the throne of the Antichrist. Zionism is spiritual suicide.

Why does God permit this? To bestow reward or punishment, God is testing every man's heart, not least our trust in Him. When the Jews convert, they will share in the visible victory over that final oppressor of the whole world, crushing the head of the snake who lied from the beginning.

Zionism: Religion without God

The establishment of the State of Israel in 1948 is highly significant. But it does not mean what many suppose. With religious fervour, Zionism takes its foundational premise from the OT but rejects the OT's authors, including God.

On the face of it, it is astounding that a people who were landless for two thousand years have regained political sovereignty over their original territory. In parallel, the resurrection of Hebrew as a living language, which a hundred years ago was all but dead, is an astonishing achievement. It all seems so unlikely that many conclude it can have only occurred with God's help.

It is true that the Zionist project requires preternatural assistance but this does not mean aid from God. It is the devil who has been working desperately to make it happen, as is made evident by Zionism's methods and *telos*. The methods are evil, as daily news bulletins show. And the end goal, even if many who are involved do not yet realise it, is the rebuilding of the Temple in Jerusalem.

The OT speaks again and again of the gathering of God's people from the ends of the earth to return them to the land, even to Mount Sion, to worship God. If misunderstood, such prophecies foster Zionist domination of other nations: *"I will bring them into my holy mount… for my house shall be called the house of prayer, for all nations"* (Is 56:7). With this verse in mind, David Ben-Gurion predicted,

> The image of the world in 1987 as traced in my imagination: …With the exception of the USSR… all other continents will become united in a world alliance, at whose disposal will be an international police force… In Jerusalem, the United Nations (a truly United Nations) will build a Shrine of the Prophets to serve the federated union of all continents; this will be the seat of the Supreme Court of Mankind, to settle all controversies among the federated continents, as prophesied by Isaiah.[113]

This dream is a nightmare. It arises from mis-reading the Scriptures, specifically by prioritising the material over the spiritual. Properly understood, Isaiah's prophecy refers to the

---

[113] *Jewish Telegraphic Agency* (4th Jan 1962), interview with *Look Magazine*. Ben-Gurion could not fit Russia into his scheme. Our Lady of Fatima has better plans.

souls entering the Church and thence the eternal Paradise, to dwell in the Temple of God.

> Behold the house increasing: behold the edifice pervade the whole world. Rejoice, because you have entered into the courts; rejoice, because you are being built into the temple of God. For those who enter are themselves built up, they themselves are the house of God: He is the inhabitor, for Whom the house is built over the whole world…[114]

This is a divine project, reaching beyond the universe. Our world is a quarry and we are the stones: here we are cut, chiselled and polished, then transported by death to that abode above to be set in place for eternity. This is a work worthy of God, greater than anything which happens on earth. The true Holy Land indicated by ancient Israel is the Church: on earth and in Heaven. God's land cannot be inherited by aggressive injustice and violence, but is reserved for *"the meek: for they shall possess the land"* (Mt 5:4).

God cannot lie. When He promises land to Israel, He means to give it. When He promises it will be forever, it is. When the Jews were expelled from Jerusalem by Emperor Hadrian after the Second Jewish-Roman War, they had already had a century's access to the real holy city — Heaven. God allowed nothing to be taken away without providing much better in its place. Christ is the way. The Jews have *not* been without a promised land for two thousand years. It is only a question of whether or not they wish to enter the Church and take possession of that which was promised.

---

[114] St Augustine, *Enarration on Psalm 95*, 9.

A time is coming, the Lord says, when I will reverse the sentence of exile against my people of Israel and Juda; I, the Lord, will restore them to possession of the land I gave to their fathers. (Jer 30:3 Knox)

The Vulgate has *"convertam conversionem"* for reversing the exile and again *"convertam"* for *"I will restore"*. This is not mere geography, but a turning of hearts to see that the Place which Jesus, not Joshua, opened up, is Heaven, which Abraham, Isaac and Jacob have already inherited (Mt 8:11).

Or else if the Jews are meant to go back to Israel, are they meant to offer the Mosaic sacrifices too? Start killing again lambs from the flock, in preference to our daily offering of the true Lamb of God? If the Old Covenant could be revived, then satan would have caught God in an apparent contradiction, for a man could protest to God: "I do not need Your Jesus, for I follow the Law You gave through Moses." However, without Jerusalem's altar of holocaust, none can even begin to believe they fulfil the Law of Moses, except by coming to Holy Mass. The Lord sifts hearts by examining how we suppose Jeremiah's prophecy is to be fulfilled.

On the one hand, it would be an error to read the *"sentence of exile"* as belonging to the past only, for example, the Babylonian exile, imagining that Jeremiah's words have no further application. The return is always spiritually relevant, pointing to the worldwide people of God being gathered into one heart and one mind, that is a spiritual nation, in the Faith that goes out from Rome.

On the other hand, it would be another error to allegorise the return from exile so completely that one denies it had a real referent the first time round in history or to deny that it has a natural referent in the future, claiming it just has spiritual meanings. For who can say the Jews will not be gathered again in Israel, even on Mount Sion, in some manner of rebuilt Temple, not as fulfilment of the prophecies, but as their dark shadow, given as a sign of the times? Not as directly willed by God, but as permitted?

The spiritual accomplishment of the prophecies does not exclude the literal sense from being satisfied again. God sets both the spiritual and the material programmes to build the Temple before us so that each can choose: life eternal won by faith or else self-will bringing everlasting death.

It is beside the point that most Zionists do not know or appear to care about building the Temple. Most of the heavy lifting so far has been done by political, not religious, actors. But the devil knows and cares where he is leading carnal minded-men. He wants the Temple. It will be his best chance to steal the worship owed only to God.

Recognising this protects Catholics from succumbing, as many Protestants do, to 'Christian Zionism', that is, to a belief that God fulfils His messianic promises by granting Middle Eastern real estate to a political power. The official policy of Israel's Likud Party is to reestablish the 'biblical borders', exploiting God's ancient works for their own godless agenda.[115]

---

[115] Israel Shahak, *Jewish History, Jewish Religion: The Weight of Three Thousand Years* (1994), p.10, "In May 1993, Ariel Sharon formally proposed in the Likud Convention that Israel should adopt the 'Biblical borders' concept as its official policy. There were rather few objections to this proposal, either in the Likud or outside it, and all were cased on pragmatic grounds. No one even asked Sharon where exactly are the Biblical borders which he was urging that Israel should attain."

The founder of the Likud Party, Menachem Begin (formerly leader of the terrorist-Zionist Irgun), stated point blank when he was Prime Minister of Israel that the Palestinians would never be granted sovereignty in Judea, Samaria [the West Bank] or the Gaza Strip, because of "our people's right to the Land; it is our Land as of right."[116] The sense of entitlement to the exclusion of others is stunning. How is it that the Palestinians have no right to their home?

If Christians accept Zionism as God's fulfilment of biblical prophecies, they are effectively apostatising from the New Covenant as the complete fulfilment of the Old and buying into Judaism's claims. This confuses countless souls.

According to [Rabbi Yehuda] Ashkenazi, things turned around after Israel's establishment. Now it was Christianity that suffered from a loss of self-identity. It's not the eyes of the Jews that are covered by a veil that prevents them from understanding the Old Testament; it's the Christians who are blind and don't understand the New Testament. The reestablishment of Jewish sovereignty proves that the Jews were right in their lengthy disputation with Christianity. Realization of the prophecies about the return to Zion proves that the Jewish interpretation of the Bible, not the Christian one, is the right one. Instead of the Jews serving as 'witnesses of faith' for the justification of Christianity, Ashkenazi says, now the Christians served as witnesses who are astonished at the resurgence of the Jewish

---

[116] Presented to President Jimmy Carter by Menachem Begin, *Israel Framework for the Peace-Making Process between Israel and its Neighbors* (July 1977). Israel's State Archives, File A 4313/1.

people. Thus a new interpretation of the creation of the State of Israel developed. Not only a 'national home' like that of other peoples, but a religious event that was meant to refute the Christian faith.[117]

Zionism is a manifestation on the political level of the rejection of the New Covenant in favour of the Old on the spiritual level. The satanic driver of Zionism is hidden. Most Christians and Jews know nothing of his involvement. While Jews never ceased dreaming of a return to the land of Israel, by what means has it actually been enabled? The methods used reveal who is ultimately behind it all.

Jewish intellectual Gore Vidal lamented that establishing the Israeli State in 1948 pivoted on a two million dollar bribe to President Truman.[118] This is of a piece with Zionism's historical development. While usurers have bankrolled wars for centuries, the Battle of Waterloo stands out as a lesson learned by bankers in utilising conflict for phenomenal profit.

After this, for whose benefit were nineteenth century French, German and English surveyors, who were invariably

---

[117] Israel Jacob Yuval, Haaretz, *Can Jews and Christians Truly Reconcile?* (2020). Professor Yuval shows a lot of good will in this article.

[118] In his Foreword for Israel Shahak's *Jewish History, Jewish Religion: The Weight of Three Thousand Years* (1994), Gore Vidal describes how the State of Israel was achieved through a $2 million cash 'donation' to Truman: "Sometime in the late 1950s, that world-class gossip and occasional historian, John F. Kennedy, told me how, in 1948, Harry S. Truman had been pretty much abandoned by everyone when he came to run for president. Then an American Zionist brought him two million dollars in cash, in a suitcase, aboard his whistle-stop campaign train. 'That's why our recognition of Israel was rushed through so fast.' As neither Jack nor I was an antisemite (unlike his father and my grandfather) we took this to be just another funny story about Truman and the serene corruption of American politics... But I will say that the hasty invention of Israel has poisoned the political and intellectual life of the USA, Israel's unlikely patron."

establishment men, competing to map out the Holy Land? How did it come to be that Australian farm boys were used, by establishment men, to ride over Turkish guns at Beersheba and thereby open up Palestine in October 1917? Given that two days later, what would become known as the Balfour Declaration was (first) communicated to Lord Lionel Rothschild, whose interests was the British government serving in WWI? How is it that Zionist terrorism is lauded, that Menachem Begin is held as a hero? Who designed the United Nations (UN), and why is the constant expansion of settlements by forced appropriation in Palestine tolerated by the UN? International law is a fig leaf, a theatre, a weapon.

How can anyone think this is God's project? Manipulation, fraud, warmongering and terrorism are not from God. Yet Zionists excuse them by a graceless reading of the OT. God is always honest with the literal sense of Scripture, as well as its spiritual senses. Attempts to return to the land and rebuild the Temple carry weighty meaning, but not from a superficial reading of Scripture. We must be awake to Heaven to understand. Adam woke up, as also did Abram, each from a momentous *"deep sleep"* (תַּרְדֵּמָה Gen 2:21; 15:12), to see God's work with new eyes. Another *"deep sleep"* is fallen on the Jews but they are not yet awoken from it. Isaiah foretold:

> *For the Lord hath mingled for you the spirit of a deep sleep* [רוּחַ תַּרְדֵּמָה, πνεύματι κατανύξεως, *spiritum soporis*]*, he will shut up your eyes, he will cover your prophets and princes, that see visions.* (Is 29:10)

St Paul quotes this verse as he explains the blindness of the Jews preceding their conversion:

καθὼς γέγραπται... As it is written: God hath given them the spirit of insensibility [πνεῦμα κατανύξεως]; *eyes that they should not see; and ears that they should not hear, until this present day.* (Rom 11:8)

The millennial attempt to build the Temple and altar will backfire, for in the very next line St Paul quotes one punishment for the Crucifixion: *"And David saith: Let their table be made a snare, and a trap, and a stumbling block, and a recompense unto them"* (Rom 11:9; Ps 68:23). This 'table', this false altar, is in preparation. The remote idea took shape among Christians with the Protestant Reformation, went further with the introduction of the *novus ordo missæ*, and Bergoglio's inter-faith efforts seem set to assist the ushering in of a one-world religion, centred on a godless altar.

There are Jews who long to have sacrifices again on an altar on Temple Mount. There are Messianic Jews and Christians who although they know the Bible well enough to realise there must be a visible sacrifice, regrettably look to a rebuilt Temple as the place to perform it. If they knew the Church, they would know this natural desire for visible sacrifice is satisfied perfectly in Holy Mass. As all the sacrifices of the Law are fulfilled and transcended in Christ, and as Holy Mass is the self-same sacrifice as Calvary, then here is the answer to everyone's deepest longings. But how many see it in the Scriptures?

The Prophet Hosea makes it crystal clear that Israel would lose their priesthood and altar and sacrifice until they receive David — that is Jesus — as King (Hos 3:4-5). But the Jews will not hear it and many are determined to reestablish the rites against God's will.

How can civilisation survive, if we do not understand the OT? Though God loved David so very much, still, He refused to let him build the Temple. Because of David's bloodshed, God chose Solomon to build it instead.[119] How, then, can the present plans to rebuild it in Jerusalem be pleasing to God, given the violence of the Israeli State? David hardly shed blood unjustly but the IDF and Mossad are indiscriminate. How can Christians imagine this project is pleasing to God?

Rejecting God's call, the Zionist project proceeds by deceit, bribery and violence. In His boundless genius, God permits it to continue as a very visible warning sign of how far the rejection of Christianity has descended, for Zionism has depended upon many perverted nations under perverted governments. In itself it cannot succeed, because its basis is godless and inhuman — namely, triumph through destruction.

Some of Zionism's Jewish opponents are sensitive to Christ's teaching, *"All things therefore whatsoever you would that men should do to you, do you also to them. For this is the law and the prophets"* (Mt 7:12). They rue Israel's cruelty. However, leading Zionists treat Palestinians as they would treat the whole world, if given the opportunity.

Again, why does God allow men to pursue this false goal? In patience and wisdom, God tests His Church through Jews who reject Jesus, to lead her to spiritual purity and maturity, so that she is ripe to receive Jesus when He returns. The restoration of Israel as a sovereign nation demonstrates the

---

[119] God said to David: *"Thou hast shed much blood, and fought many battles, so thou canst not build a house to my name, after shedding so much blood before me: The son, that shall be born to thee, shall be a most quiet man... He shall build a house to my name."* (1 Chron 22:8-10)

determination of men, not the fulfilment of God's Promises. The restoration of the Temple contains a parallel meaning. The closer the rebuilding of the Temple seems to be, so much clearer is the measure of the world's rejection of Jesus as the true Temple. Thereby all who have eyes to see the signs of the times can be comforted that the harvest is near.

Globalism — the Jewish Dream

Zionism's progress has depended upon reducing and steering other nations against their own interest. It has been a very long-term project, befitting not just a political purpose (which for centuries could have no conceivable roadmap), but a spiritual goal which perdures even without visible hope.

If it were only about land, then local political power and military force would be enough. But the aim is deeper than soil, deeper than man. The demonic aim requires a one-world order, because it is about finalising the rejection of Jesus, the King of Kings. To satisfy man's instinct for religion, it needs a Temple with global appeal. It amounts to a rebuilding of the Tower of Babel. For this satan can use Judaism as a spearhead, largely thanks to its rejection of Jesus.[120]

Though God's plan is for diverse nations to live under Christ, satan wants a single world order under himself. We see it arising. What are its roots?

The Knights Templar, the first of the military orders, began as an international Christian elite. Their purpose was to

---

[120] Yuri Slezkine, *The Jewish Century* (2019), p.1, "Modernization, in other words is about everyone becoming Jewish… but no one is better at being Jewish than the Jews themselves. In the age of capital, they are the most creative entrepreneurs; in the age of alienation, they are the most experienced exiles; and in the age of expertise, they are the most proficient professionals."

defend the Christian Kingdom in the Holy Land, especially for pilgrims. Their financial resources became immense, and were soon managed by Jews. Though clichéd reports purporting to be history are not to be trusted, it seems that the organisation did become diabolically corrupted. They were dissolved in 1312. Note their full title was *Pauperes commilitones Christi Templique Salomonici*, that is, The Poor Fellow-Soldiers of Christ and of the Temple of Solomon. The first half of their title is solidly Christian, the second half betrays strong Jewish influence.

Skipping forward four centuries, we see the formation in 1717 of another fraternal order of the elite, the Freemasons, also named in relation to Solomon's Temple. The masons' purpose is to cut and assemble stones for a new world order at the behest of the 'Grand Architect of the Universe', an ill-defined 'Supreme Being' who certainly is not God. From God the masons think they are free.

Following their spread, secret societies became fashionable. Even if most members join from self-interest, rather than any grand vision, these organisations which sideline Jesus are the furthest thing from a joke. British Prime Minister Benjamin Disraeli wrote that the revolutions which swept Europe in 1848 were organised by

> the secret societies who form provisional governments, and men of Jewish race are found at the head of every one of them. The people of God co-operate with atheists; the most skilful accumulators of property ally themselves with communists; the peculiar and chosen race touch the hand of all the scum and low castes of

Europe! And all this because they wish to destroy that ungrateful Christendom which owes to them even its name, and whose tyranny they can no longer endure.

When the secret societies, in February, 1848, surprised Europe, they were themselves surprised by the unexpected opportunity, and so little capable were they of seizing the occasion, that had it not been for the Jews, who of late years unfortunately have been connecting themselves with these unhallowed associations, imbecile as were the governments, the uncalled-for outbreak would not have ravaged Europe. But the fiery energy and the teeming resources of the children of Israel maintained for a long time the unnecessary and useless struggle. If the reader throw his eye over the provisional governments of Germany and Italy, and even of France, formed at that period, he will recognise everywhere the Jewish element.[121]

Disraeli was Jewish, no less so for becoming Anglican too. He disapproved the violence and chaos of the revolutionaries but could not conceal his pride at their Israeli energy. He put the blame for their outbursts on Christian oppressors. This is a red herring, a distraction from the Jewish revolutionary spirit.

Another British Prime Minister, Winston Churchill, picks up the story of revolution in the following century.

The adherents of this sinister confederacy are mostly men reared up among the unhappy populations of countries where Jews are persecuted on account of their

---

[121] Benjamin Disraeli, *Life of Lord George Bentinck* (1852), X.

race. Most, if not all, of them have forsaken the faith of their forefathers, and divorced from their minds all spiritual hopes of the next world. This movement among the Jews is not new. From the days of Spartacus-Weishaupt [d.1830] to those of Karl Marx, and down to Trotsky (Russia), Bela Kun (Hungary), Rosa Luxembourg (Germany), and Emma Goldman (United States), this world-wide conspiracy for the overthrow of civilisation and for the reconstitution of society on the basis of arrested development, of envious malevolence, and impossible equality, has been steadily growing. It played, as a modern writer, Mrs. Webster, has so ably shown, a definitely recognisable part in the tragedy of the French Revolution. It has been the mainspring of every subversive movement during the Nineteenth Century; and now at last this band of extraordinary personalities from the underworld of the great cities of Europe and America have gripped the Russian people by the hair of their heads and have become practically the undisputed masters of that enormous empire.[122]

It is scarcely conceivable that today's public figures should speak so openly about Jews. Churchill, like Disraeli, stresses that the Jews involved have mostly fallen away from Judaism. This is because Judaism is untenable. When men fall away from it, if they have not Christ, they are utterly unmoored.

A contributing factor to their spasmodic spirit may have been the unexpected release from the long oppression

---

[122] Winston Churchill, *Illustrated Sunday Herald*, *Zionism versus Bolshevism* (London, Feb 1920), p.5.

suffered by Jewish communities under their own leaders during the period of classical Judaism (the second to the eighteenth century). Israel Shahak describes how

> once the modern state had come into existence, the Jewish community lost its powers to punish or intimidate the individual Jew. The bonds of one of the most closed of 'closed societies', one of the most totalitarian societies in the whole history of mankind were snapped. This act of liberation came mostly from *outside;* although there were some Jews who helped it from within, these were at first very few.[123]

I hesitate to accept everything Shahak writes about Judaism's totalitarian character. He seems fundamentally opposed to any doctrinal or moral absolutes taught by organised religion. Thereby he throws the baby (Jesus) out with the dirty bathwater (Judaism). But in this he demonstrates a crucial dynamic: rejecting Judaism as impossible, he turns not to Jesus Christ and true religion, but instead voices a superficially attractive humanism which, for all its searching, cannot get anyone into Heaven. The rabbis rarely strike us as being revolutionary, even so, by being "totalitarian", they provoke social revolution in the people, who seek escape from their suffocating control. In fact, this is a spiritual consequence of the rabbis' rebellion against God.

That said, Shahak's observation stands: it cannot have been easy for poor Jews of the classical period, who, unlike their leaders, were so powerless and cut off from the world.

---

[123] Israel Shahak, *Jewish History, Jewish Religion: The Weight of Three Thousand Years* (1994), p.15.

No wonder, once emancipated, they have been among the most fervent and psychotic of revolutionaries.[124]

Bringing the revolutionary spirit from Russia to Germany, Nahum Goldmann, in his 1915 pamphlet, *The Spirit of Militarism*, praised and expanded on Karl Marx, zealously predicting that German victory in WWI was inevitable.

> The meaning and historical mission of our time can be summed up… to reorganise human culture, to replace the existing social system with a new one. All restructuring now consists in two things: the destruction of the old order and the construction of the new…
>
> Thus, the first task of our time is destruction: all social strata and societal formations created by the old system must be annihilated, individuals must be torn from their ancestral milieus; no tradition can be considered sacred

---

[124] Gershom Scholem, *Redemption Through Sin* (1971), I, "The nihilism of the Sabbatian and Frankist movements, with its doctrine so profoundly shocking to the Jewish conception of things that the violation of the Torah could become its true fulfillment (*bittulah shel torah zehu kiyyumah*), was a dialectical outgrowth of the belief in the Messiahship of Sabbatai Zevi… [W]ithin the spiritual world of the Sabbatian sects, within the very *sanctum sanctorum* of Kabbalistic mysticism, as it were, the crisis of faith which overtook the Jewish people as a whole upon its emergence from its medieval isolation was first anticipated, and how groups of Jews within the walls of the ghetto, while still outwardly adhering to the practices of their forefathers, had begun to embark on a radically new inner life of their own. Prior to the French Revolution the historical conditions were lacking which might have caused this upheaval to break forth in the form of an open struggle for social change, with the result that it turned further inward upon itself to act upon the hidden recesses of the Jewish psyche; but it would be mistaken to conclude from this that Sabbatianism did not permanently affect the outward course of Jewish history. The desire for total liberation which played so tragic a role in the development of Sabbatian nihilism was by no means a purely self-destructive force; on the contrary, beneath the surface of lawlessness, antinomianism, and catastrophic negation, powerful constructive impulses were at work, and these, I maintain, it is the duty of the historian to uncover."

anymore; old age is only regarded as a sign of illness; the slogan is: what was, must go.[125]

Goldmann identified capitalism and democracy as the two weapons of destruction. Once their work was complete, a new order was to be established on the twin principles of uniformity and subordination. Those who are fit to be ruled (the vast majority) were to subordinate themselves to a life of grey uniformity, while those who prove themselves capable of seizing leadership simply dominate. The system was to be secured so that no further rebellion would ever be possible.

Such was the spirit of the twenty-year-old Goldmann. Later, he moved to New York, founded the World Jewish Congress (1936) and became President of the World Zionist Organisation (1956). He had been born in Tsarist Russia. Churchill recounts its demise:

> There is no need to exaggerate the part played in the creation of Bolshevism and in the actual bringing about of the Russian Revolution by these international and for the most part atheistical Jews. It is certainly a very great one; it probably outweighs all others... [T]he majority

---

[125] Nahum Goldmann, *The Spirit of Militarism* (1915), p.37-38. He continues: "The forces executing this negative task of our time are capitalism in the economic-social realm and democracy in the political-spiritual realm. We all know how much they have already achieved, but we also know that their work is not yet entirely finished. Capitalism still battles against the forms of the old, traditional economy, and democracy continues a fierce struggle against all reactionary forces. The military spirit will complete the work. Its principle of uniformity will carry out the negative task of the time completely: once all members of our cultural sphere are uniformed as soldiers of our cultural system, this task will be solved. Then arises the other, greater and more challenging task: the construction of the new order. The members who have now been uprooted from their old foundations and layers, lying disordered and anarchic, must be organised into new formations and categories... A new, pyramidal, hierarchical system must be erected."

of the leading figures are Jews. Moreover, the principal inspiration and driving power comes from the Jewish leaders… In the Soviet institutions the predominance of Jews is even more astonishing. And the prominent, if not indeed the principal, part in the system of terrorism applied by the Extraordinary Commissions for Combating Counter-Revolution has been taken by Jews, and in some notable cases by Jewesses.[126]

Besides killing millions of men, WWI brought down four empires: those of the Russian Tsar (Orthodox), the Austro-Hungarian Habsburg monarchy (Catholic), the Prussian monarchy of Kaiser Wilhelm (Protestant), and somewhat delayed, the Ottoman Empire (Islamic). *Cui bono*? Amid this overturning of order, something progressed. The war saw the Balfour Declaration issued and the Mandate for Palestine instituted. To defeat the Turks, Jews used the English, or rather the colonials, for Churchill, as First Lord of the Admiralty, sent Australian and New Zealand Army Corps (ANZAC) into Gallipoli, their blood poured out for Zionism.

In another world war, costing more millions of dead, Churchill, a Freemason, played his part again. After this, England's bleeding and bankrupt empire dissolved. More important for Israel was America. Truman, a more dedicated Freemason, also played his part for Israel, being persuaded, as we have heard, by two million arguments from the Jews. Where did they get the chutzpah and the money? Did not the Rothschild family make its fortune fixing a bet on Waterloo,

---

[126] Winston Churchill, *Illustrated Sunday Herald, Zionism versus Bolshevism* (London, Feb 1920), p.5.

arbitraging on war? Did this mis-directing of military force not emerge much earlier, even with the Templars?

For the record: I do not believe that anybody can plot in advance a strategy from the Templars to Truman. It is beyond human calculation. It is the devil. See how Iraqis have suffered since their sick tyrant Saddam was taken down. They were not liberated but deliberately ruined. The destruction of Iraq was fanatically driven by a generation of American Jews, this time called Neoconservatives.[127] They lie, kill, retire and die. They can hardly know the full evil they serve. But it is becoming apparent as globalism climaxes.

President Vladimir Putin, in 2012, and President Donald Trump, in 2017, met with the Sanhedrin in Jerusalem, and both responded favourably to their plans to rebuild the Temple.[128] Putin was told by a Russian immigrant about the importance of the *Kotel*, "the western wall", the place for Judaism's most intense prayers. Reportedly he responded: "It is exactly for this that I came here, to pray that the Temple will be rebuilt. I wish that all your prayers be answered."[129] If America or Russia, or any other nation, will not serve Christ the King with all its mind and heart and strength and soul, then it will serve Christ's enemy. Spiritual warfare is total.

---

[127] See *A Clean Break: A New Strategy for Securing the Realm* (1996), a policy document written by prominent Zionist neoconservatives, led by Richard Perle, who would later become a key architect of the Iraq War as an advisor to Secretary of Defense Donald Rumsfeld. The paper called for the removal of Saddam Hussein from power in Iraq and the rolling-back and destabilisation of Syria. Both objectives have transpired in the decades since.

[128] In 2004, after 1,600 years of non-existence, the Sanhedrin was ostensibly reconstituted (albeit without asking God).

[129] *The Jerusalem Post, Putin wishes us a rebuilt Temple* (26th June 2012).

To survive, Zionism requires globalism. This is more than acquiring influence over multiple governments. Globalism is an artificial homogenisation of culture and a destruction of identity so that objections to Jewish exceptionalism can be stifled. It begins with multiculturalism, which is not about tolerance but about perversely setting the minority over the majority. The preposterous aim is world domination. Preposterous, except it is foretold again and again in the OT. Recently we have seen the desire of megalomaniacs to lockdown and subjugate is approaching a crescendo.

How can we understand the world, with all its contingent detail? Sacred Scripture gives us the principles from which history and politics flow. They tell us what has been and what is coming (often each single story telling both, for God's Word is eternal). God made the various nations of the world and set their times and boundaries (Acts 17:26; Dt 32:8), with angelic powers assigned to guard them (Dan 10:13,20). Scripture gives the number of nations as seventy (Gen 10). In realpolitik this fluctuates, but symbolically it is why Jesus sent seventy disciples to preach the Gospel ahead of His coming (Lk 10:1). They were to reach the entire world. Pointedly, they returned to Him rejoicing to have overcome the demons (Lk 10:17), which is prophetic of the mission of the Church.

Saliently, some early manuscripts record *"seventy"* and others *"seventy-two"*. A similar ambivalence occurs several times in the OT. Might it mean that after the seventy natural nations created by God, there arise two more nations: a priestly, holy nation, the City of God, in contrast to an unholy, worldly nation, the City of Man?

Counting seventy nations in Genesis 10 is not easy, for extra names are listed. Among them are Heber (father of the Hebrews) and Nimrod (founder of the doomed city of Babel, whom legend tells hunted men to eat them, though Abraham outsmarted him). Hence among all the nations we have these two figureheads for the Holy Nation and for the Antichrist.

In Exodus we read of Moses forming the early Sanhedrin when God instructed him to bring *"seventy of the ancients of Israel"* up the mountain with him, *"and they saw God, and they did eat and drink"* (Ex 24:1,11). They represent all the nations of the world to whom Holy Mass should come.[130] But besides the seventy, there are also named two pairs of brothers: Moses and Aaron, and Nadab and Abiu (sons of Aaron). Moses and Aaron represent the City of God, standing respectively for the Divinity and Humanity of Christ. They are a saving team. Nadab and Abiu represent the opposing City of Man, being killed by God for *"taking their censers [and] offering... strange fire"* (Lev 10:1), false religion.[131] Their fall shows satan and the Antichrist, a destroying team.

The Book of Judges gives numerous prefigurations of the Antichrist being defeated by the Christ. The first was the Canaanite king, Adonibezec. The armies of Juda and Simeon defeated him, captured him and *"cut off his fingers and toes"* (Jdg 1:6). Why so gruesome? Because, as he confessed, he was repaid just as he himself had done. Adonibezec said:

---

[130] Fittingly, the college of cardinals in the Catholic Church was never to exceed seventy members, showing it to be the successor of the Sanhedrin. In the 1970s, Pope Paul VI set a new limit at 120. This was yet another break by the Church hierarchy from God-given OT roots especially meaningful to Jews.

[131] Recall censers in the hellish rebellion of Core, Dathan and Abiron (Num 16).

Seventy kings, having their fingers and toes cut off, gathered up the leavings of the meat under my table: as I have done, so hath God requited me. (Jdg 1:7)

A cruel murderer of kings, Adonibezec died as he deserved. The *"seventy kings"* represent the world (or UN member states), crippled and stripped of sovereignty (*"fingers and toes cut off"*). Adonibezec's name means 'My Lord of Lightning', reflecting subjection to Lucifer. The victorious Juda and Simeon stand for the dual natures of Christ.

Later we read that Jerobaal had seventy sons (Jdg 8:30). One of his sons, Abimelech, vying to be king, *"slew his brethren, the sons of Jerobaal, seventy men, upon one stone"* (Jdg 9:5). Here Abimelech prefigures the Antichrist, symbolically seeking world domination by destroying the sovereignty of all countries so that he can rule alone. But the verse continues: *"And there remained only Joatham, the youngest son of Jerobaal"*. Are there seventy or seventy-two sons? Seventy were killed, one was the killer, one survived. The killer, Abimelech, would later have his head crushed by a woman. The prophetic survivor, Joatham, is the City of God.

The last Book of Kings recounts how seventy sons of the idolatrous King Achab, signifying world leaders who follow God's enemy, end with their decapitated heads in baskets outside the city gate, while the unstoppable Judgement of Jesus is prefigured in their nemesis, King Jehu, whose name means 'Yahweh Himself' (4 Kgs 9-10). These accumulating references to *"seventy"* become hard to overlook. Achab and Jehu stand for the Antichrist and Christ, making seventy-two.

While the OT Scriptures often portray the aspect of the Antichrist as an outsider, a foreign power, the prophets show him rising from within. In a vision given to Ezekiel, an Angel of the Lord shows him the Temple, and says:

Go in, and see the wicked abominations which they commit here. And I went in and saw, and behold every form of creeping things… the abominations, and all the idols of the house of Israel… And seventy men of the ancients of the house of Israel, and Jezonias the son of Saaphan stood in the midst of them… and every one had a censer in his hand: and a cloud of smoke went up from the incense. And he said to me: Surely thou seest, O son of man, what the ancients of the house of Israel do in the dark… for they say: The Lord seeth us not, the Lord hath forsaken the earth. (Ezek 8:9-12)

The seventy ancients had abandoned the worship of God in His House for idolatry, offering incense to animalistic abominations. *They* had *"forsaken"* God. In addition to the seventy was their antichrist leader, Jezonias son of Saaphan. Also mystically present is Ezekiel representing the Humanity of Christ and the Angel representing His Divinity. The seventy stand for the Sanhedrin which, in service of satan, took control of the Temple and crucified Christ. We may think of an anti-pope abusing the Church. They will not prevail: *"Surely thou seest, O son of man"*, says the angel, Jesus' Divinity illumining His Humanity ahead of His final victory.

Each of these OT stories is easy to pass over on its own. But they are threaded together by the theme of seventy plus two in order to serve as a warning. Besides appropriating sovereignty worldwide, globalism will require its own religion. The Abrahamic Family House in Abu Dhabi and the

House of One in Berlin are preparatory steps for a one-world cult.[132] To complete it will require a man more charming, deceptive and ruthless than any other has ever been.

The Jewish Antichrist

The Antichrist, opposing and denying Jesus Christ, will declare of himself, "I am the Christ", or in Hebrew, "I am the Messiah", God's anointed, the saviour of the world. His moment will be brief. His collapse will be complete.

Privately, Jesus warned His disciples: *"For many will come in My name saying, I am Christ: and they will seduce many"* (Mt 24:5; cf. 24:23-25). The final Antichrist will be the most convincing and brutal of many false messiahs. To have any credibility in claiming to be the one promised of old by the Scriptures, he must pass himself off as the *"seed of Abraham"* (Gen 22:18), the *"expectation of the nations"* of the tribe of Judah (Gen 49:10), more specifically a son of David (2 Kgs 7:12-13). All that is to say, he will have to pass himself off as being Jewish.[133]

---

[132] Pope Leo XIII, *Humanum genus* (20th April 1884), 16, "Freemasons… teach the great error of this age… that all religions are alike. This manner of reasoning is calculated to bring about the ruin of all forms of religion, and especially of the Catholic religion, which, as it is the only one that is true, cannot, without great injustice, be regarded as merely equal to other religions."

The interfaith Abrahamic Family House (opened 16th February 2023) on Saadiyat Island in Abu Dhabi includes the St Francis Church, Imam Al-Tayeb Mosque and Moses Ben Maimon Synagogue. The project was the fruit of the mutual efforts of Francis and Ahmed El-Tayeb who co-signed the Document on Human Fraternity for World Peace and Living Together (4th February 2019). Christians, Jews and Muslims have built Berlin's House of One as an interfaith religious centre. The Protestant minister, Rev Gregor Hohberg, Rabbi Andreas Nachama and Imam Kadir Sanci set the cornerstone on 27th May 2021.

[133] St Hippolytus, *Discourse on the End of the World*, 23-25.

Moreover, he must claim to be the *"prophet"* promised by Moses (Dt 18:18), perhaps even a rabbi to succeed *Moshe Rabbeinu* ('Moses our Teacher'). He will take his seat *"in the Temple of God"*, suggesting Jerusalem (2 Thess 2:4), and seem to *"restore again the Kingdom of Israel"* (Acts 1:6).

The Gentile world produces megalomaniacs, but they cannot get traction in claiming to be the biblical Christ. Meanwhile, there has been no shortage of Jewish applicants. Sabbatai Tzevi (d.1676) made a big splash in Smyrna, gaining a massive following. A raving kabbalist, no saviour, he converted to Islam to save his own skin.

More insanely, the Polish-Jew Jacob Frank (d.1791) claimed to be Tzevi reincarnate. Travelling to Turkey as a merchant, there he picked up (Tzevi's) Sabbatain Kabbalah, an orgiastic rebellion against the Law. Frank, too, abandoned his movement, unconvincingly becoming Catholic.[134] It smells of satan sowing seeds for syncretism. Nobel Prize winning novelist Olga Tokarczuk effuses over Jacob Frank's religious emanations:

Jacob gives a lengthy talk to those assembled, full of parables. He proclaims a new religion, one accessible

---

[134] A few months after being baptised (twice, which is impossible), Frank was convicted of heresy in 1760, spending 13 years in prison. Decades later he said: "I tell you: As Christ, as you know, said that he came to free the world from the hands of Satan, but I came to free it from all laws and statutes which have been till now, for all that was the work of the hands of Satan, and by that all fell into his hand. I must destroy all that, and only make that which is black look utterly white. At that time the good God will reveal himself." And, "The first man Adam, at every place he trod a city was built, but I, wherever I only tread all will be destroyed. Because I came only for that, so that everything would become spoiled. But then I will build, so that it will endure forever." *The Collection of the Words of the Lord*, [Jacob Frank], translated by Harris Lenowitz (2004), 2142 & 2145.

exclusively through Esau, meaning Christianity, just as Sabbatai crossed over to Ishmael, meaning the Turkish faith. The progress of salvation depends upon extracting from those religions the seeds of revelation and sowing them in one great divine revelation… the Torah of the World of Emanations. In this religion of the end of days, all three religions will be braided into one.[135]

There is a profound confusion of religion here. Tzevi went from Judaism to Islam, and Frank from Judaism to Catholicism. Threads are being sewn together. What they had in common during their messianic phases was not *prima facie* Judaism, for they both despised the Law. Rather, their sects were mired in Gnostic insanity. In place of theology they trip out on an indescribable demonic abyss.

Tokarczuk's confusion over Esau is telling. She follows the rabbis in identifying Esau with Christians, whereas the Bible as a whole shows he represents the Jews. Using some modern imagination, Tokarczuk portrays Frank's messianism:

It is a question of uniting the three religions: Judaism, Islam, and Christianity. Sabbatai was the First, and he opened the door to Islam, while Baruchiah paved the way to Christianity. What appalls everyone and makes them stomp and shout? It's the fact they have to ford the Nazarene faith as they would a river, and that Jesus was a shell and a shield for the true Messiah.

The satanic putsch to dethrone Jesus will not be attempted by Jews who love Torah and tradition. It will come from

---

135 Olga Tokarczuk, *The Books of Jacob* (2014).

those who pretend all religions are one. None who subscribe will be free, for the Antichrist will demand to be worshipped.

Does this mean Orthodox rabbis, averse to syncretism, are not culpable? No. For it is their attempt to hold onto the Old Covenant while rejecting the New that creates the impossible culture of Judaism. Jews who reject this often retain the catastrophic mindset: materialistic, legalistic, chauvinistic, kabbalistic. They become humanist, atheist, and all too often, messianic. These are the ones satan uses, paradoxically, to advance the rabbis' goal. They corrupt Christendom, amass wealth, sponsor Jewish nationalism. So the Temple project advances beyond the possibilities of human co-ordination.

This is made explicit by St Hippolytus of Rome (✝235), who wrote that as Jesus raised the Temple of His Flesh, so the Antichrist will "raise a temple of stone in Jerusalem".[136] The marvel of such a sign is that it will grow by the efforts of those who reject Jesus' Divinity. What passes for the rebuilt Temple will serve as a definitive sign of Jesus' return. *"Salvation is from the Jews"* (Jn 4:22) — willingly or unwillingly! Jonah shows how fleeing from God's call only serves it with greater scope.

Followers of Judaism seek a political messiah because they underestimate God. Given that poverty and wars continue, they conclude that Jesus could not be the Saviour. But for Jesus to bring worldwide peace in one day is too easy — He Who multiplied bread for the multitudes, more than they

---

[136] St Hippolytus, *Treatise on Christ and the Antichrist*, 6; 14; 49.

St Irenæus, *Adversus Hæreses*, V, 30, 4 "when this Antichrist shall have devastated all things in this world, he will reign for three years and six months, and sit in the temple at Jerusalem…"

could eat; Who cured the sick at a distance; Who raised the dead; Who could summon twelve legions of angels to bring every mob into order. God can bring peace to the whole world in an instant — but it would require reneging on our free will.

Instead, Jesus was sent to defeat sin and death, to build an everlasting City of Peace, a heavenly Jerusalem. This is a mission fit for our Saviour, which sublimely He chooses to achieve with our cooperation, by teaching us how to love. As the population of Heaven grows ceaselessly, we cannot dispute His success.

By no means does this neglect the present world. God invites us to full engagement with His Plan. Finally, on earth man will see that nothing but God's Way could ever have succeeded, and it will include the conversion of the Jews.

Meanwhile, through the unfathomable mess of history, fuelled by usurious greed and kabbalistic depravity, using the hard-heartedness of men who search the Torah for Christ but fail to find him, God permits satan to approach, but not reach, his ultimate goal. In 2016, Israel National News carried the stunning headline: *Sanhedrin to Trump-Putin: Fulfill Cyrus-like role in Jerusalem.* The article reported:

With the two top world leaders supporting Jewish right to Jerusalem, Sanhedrin asks that they build Third Temple… Prof. Rabbi Hillel Weiss, spokesman for the Sanhedrin, said, 'The political conditions today, in which the two most important national leaders in the world support the Jewish right to Jerusalem as their spiritual inheritance, is historically unprecedented'.[137]

---

[137] Israel National News (5th Nov 2016).

This hopeless dream rising on everyone's radar indicates the power of the Jews is waxing and the time of the Antichrist approaches: *"The man of sin... sitteth in the temple of God, shewing himself as if he were God"* (2 Thess 2:3-4). If the building be completed, we will see the *"abomination of desolation standing in the holy place"* (Dan 11:31; Mt 24:15). Scenes broadcast from Jerusalem in those days will prove that generations of Catholic hierarchs left the Lord for the sake of the world. Had Churchmen been faithful, Zionism could not succeed (2 Thess 2:7).

In the last days, ignorance of Scripture will leave Christians vulnerable to deadly deceit. A prophet of the Last Day, St Vincent Ferrer, O.P. (✝1419), preached:

> The disputations of the antichrist with the learned will be based entirely on the text of the Old Testament, and these doctors, far from being able to answer him, will not even be able to speak. Then the stars — the masters — will fall from heaven, that is, from the heights of the Faith.[138]

Jews unlearned in the NT cannot recognise Jesus' approach, even if on the OT they might be articulate enough to demolish Christian 'experts'. Meanwhile, Christians who do not know that the OT is all about Jesus, Mary and Holy Mass, have fallen for the false exegesis of Zionists. Without a true sense of the Scriptures, such Christians are immeasurably more vulnerable to being deceived by the rhetoric of the Antichrist, who will quote the Bible like satan (Mt 4:6).

---

[138] St Vincent Ferrer, *Sermon on the Last Judgement.*

There are unexpected layers to the Scriptures. Abraham's great-grandson, Joseph, prefigures Jesus Christ in the richest of ways. Surprisingly, the very same man, in the very same book, prefigures the Antichrist, too. I recoiled from this the first time I heard it. But on investigation, the conclusion can scarcely be denied. Genesis 47 outlines the methodology of multi-generational evil taking control of all the world's resources and enslaving mankind. It forewarns us of the mechanics of world domination, that unspeakable power should fall into the hands of one man. None of this impugns Joseph's holiness and exceptional virtues. The applicability of the prefiguration as Antichrist is God's mysterious work (a heavily-filtered angle on the events He arranged).

Joseph was young, *"thirty years old"* (Gen 41:46), when his astounding rise to power took off.[139] His experience as bursar for Potiphar and as administrator for the prison prepared him to acquire everything in Egypt. Today, the Bank of England, Federal Reserve and Bank of International Settlements, along with high political office, have so unified finance that the likes of BlackRock and Vanguard aspire to own the world.[140] How did Joseph do it?

---

[139] As background, Jacob's sons, representing in this reading the Gentiles, lived in varying degrees of vice. Then arose their younger brother, Joseph, who thought himself better than all the rest. (Seeing Jesus Christ here this is plain truth; but for such as claim Christ's place it is empty pride.) Joseph was his father's favourite, gifted with a wonderful coat, as the Hebrews were God's chosen people, made resplendent with blessings. But Joseph was cast out by his brothers and suffered a long imprisonment. So the Jews have been expelled from land after land, set apart and have suffered greatly. Joseph finally emerged from prison by interpreting dreams (perhaps suggestive, in this particular reading, of medieval Kabbalah).

[140] Roger Lowenstein, *The Jewish Story Behind the U.S. Federal Reserve Bank* (Nov 2015). Also Heike Buchter, Handelsblatt (Dec 2015): "No government... has such a... deep insight into the global financial and corporate world as BlackRock."

Joseph exploited his inside knowledge of the boom-bust cycle of seven years of plenty followed by seven years of famine. By buying cheap during the abundance, storing, and selling during the famine, he took advantage of people's desperation as usurers do. He used his connections with Pharaoh (Gen 45:6-8) to arrange for his family to gain a *"possession in the land of Egypt, in the best of the land"* (Gen 47:11) — think Zionism.

Having amassed all the money, Joseph did not give out food to help others avoid starvation, but demanded all their cattle and herds as the price (Gen 47:16). The worsening scarcity pressured the people to go, as it were, to plead with the Antichrist and sell their souls to satan:

[They] said to him: We will not hide from our lord, how that our money is spent, and our cattle also are gone: neither art thou ignorant that we have nothing now left but our bodies and our lands. Why therefore shall we die before thy eyes? we will be thine, both we and our lands: buy us to be the king's servants. (Gen 47:18-19)

Biblically, one's inheritance, or possession, means one's place in Heaven. If you lose it, that means hell. We read of *"every man selling his possessions"* to Joseph *"because of the greatness of the famine. And he brought it into Pharao's hands"* (Gen 47:20) and *"as for the people, he made slaves of them from one end of Egypt to the other"* (Gen 47:21 RSVCE). This is the blueprint for global finance, subjugating all whom it can reach with crippling debt. Joseph enslaved the population with a twenty per cent tax rate (Gen 47:24-26). Today, taxes are higher. Joseph used *"the greatness of the famine"* for leverage.[141] That time, the scarcity was sent by God. Today, the enemies of mankind (1 Thess 2:15) are adept at engineering depressions and busts.[142]

God knows I love Joseph! But here he prefigures evil. He is second only to Pharaoh, as the Antichrist is second to satan. Employing state propaganda, we hear the *"crier proclaiming that all should bow their knee before him"* (Gen 41:43), as all will be commanded to honour the final imposter. After a meteoric rise from nowhere, he marries a daughter of the priest of the Sun-City (Gen 41:45), a suitably pagan arrangement for the Antichrist's false religion. He is called *Tsaphenath Paneach, "Saviour of the World"* (Gen 41:45), a title the Antichrist seeks to steal from Jesus. It is an alien term, ancient Egyptian, not at home in Hebrew, Greek or Latin. The unfamiliar sound of it hints at the Antichrist's occult spirit. Yet he will appear to be one of us.

Distilling the themes touched upon in this chapter, the Antichrist is one who claims to be Christ but is not, who opposes God, who seduces and terrorises the world so that he "be adored as God. [In] the temple in Jerusalem… endeavouring to show himself as Christ."[143] 'Christ' is Greek for 'Messiah'. The Messiah is the Anointed One, the Chosen One, sent by God to save Israel, to save the world. The final Antichrist, the Anti-messiah, must be Jewish, or few would

---

[141] The *"priests"* escaped this enslavement and land loss. Due to a previous contract, they *"were not forced to sell their possessions"* (Gen 47:22). These priests stand for all the saved: *"A kingly priesthood, a holy nation, a purchased people"* (1 Pet 2:9), purchased not by the Antichrist but by the Blood of Christ.

[142] Stephen Mitford Goodson, *A History of Central Banking and the Enslavement of Mankind* (2014), *passim.*

[143] St Irenæus, *Adversus Hæreses*, V, 25, 1-5.

buy into his claims. But if a Jerusalem-based Jew were to convince much of Israel that he is the promised Messiah, he will go on to convince much of the world. Without globalism, he would not have the necessary reach for this. And he would have no base, no place, without Zionism. Even if very few humans calculate so many generations ahead, satan does. He is ruthless and determined. So are his protégés.

St Jerome divides the Jews into those who serve Christ and those who serve the coming Antichrist. Finding these two leaders spoken of by Solomon's saying: *"Better is a poor but wise youth, than an old and foolish king who no longer knows how to take care of himself"* (Eccles 4:13), he comments:

> The two nations of Israel are to be understood here. The first, which was before the arrival of the Lord, and the next, which will support the Antichrist in place of Christ.[144]

Jesus warned this would happen. After being received by Samaritans, Galileans and Gentiles (Jn 4:42,45,47), He stated to the Jews of Jerusalem:

> *I have come in My Father's name, and you do not receive Me; if another comes in his own name, him you will receive. How can you believe, who receive glory one from another: and the glory which is from God alone, you do not seek?* (Jn 5:43-44)

The one who comes in his own name is the Antichrist. As the Antichrist apes Christ darkly, so the beautiful humility of Jesus in His hidden life before revealing Himself will be

---

[144] St Jerome, *Commentary on Ecclesiastes* 4:13-16.

mirrored in the deceptive concealment of the Antichrist before he is revealed.[145]

The machinations of the Antichrist will be overcome by charity, by grace. It is hopeless trying to oppose him by treating anyone with cruelty or injustice, including one's enemies, for all sinful acts serve his coming. At first, he will appear to favour the Mosaic law. This is how he will win Jews to his side. But he deceives. He betrays. Before one Passover lamb has its throat cut in the modern Temple (which I do not believe God will allow), the Antichrist will demand that he himself be worshipped. The good Jews will not hear this. They will convert.

Then comes the Antichrist's defeat, *"whom the Lord Jesus shall kill with the spirit of His mouth; and shall destroy with the brightness of His coming"* (2 Thess 2:8). The *"spirit of [Jesus'] mouth"* comes in bishops preaching the Truth; the *"brightness of His coming"* may describe the holiness of His saints in the last generation. God's Word does not fail.[146]

---

[145] Gershom Scholem, *Toward an Understanding of the Messianic Idea in Judaism* (1971), II, describes how the Messiah "continually waits in hiding... This symbolic antithesis between the true Messiah sitting at the gates of Rome and the head of Christendom [the pope], who reigns there, accompanies Jewish Messianic thought through the centuries. And more than once we learn that Messianic aspirants have made a pilgrimage to Rome in order to sit by the bridge in front of the Castel Sant' Angelo and thus enact this symbolic ritual."

[146] This Word, God's Son, chooses to accomplish His mission with Mary, her victory over the Antichrist being prefigured in Eve, Jael, the woman of Thebez, Jephthah's daughter, the wise woman of Abel, Judith, Esther and Susanna, also by Thamar, Rahab, Ruth and Bathsheba, as well as by Sarah, Rebekah and Rachel. From all these, and especially with Sephora, spouse of Moses, we can be sure that Our Blessed Lady will be key to the conversion of the Jews.

Judaism's Endgame is Totalitarian Domination

Instead of thy fathers, sons are born to thee: thou shalt make them princes over all the earth.

Psalm 44:17

The idea of world domination sounds ridiculous because nobody can yet know what it will look like. We can scarcely imagine a realistic roadmap to achieve it. But we can see the political architecture to enable it is being erected. Distant international bodies, run by hidden forces, determine national policies globally. The brutally orchestrated and obviously harmful response to Covid-19 revealed this with clarity; prime ministers and presidents are puppets.

It is a theological fact that satan (lying) offered Jesus control of all the kingdoms of the world (Mt 4:9 ‖ Lk 4:6). While satan can confer advantage power to his worshippers, evil never constructs good, as the Church has done for two thousand years. Rather, evil usurps what others have built. Jesus rejected satan's temptation. The kabbalists have not.

Because Jews have been hated by genocidal men (Pharaoh, Amalek and Haman are figureheads), many Jews react with a deadly disdain for non-Jews and, misreading their unique history, some plot for Jewish world rule. These two disorders are spectacularly evident in the Manhattan businessman, Theodore N. Kaufman. In a 1941 interview, he declaimed:

> I believe that the Jews have a mission in life. They must see to it that the nations of the world get together in one vast confederation. 'Union Now' is the beginning of this. Slowly but surely the world will develop into a paradise. We will have perpetual peace. And the Jews will do the most to bring about this confederation, because they have the most to gain.[147]

How this great leap forward should be accomplished, Kaufman proposed in his booklet, *Germany Must Perish*.[148] Summarising it, journalist Harold Ribalow wrote: "Kaufman is convinced that the solution for the ills of the world lies in the sterilization of the German people", with Kaufman calculating that if 20,000 surgeons were to perform 25 operations daily, then "it would take no more than one month at the maximum, to complete their sterilization."

Kaufman's excesses were immediately used by Nazis to justify deporting Jews from Hannover. Unabashed, the 31-year-old Kaufman continued,

> The trouble with democracies [is failure to] understand German psychology. Germanism, since the days of the first German conquests, 500 years ago, *planned to take over the world*... Germany insists on total victory.[149]

---

[147] Harold Ribalow, *The Canadian Jewish Chronicle, One Man's Plan for Peace Forever* (26th Sep 1941), 5.

[148] Theodore N. Kaufman, *Germany Must Perish* (New Jersey, 1941).

[149] Harold Ribalow, *The Canadian Jewish Chronicle, One Man's Plan for Peace Forever* (26th Sep 1941), 5.

This accusation, or projection, comes from a man who believed "the Jews have a mission" to unite all the world "in one vast confederation" to bring "paradise" on earth and "perpetual peace". Perhaps the most astonishing part of all this is that he is right! Except of course, that unless this be done through Jesus Christ, it will not develop *"on earth as it is in Heaven"* (Mt 6:10), but on earth as it is in hell. And it cannot be achieved in a political unity but only in a spiritual unity, namely, the Church.

Universal Service versus World Domination

If one rejects Jesus Christ, who else can be the Messiah? Gentile claimants cannot get far, for reasons already explained. Jewish claimants do not get much further, being unable to fulfil the prophecies. Because this latter point has become increasingly evident, a more dangerous derangement has developed, one which is widely received among Jews. It is that Israel itself is the Messiah, the people taken as a whole, raised up by God to lead all the nations of the world, even to dominate them as lord. This lordship is not service as of Jesus but subjugation as in Palestine. Such insanity arises from reading the OT without the light of Christ.

What do the Psalms promise for God's chosen? *"Instead of thy fathers, sons are born to thee: thou shalt make them princes over all the earth"* (Ps 44:17). These words of God are directed to the Messiah. He, Jesus, *"shalt make them princes over all the earth"*, to judge and govern. Who? Not *"thy fathers"*, not Abraham, Isaac or Jacob. Rather, *"sons are born to thee"*, the Apostles. These are literally God's chosen (Lk 6:13). And so *"thou shalt make them princes over all the earth"* is selected as a text for the Divine Office on feasts of the Apostles. By apostolic succession, more princes are appointed after them. It is vital that this be understood spiritually, from the altar, not politically (Lk 22:30).

Kaufman sought Jewish domination, but no racial group ought to rule politically over another, which inevitably involves exploitation. This is what Kaufman missed: the Jews do indeed "have a mission" to bring worldwide peace. Spiritually understood, when the Jews lost their homeland, God in His goodness opened the offer to inherit a better one (cf. Mt 8:20). As super-abundant compensation for the loss of Israel, Christ chose Jews to gloriously lead His Church. This the Apostles did. This, after conversion, the last generation of Jews, we may hope, are also set to do.

After Christ's Ascension, His Apostles served with boldness. They did not bind themselves to the land of Israel but baptised all nations (Mt 28:16-20). With reason, God placed the Holy Land at the natural geographical join of Asia, Africa and Europe. This afforded the most rapid spread of the Gospel. Misunderstood, the place is taken by Zionists as the fortuitous nexus of geo-politics. Such a worldly view drives out spiritual understanding.

Jews aim high. If their sights are on Jesus, then the Church can only benefit from a strong influx of Jewish leadership (provided she guard against false conversions). By no means am I suggesting an exclusive Jewish leadership. It is proper and desirable that the college of cardinals be characterised by internationality, even if, as in the Roman Curia, there is a high representation of Italians, Rome being the location on earth where the Church is planted. Converted Jews would probably not be the majority in any local hierarchy, or the Vatican either, but having been dispersed all over the world, the Jews are in a unique distribution to serve unity: *"A little leaven leavens the whole lump"* (1 Cor 5:6 RSVCE).[150]

Why should Jews, on fire with love for Jesus, be disposed to ecclesial leadership? Because the perennial vigour to utterly eradicate the 'Amalekites' (i.e. any mortal enemy), when spiritualised and turned against sin, is what the Church needs. But if it remains worldly, against *"flesh and blood"* (Eph 6:12) enemies, it explains Kaufman's genocidal mania. And the magnificent tenacity in holding onto Tradition, if done for the Deposit of Faith, is what the Church needs. But if this stubbornness be for the pharisaical *"traditions of men"* (Mk 7:8), it breeds totalitarianism. And if the sense of being one of the Chosen People is infused with an evangelical desire to bring all who will hear into Heaven, then this is the ardour which should govern the Vatican. But if confined to Jewish racial chauvinism, then it explains much of the catastrophic state of the Middle East today.

If someone is unconvinced that there is something unique about the Jewish trajectory, then the ancient history of the Hebrews gives clear data. Is it not remarkable that a Hebrew, Joseph, rose to run Egypt, in his day the world's most

---

[150] Though the number of Jews is low in absolute terms, their representation in the hierarchy and Curia could be high in relative terms. Over-representation of Jews is a phenomenon of secret societies, revolutionary movements and globalist conclaves — as Disraeli, Churchill, Solzhenitsyn and a glance at the World Economic Forum attest. In this respect, to take an alternative translation of the verse above: *"a little leaven corrupteth the whole lump"* (1 Cor 5:6; cf. Gal 5:9 DRB). This is a valid translation of the Latin *"corrumpit"* and the Greek "ζυμοῖ", in harmony with the interpretation of חָמֵץ, meaning to "leaven", or in the idiom, to be sour, ruthless and *"unjust"* (cf. Ps 71:4).

powerful dominion? Is it coincidental that Daniel did the same in Babylon? His closest collaborators in running this unprecedented empire were three more Jewish boys: Sidrach, Misach and Abdenago. They were freely appointed by King Nabuchodonosor, as Joseph was by Pharaoh. Each was sent for the task by God. So were Mardochai and Esther, who ended up wielding all the influence they needed with the Persian Emperor, Xerxes I (whose dominion extended from India to Ethiopia), to turn around a genocidal threat against the Jewish people, such that instead the demise and slaughter of their enemies was accomplished. In the next generation, in the same city of Susa, Nehemiah was appointed cupbearer to Artaxerxes I, placed there by God to gain all that he needed for resurrecting the walls of Jerusalem, despite the savage machinations of lesser potentates against him.

All these Jews had power next to the throne, reaching the top of foreign governments. For His own purpose, God has given Jews great gifts and talents for leadership and administration. They do not lose this natural gift if they reject God's call. But anybody, Jew or Gentile, who goes against God, cannot avoid still serving His overall Plan. Confidently, God chose a people who were *"stiff-necked"* (Ex 34:9), compared to a discarded baby weltering in its afterbirth, not *"washed"* or *"rubbed with salt"* (Ezek 16:4). God chooses what appears to be *"least"* (Dt 7:7) to do His greatest works.

What happens when Jews do not lead God's way? They lead astray. Gentile Freemasons enjoy their exclusive club, network to great advantage, delight to accumulate wealth and, when it can be arranged, dodge prosecution. Some dream of a one-world order, though it is not clear they have the drive to bring it about. Once infused, however, with a more aggressive spirit, the 'Judeo' of 'Judeo-Masonic' provides the messianic principle to the self-interested Masonic network.[151] This hybrid is a far more dangerous beast.

If it is difficult to see through the lies and misdirection of the modern scene, telling facts emerge from the long sweep of history. Active denial of Jesus, His Gospel, divine charity involves giving way to a spirit inimical to all.

Had the Jews been expelled from one or two lands, then the contemporary trope of antisemitism might be a credible explanation. But the facts tell otherwise. The Jews were expelled from Jerusalem, not for the first time, around AD 135. They had already been banished, not for the first time, from Rome. In the centuries which followed, Jewish communities were ordered to leave from various Middle Eastern cities, then regions of Germany, France, Italy and Switzerland, then from entire countries, including England (1290), Hungary (1360), Austria (1420), Spain and Sicily (1492), Portugal (1496) and, after the Reformation, from certain Papal States (but not Rome) and Russia (1727).

The narrative today explains all this misery by positing an innate antisemitism in Europeans or non-Jews. The suggestion that the Jews themselves might have something to do with it only increases the temperature of the accusations.

We know that if in his relationships someone is always running into trouble, and if he finds grievous fault in every other person, and if questioning the completeness of his account is met with angry counter-accusations, then such a

---

[151] *The Jewish Tribune* (New York, Oct 1927), "Masonry is based on Judaism. If you eliminate Judaic teaching from the Masonic rite, what remains?"

person has a personality disorder. One should be charitable toward him, for he suffers, but set clear boundaries so as to avoid being dragged down into his mental crises with him. Where one can, it is often best to walk away. But within a family, one cannot walk away. One needs to work out a *modus vivendi.*

On a bigger scale, while Jews and Christians in cities and states kept running into crises, the medieval Church imposed a formula which worked, barring Jews from public office but protecting them from molestation. These were the boundaries.

Alas, failure to maintain this rational and just policy gravely exacerbated the disintegration of the godly world order, Christendom. This capsizing Karl Marx explained:

> The Jew has emancipated himself in a Jewish manner, not only because he has acquired financial power, but also because, through him and also apart from him, *money* has become a world power and the practical Jewish spirit has become the practical spirit of the Christian nations. The Jews have emancipated themselves insofar as Christians have become Jews.[152]

This did not happen overnight. The Renaissance is presented as wholly beneficial; it was not. The Reformation, the mainstream claims, was for God; it was not. The Revolutions following from the French, we are told, are about liberty; they are the opposite. A beast has been incubated, and hatched, and nourished. Now it is a monster clawing for world domination. Its name is mammon. It feeds on debt.

---

[152] Karl Marx, *On the Jewish Question* (1943), II.

Mammon — Demon of Global Finance

Shortly after the Norman conquest of England in 1066, Jews were brought in to assist the new rulers with administration, governance and finance. Generations later, large numbers of Jews in England were accused of coin clipping. It is a financial crime which, creating money as if from nowhere, devalues the currency, causes inflation and effectively robs everybody. It became so extreme that, in 1279, King Edward I had hundreds of Jews arrested and, as it was a capital offence to steal people's livelihood, 280 culprits were hanged. In 1290, Jews were expelled from England altogether.[153]

Today we are told the hangings of coin clippers were because of antisemitism. We are told Jews would not commit such harmful financial crimes. But considering world finance (especially fractional lending, loans 'without risk', quantitive easing and the baseless printing of money by central banks), that simple brush off is risible. The consuming greed resonates with the exorbitant rates of Jewish money-lenders later in Spain, Venice, Russia and elsewhere. Time and again, cannibalistic usury has left despairing families starving.[154]

The dominance of Jews in finance can be traced back to the diaspora following the Babylonian captivity. Jews were dispersed far and wide. They had the deepest identity of any people on earth and so preserved their communities, looking after each other with great solicitude and sacrifice (see Tobit). This resilient network facilitated money management for

---

[153] Though some came earlier, Jews were officially readmitted into England in the mid-seventeenth century, once Cromwell's Judaizing Puritans seized power.

[154] For a favourable account of Jews accumulating great wealth through usury, see Robert Chazan, *The Jews of Medieval Western Christendom*, 1000-1500 (2006).

traders. Instead of risking being robbed on long journeys or losing treasure on hazardous voyages, promissory notes were exchanged between distant but related Jews, who trusted each other, affording a great advantage for merchants.

This trading-finance-banking network was based on a deeper cultural identity whose hero was Moses. That interconnectedness is meant to serve a more positive goal than personal profit. For a dispersed people to look after each other and retain their identity is admirable. With the Jews it is germane to God's plan for the salvation of the world.

When economics becomes religion, when mammon is chosen for god, then money inverts nature and becomes the hidden force governing politics. Mayer Amschel Rothschild (d.1812), founder of modern international finance, purportedly said, "Give me control of a nation's money supply, and I care not who makes its laws." What passes in public for politics is irrelevant to long-term power plays. The political scene becomes theatre, staged to distract from gradual enslavement.

Today we see financiers living like pagan gods in their contempt for whole populations, ready to drain nations if for them it means profit, as in the 1990s George Soros happily did to England and tried to do to Malaysia. In his own words:

> I fancied myself as some kind of god... If truth be known, I carried some rather potent messianic fantasies with me from childhood, which I felt I had to control, otherwise they might get me in trouble.[155]

---

[155] *LA Times, George Soros: The 'God' Who Carries Around Some Dangerous Demons* (Oct 2004).

It is a sort of disease when you consider yourself some kind of god, the creator of everything, but I feel comfortable about it now since I began to live it out.[156]

Soros steals money 'legally' in order to shape politics, with his motto, "If I spend enough, I will make it right". Determined to prevent President George W. Bush's re-election in 2004, but failing, Soros was more determined to prevent President Donald J. Trump's re-election in 2020, and evidently succeeded. This he predicted with sinister arrogance when addressing the World Economic Forum (WEF) two years before. Soros' Open Society Institute (OSI) purports to spread freedom, but actually promotes abortion, contraception and sodomy — all anti-life. With Klaus Schwab, a protégée of Henry Kissinger, the WEF and the OSI serve as streamlined versions of the UN, which promotes sterilisation programmes to reduce unwanted populations. The UN is one of a plethora of supra-national organisations which hyper-legalistic Jews design, and whereby, under the guise of humanism, sovereignty is sucked out of individual nations.[157]

---

[156] *The Independent, The billionaire who built on chaos — the rise of a speculator who considers himself 'some kind of god'* (June 1993).

[157] The realisation of this plan goes back a century. *The Democratic Messenger, Jerusalem World's Capital — League of Nations Jews Idea* (MD, 2nd Sep 1922). Dr Nahum Sokolow, Chairman of the Executive Committee of the Zionist Conference, said of the predecessor to the UN, "The League of Nations is a Jewish idea, and Jerusalem will some day become the capital of the world's peace." See also the formative work of Moses Moskowitz, Harold Laski and Bernard Baruch.

Francis supports this globalist vision, quoting his encyclical *Fratelli tutti* in *Laudate Deum* (4th Oct 2023), 35, "We are speaking above all of 'more effective world organisations, equipped with the power to provide for the global common good, the elimination of hunger and poverty and the sure defence of fundamental human rights'. The issue is that they must be endowed with real authority."

Douglas Reed, *The Grand Design of the Twentieth Century* (1977), *passim*.

The International Criminal Court (ICC) is another striking example.[158] It used to be understood that a sovereign was immune from criminal charges. This is wisdom. But in the name of 'human rights' (another lie), with shameless moralising and hypocrisy, stronger nations now indict leaders of weaker nations and subject them to trial. This is a facade. It is about global control, a mechanism to bring down the minor despots who refuse to serve the global despots.

The ICC is a precedent for the establishment of an entity with global jurisdiction. Putting sovereigns on trial is against nature. There are last resort methods to deal with tyrants, lawful but not legalistic, which are far safer for mankind than erecting a supposedly supra-sovereign power which knows no borders. It is true that a lawless leader is an evil not only for those he subjugates but invariably for the international order as well. Yet the establishment of a supra-national jurisdiction, to try and depose national leaders, is designed with evil intent and tolerated by short-sightedness. What happens when this structure is in the hands of a beast? Then there will be global totalitarianism and no human way out.

The order of nature teaches us wisdom. The spiritual order is above the political order just as the soul is more than the body. Both are good, but whereas each of us lives by a soul that is simple, not composed, our bodies are necessarily made up of multiple organs with particular specialities. In God's analogy, the only way for the world to be healthy, to flourish, is under a single spiritual order, that of Christ, the life, or soul, of the world. Universal truth is truth for everyone alike

---

[158] The International Criminal Court was founded by German Jew Robert Kurt Woetzel and Hungarian-American Jew Ben Ferencz.

and does not diminish by being shared across borders and centuries. In contrast, political decisions are by nature prudential judgements. They depend upon time and place, upon resources and opportunities, upon weighing the prevailing circumstances. This cannot be done at a distance but requires familiarity, closeness to the situation. Providentially, God made the various nations, awarding them sovereignty over themselves. It is a crime against the natural order to pool sovereignty.

With national sovereignty so vital, what does this leave for the Jews, since they lost their land two thousand years ago? God did not punish faithful Jews by taking away their Temple and Promised Land. Rather, He gave them realities infinitely better in the Body of Christ and the Catholic Church. It is here that Jews can use their gifts for prayer, administration and leadership, to the advantage of literally everyone. They can tell mankind's story. But if they decline this calling from God, if they are determined to assert themselves among and then over others, while chasing false messiahs, then they become the enemies of Christendom and mankind.

Whence this terrible reach? By their nature, information and finance networks (spies and banks) inevitably interweave because they serve the same master: despotic control. In train with the misnamed Enlightenment came a phenomenal growth of secret societies, of anti-Christian revolutions. The damage has been accelerated by Jewish infiltration of multiple secret services. Bismarck reputedly remarked: "God created the Hebrew in order to serve the man who needs him as a spy." Operating in darkness, secret services are the ideal instrument for evil, combining unaccountability with the full authority of the State. The intelligence alliance of the Anglosphere, Five Eyes (FVEY), has a sixth: Mossad, spying on the spies to surveil the whole world. Coming from below, not above, this is the perspective of satan.

Unless there has been an inversion of power, how did England get from hanging coin clippers to being defenceless when robbed by George Soros, given that their crimes are the same, multiplying money from nowhere? Has the world not fallen for false messianism? Christians, seduced or drifting from their faith, have been so brainwashed that we, too, have applauded the dreadful stages of decline. The mainstream lies to us that the Renaissance was all good, the Reformation a boon, the Enlightenment progress, Revolution a happy leap. Josué Jéhouda identifies where the deepest credit is due:

> The Renaissance, the Reformation and the [French] Revolution (of 1789) constitute three attempts to rectify Christian mentality by bringing it into tune with the progressive development of reason and science.[159]

The key term is "progressive". Since 2020 it is obvious that "science" is abused as a cover for tyranny. While Jesus assures *the truth will set you free* (Jn 8:32), Jéhouda equates Christianity with oppression, as he further writes:

> As dogmatic theology began to yield its oppressive control over man's conscience, the Jews began to breathe more freely. The three breaches opened in the decrepit fortress of Christian obscurantism extend over

---

[159] Josué Jéhouda, *L'Antisémitisme Miroir du Monde* (1958), p.161.

roughly five centuries, in the course of which the Jews were still considered the pariahs of history.

If the Jews were still removed from all the intellectual and social activity of the Christian peoples, nevertheless, despite the ostracism to which they were subjected, their thought played a preponderant though unacknowledged role in the Renaissance, the Reformation and the Revolution, which are all indirectly stamped with its mark and it is certainly not by chance that these attempts to rectify Christian mentality were inspired by the assiduous study of Jewish sources at a time when the Jews were still looked upon with suspicion and mistrust.[160]

Jéhouda is telling us that generations of Jews had to work in obscurity, for they were mistrusted. Now they are powerful, he can tell us openly that for centuries they have worked to recalibrate the thinking of Christendom with Jewish thought. That means, essentially, dismissing the Crucifixion of the Son of God.

With help from below, that is Kabbalah, Jews have had such phenomenal success that they can write and publish openly about undermining, or buying off, Christendom. Replacing God with impersonal mammon has a very personal target, the Most Blessed Trinity, by destroying man made in God's image. Modern man appears to accept that civilisation can grow even while ignoring the killing of Jesus, as if He is irrelevant to society, as if it does not matter whether we keep the ancient memorial of Calvary, the apostolic liturgy.

---

[160] Josué Jéhouda, *L'Antisémitisme Miroir du Monde* (1958), p.161-62.

Can we make the connection now as to why the traditional Mass is under relentless attack and in parallel the world is falling away from God? Is it not clear that the humanist lie 'Liberty, Equality and Fraternity' is the prototype slogan for 'Build Back Better'? The fall from Catholic Christendom to deism, then to humanism, is sliding toward transhumanism and the ultimate cancellation of creation, of everything given in Genesis 1. The Creator made man and woman to marry and multiply. The globalists desire decimation.

This is the Great Reset, the alternative to entering a new Creation in Christ. They lie to us: "You will own nothing, and you will be happy". To which comes the reply: "You will own everything, yet you will be miserable".

Covid-19 gave a taste of the inhumanity of the encroaching one-world system. It has been engineered over centuries by purposefully drowning persons and nations over their necks in debt. Now world finance is strategising for digital currencies. CBDCs are planned to merge with artificial intelligence, total surveillance, data mining, genetic manipulation, bio-digital convergence and weaponised robotics, such that complete domination will apparently fall to whoever can maintain a will to deceive which matches their developments in computing power. Renowned for his contempt both for Jesus Christ and for Orthodox Judaism, Yuval Noah Harari boasts:

> We are really acquiring divine powers of creation and destruction. We are really upgrading humans into gods. We are acquiring… the power to re-engineer life.[161]

---

[161] Yuval Noah Harari in conversation with Sara Pascoe (2020), YouTube.

These are not the rantings of an isolated man but a consultant to the World Economic Forum. More recently, he has expressed that religion can be "useful", meaning in drawing populations toward globalist thinking.

Striking a more sober tone, Prime Minister Benjamin Netanyahu has repeatedly boasted of the unheard of capacities to which Israel is aiming through the above-listed technologies and is unabashedly ambitious for Israel to lead the whole world.[162]

The rise of Zionism, its methods and fruit, provide a lens to perceive that Israel's progress in relation to Gentiles, overtaking them in everything materialistic, is done by evil and for evil. The dominated world will look like Gaza.

Jewish Revenge on the Goyim

The Jews were born in a divinely ordained struggle to obtain land. Their relationship with the land is deeper than that of other nations because it is the model and meaning of every person's attachment to home: it signifies our portion in Heaven. But having spent two millennia without land, resenting the nations who had homes, detesting them as antisemitic, once Israel was regained for Jews, the opportunity arose to let other peoples know what it is to be landless. The idea of multiculturalism was always a cover to advance Jewish interests wherever they were a minority. That was until the State of Israel was re-founded. Now ardent

---

162 Benjamin Netanyahu, Address, Cybertech Conference, Tel Aviv (Jan 2019). Address at the Adelson School of Entrepreneurship at IDC Herzliya (Oct 2016). See also, Times of Israel, *Israeli startups to play key role in the fourth industrial revolution* (Aug 2023).

multiculturalism is pushed everywhere except Israel. In parallel, Israel favours for itself immigration only from Jews while zealously promoting mass immigration everywhere else in a global attempt to rob *everyone* else of his homeland.

Israel found it could not survive without making war against its Arab neighbours. Succeeding in the Six Day War of 1967, Israel has never ceased destabilising Middle Eastern nations and using America to crush them. Now the programme of mass immigration into Europe and North America further destabilises these destination nations, as well as the poor places from where the young immigrants come, for a country which loses its youth loses its future. From being the only people (but Gypsies) without land, will Israel become the only homogenous people (with China) to have it?

With Temple Judaism theologically and practically insupportable, many Jews fall into atheism. The worst of these retain such a contempt for God and Goyim that they turn to dark arts for success.[163] These megalomaniacs, who mean to rule us all, will enlist false religion to achieve it. The dedicated kabbalist Elia Benamozegh wrote that Christians are in error to dream that Jews will be reconciled to them before the final coming of Jesus Christ. Instead,

---

[163] Israel Shahak, *Jewish History, Jewish Religion: The Weight of Three Thousand Years* (1994), p.16, "Nor can one find in the numerous English-language 'Jewish histories' the elementary facts about the attitude of Jewish mysticism (so fashionable at present in certain quarters) to non-Jews: that they are considered to be, literally, limbs of Satan, and that the few non-satanic individuals among them (that is, those who convert to Judaism) are in reality 'Jewish souls' who got lost when Satan violated the Holy Lady (*Shekhinah* or *Matronit*, one of the female components of the Godhead, sister and wife of the younger male God according to the cabbala) in her heavenly abode."

this return, we say, will take place not... as it is expected to happen, but in the only genuine, logical and lasting fashion possible, and above all in the only way in which it will benefit the human race. It will be a reunion between the Hebrew religion and the others that have sprung from it and 'the return of the children's hearts to their fathers'.[164]

This multi-generational audacity to overthrow Christ could be discounted except that we see it happening before our eyes. The early Zionist Andre Spire concurs that for reconciliation it is the Church who must repent and change:

Beyond every confession, above every dogma, the Jew has remained anchored to the spirit of the Scriptures. By an original twist of thought, he incorporates the most attractive features of Christianity into Judaism and, leading the Church back to the synagogue, reconciles the mother with her daughter in an ideal Jerusalem. But it is the daughter, as one would expect, who recognises her wrongs and confesses her errors.[165]

Catholicism proclaims that Jesus is subjecting everything to Himself (Phil 3:21). Jews are telling us that they will subject all to themselves. There is a monumental asymmetry between bowing to God Who makes Himself Man and submitting to man who makes himself god.

---

[164] Elia Benamozegh (died 1900), *Israel et Humanity*. Cited by Vicomte Léon de Poncins, *Judaism and the Vatican* (1967), p.122.

[165] Andre Spire, *Quelques Juifs et Demi-Juifs* (1928), p255. Cited by Vicomte Léon de Poncins, *Judaism and the Vatican* (1967), p.120.

God created Adam to *"have dominion"* (Gen 1:26) over the world, literally to dominate other creatures. Jesus showed that to be *Dominus*, Lord, means to serve the weak, not to exploit them (Mt 20:25-28). God formed the Jews so that, in the fullness of time, embracing Christ, they lead the Church. They have the vision, the great talents, the natural disposition suited to the graces required for so mammoth and holy a task.

This is not a dream for the end times only. It has been constant since Pentecost. The Church began wholly Jewish. As the number of Gentiles exponentially increased, there has always been a trickle of Jewish converts. Some rise high in the hierarchy, some influence the world through their sanctity. God knows. But the Church has always been open to Jews — not as infiltrators, but as loyal and fruitful servants of God.

It is Jacob's calling to come through unexpectedly, according to God's design, to acquire an elevated identity, so that Israel may enter Israel (Gen 25:25; 27:36; 32:28). By converting to Christ, Jews stand to lose everything, and thereby to gain everything.

Whosoever shall lose his life for My sake and the Gospel, shall save it. For what shall it profit a man, if he gain the whole world, and suffer the loss of his soul? (Mk 8:35-36)

The world is not enough. Judaism's last son, the Antichrist, may be such a godless, murderous liar, as to inadvertently provoke the Jewish people to convert to Jesus in full. All satan's machinations will backfire — the usurper usurped.

GENTILES AND JEWS CANNOT SHARE SOVEREIGNTY

Bring not every man into thy house: for many are the snares of the deceitful… Receive a stranger in, and he shall overthrow thee with a whirlwind, and shall turn thee out of thy own.

Sirach 11:31-36

What some call simply the 'Jewish Question' might seem intractable. Peace in Palestine seems impossible, and that is just one element of the whole. But there is a clear solution given by God in his dealings with Cain and practiced by the Catholic Church until she fell sick with modernism. It is truly to the benefit of all parties.

Who is Cain? He is the one who kills his younger brother out of envy of his perfect sacrifice to God. God engages with him, showing that he can overcome sin. Instead, Cain throws off God's admonition and slaughters his innocent brother. Instead of repenting, Cain complains he will be victimised. How does God treat him? After appealing to Cain's conscience (*"Where is thy bother Abel?"* Gen 4:9), which Cain again refuses, God curses him and decrees his penance will not be tilling the earth like all other men, but will be to wander, rootless, a vagabond (Gen 4:12). Cain could not escape his penance any more than Adam could escape his. Penance always catches up with us.

God ordains that whosoever harms Cain will suffer a sevenfold punishment, and thus He marks Cain for his protection (Gen 4:5). Cain perished, but no one is forced to follow. We see analogies in God's care for Ishmael, for Esau and for Joseph's brothers, each of them resentful aggressors. David safeguarded Saul and punished those who took vengeance on Saul's household. All this is instructive for how Catholic nations should treat Jews.

This requisite divine restraint was encapsulated in the Church's medieval policy laid out in an AD 1120 papal bull titled *Sicut Judaeis*. After the Church escaped from Roman torments and grew strong, rather than seek vengeance on Jews who had encouraged persecutions, Pope St Gregory the Great (✝604), and numerous popes following him, issued instructions forbidding Christians from harming Jews, or from forcing Jews to convert, taking their property, disturbing their festivals or damaging their cemeteries.[166] This broad and humane protection involved grave penalties, including excommunication, for Christians who violated its terms.

Besides protecting Jews from the nations, this policy had a necessary counter-balance to safeguard the nations from the Jews. The complement to protection for them was that unless

---

[166] AJC, *The Image of Jews in Catholic Teaching* (1961), I, "On one hand, the Church has protected them; popes and Church Councils, in medieval and modern times, have condemned anti-Jewish propaganda, violence and persecution, and for five hundred years (from the 11th until the 16th century) Jews enjoyed safety in the Papal states. But, on the other hand, Jews in nearly every century have undergone untold suffering and degradation at the hands of supposed Christians, sometimes with the acquiescence of ecclesiastical authorities."

they converted to Christianity, Jews should not be granted full citizenship in the countries where they resided. Without citizen rights, Jews could not attain formal political power or undue influence. This preserved Christendom.

However unaccustomed we are to thinking this way, it is wholly congruent with natural law and divine law, and so long as it was maintained, it has been the only approach proven to work. A Christian society can only exist with the Cross at the top, to reign in Christendom's every school and hospital, on the banner of every army and the centre of every legislature. Christ's reign is total. To remove the Cross is to invite satan to rule instead. There is no other party who can come between these two. There is no equilibrium in a schizophrenic society which makes space both for the Holy Sacrifice of the Mass and the satanic sacrifice of abortion. Only one of these will prevail.

One could object that the American system, or an 'open society', works. But Karl Marx saw further than this, realising that a non-confessing state such as America was simply a useful step toward abolishing religion altogether.

> The most rigid form of the opposition between the Jew and the Christian is the *religious* opposition. How is an opposition resolved? By making it impossible. How is *religious* opposition made impossible? By *abolishing religion*.[167]

Meanwhile, America has not worked well for Iran, or Iraq, or Afghanistan, or Libya, or Syria, or other countries that Israel decides to target. Instigating Christians and Muslims to

---

[167] Karl Marx, *On the Jewish Question* (1943), I.

fight each other has not worked out for the US either, seeing as it is American money and blood which must pay for Israel's foreign policy. Self-defence is never a problem. Subverting sovereignty is always a problem. It is the biggest problem in international politics, utterly against God's order.

Jews make up some two per cent of the US population but hold about one third of the appointments in the Biden Cabinet.[168] They are similarly over-represented in the State Department's senior ranks. This explains the inexplicable, the insane campaign through Ukraine to cripple Russia. It is impoverishing Americans, has displaced millions of Ukrainians, and killed hundreds of thousands of Ukrainians and Russians. The long-provoked war reeks of Jewish revenge and globalist reconstruction.

Dr E Michael Jones observes that unless you deny political power to Jews, they will end up ruling you. This conclusion may strike us as outlandish, except its veracity is demonstrated again and again. And now the whole world is tasting the truth of it. More precisely, Dr Jones wrote:

> Any country which turns away from laws based on the teaching of the Catholic Church and God's eternal law will end up being ruled by Jews.[169]

Depending upon one's bias, one can find a positive, negative or neutral explanation for this phenomenon.

---

168 Jacob Kornbluh, Forward, *Enough for a minyan: A Jewish Who's Who of Biden's Cabinet-to-Be* (Jan 2021). Shalom Maital, The Jerusalem Report, *Biden's Jewish A-Team* (Feb 2021).

169 Here Dr Jones summarised a three-part series, *The Jewish Question in Europe*, which originally appeared in 1890 in *La Civiltà Cattolica*.

One could say it is because the Jews are gifted that they rise to the top. They are diligent, study hard, have an affinity for the law, and possibly have the highest IQ of any race. God gave natural and supernatural blessings to Abraham and his descendants. Perhaps these are fruits of the natural blessings even when Judaism rejects the supernatural blessings?

Or one could opt for a negative explanation, saying it is because Jews are more ruthless, they look down on non-Jews, exploiting them financially and stirring us up in wars against each other so that they can come through the middle (for example, increasing the debts of both sides). Worse, it could be with the edge granted by demonology, by Kabbalah, albeit these are no match for the Sacraments.

Or one can find a neutral explanation. Whichever group of people is best distributed will end up ruling, for all other things being equal, it is the distribution through a society, or the world, which provides the most useful network for information, for perceiving the big picture, for influence and finally, control. The ideal distribution is that of the Church, raising the whole loaf with charity and truth. But if the Church surrenders her identity, then the next best distribution is that of the Jews. Both have a global presence. A thin distribution takes time to bear fruit, even centuries. But history affords plenty of time.

Yet weighing these three possibilities, can we ignore what Rabbi Moses ben Maimon taught?

If a Jewish male enters into relations with a Gentile woman, when he does so intentionally, she should be executed. She is executed because she caused a Jew to be involved in an unseemly transgression, as [is the law with regard to] an animal. [This applies] whether the gentile women was a minor of three years of age, or an adult, whether she was single or married.[170]

The Rambam, one of the most influential Jewish philosophers of the past, considers Gentile women, even three-year-old girls, as a temptation to bestiality for Jews. Though the majority of Jews reject this level of psychopathy, the irrational contempt for Gentiles is deeply wired.

Part of the reason such Jews bristle when their contempt for Gentiles is exposed is that they think we must be like them. They think we must contemn them (Ps 49:20-21), want to dominate and destroy them. There are Gentiles who think this way. But Christ dispels this, showing a more excellent way. This way of the Cross is inconceivable to Jews unless they convert. We heard above from Albert Memmi, despising Jesus and the Cross. In his 1962 book, he describes the Jewish sense of alienation from all other peoples:

What we felt confusedly, what we were trying to suppress by rejecting the society of those days, I neither can, nor do I wish to make a secret of any longer. The religious state of nations being what it is, and nations being what they are, the Jew finds himself, in a certain measure, outside of the national community.[171]

Memmi goes on to write how, under this alienation, Jews inevitably work against other peoples. The Jewish proclivity

---

[170] Maimonides, *Mishneh Torah, Issurei Biah*, Chapter 12:10. Maimonides is also referred to by the acronym Rambam (רמב״ם, Our Rabbi, Moshe son of Maimon).

[171] Albert Memmi, *Portrait of a Jew* (1962), p.195-96.

for steering nations toward Jewish interests and coordinating an international system which they dominate need not be held against them. It needs to be recognised as a fact and dealt with accordingly — not with injustice. Each nation has a duty to protect its sovereignty from exterior and interior threats. This means refusing to surrender sovereignty to outsiders when enticed or pressured to pool it under exaggerated internationalism. And it means limiting the internal political rights of all foreigners according to natural law. Those who identify as Jewish have no claim to be an exception here.

The notion that everybody present in a country should have full rights is a deception. Prisoners used to lose voting rights because they cared not for the common good. Foreigners had limited rights, not because they are guilty of anything, but because that is what foreign means: they are guests, not householders. Their loyalty lies elsewhere, which is perfectly normal. But we have been brainwashed to believe that a stable national identity is a harmful deviation rather than a natural good. Diluting national sovereignty from within is a self-serving device of Jews contrary to natural law. This is made evident by considering three natural unities: the person, the family, the nation.

Each person must love God and neighbour, in that order. But each has a spiritual duty to love himself before his neighbour. If he does not love himself, then he will be metaphysically incapable of loving any other human being. Aristotle explains healthy self-love to be a basis of friendship.

For a family, it is absolutely proper to share some goods with others less fortunate. But it would be a sin for parents to care for orphans disproportionately, to the detriment of their own children. Their duties of state require seeing to the welfare of their own first, which is also the route to giving the best care for others.

In like vein, a nation must care for its own subjects before aliens. Moses taught that a nation should offer hospitality to sojourners, refuge to the needy, even work to immigrants in as far as it can. Even so, the award of citizenship depends upon an assimilation of cult.[172] They have to adopt the religion of the country they come into before they can be considered citizens. Aristotle reported on an opinion of antiquity that it took two or three generations for immigrants to assimilate.[173] St Thomas, arguing from Revelation as well as reason, added that there are some peoples who, by reason of hostility to the culture, can never become citizens.[174]

The Jews who reject Christ cannot be integrated into Christendom. Like Cain, their concern remains for themselves, not for their host countries. In their sojourn, they must be treated with charity, even protection, but they are not owed political rights of governance, nor liberty to accrue out-sized influence. Certain rabbis are sympathetic with these limitations (for example, Rabbi Yisroel Dovid Weiss, of Neturei Karta, Orthodox Jews against Zionism).

Today this is rejected as xenophobic, white-supremacist, bigoted, alt-right fascism because we have been indoctrinated by globalists to reject nature. The same people lead our populations into silently assenting to transgender surgery for

---

[172] Ex 22:21; Lev 19:34; Dt 1:16; Ex 12:43-49; also Ezek 47:22-23.

[173] Aristotle, *Politica*, III, 2.

[174] St Thomas, *S.Th.* I-II, Q.105 a.3.

children. We must answer to God for that, but why is this mutilation mainstream? The psychological catastrophe of being an unconverted Jew, which is a profound existential contradiction, is being projected outward, shared around the world for everybody to experience. Our societies are hurting and will hurt much more until we face up decisively to the Jewish Question. For the sake of our salvation and theirs, God will not permit us to ignore it.

Jews who have not converted to Christ confront us with a question from which there is no escape. Eventually, all the world will have to answer: was it OK to crucify Jesus? Any response will end in disaster which suggests this is a purely private question. No. If it is OK to pretend Calvary does not matter, or if it is OK to be unrepentant for the Crucifixion, then one has a psychotic society which will turn to hell. Certainly, nobody can have their conscience forced. But we cannot pretend that any who justify the Crucifixion are spiritually balanced, for they are unfit to govern or wield influence. Their spirit is dangerous.

'Judeo-Christian' is worse than a misnomer; it is a self-contradiction. The two are essentially antagonistic. By definition they differ on the single most crucial matter: the Christ. They are two different religions from the time of Jesus' Sacrifice. Judaism is not the continuation of the Old Covenant: it is new, it is the Pharisees, it is the law of man, and it approves the Crucifixion.[175] Christianity laments it. So how can anyone talk of Judeo-Christian culture?

---

[175] Israel Jacob Yuval, Haaretz, *Can Jews and Christians Truly Reconcile?* (2020), "Judaism is not the religion of the Bible but the religion of the Talmud, the rabbinical literature, the kabbala and prayer."

Whatever passes as 'Judeo-Christian' is guaranteed to have demoted and sidelined the Crucifixion, in which case it is no longer Christian, just Judeo, for without the Cross Christianity is nothing, powerless, empty (1 Cor 1:18).

A society is either governed by love of God, of Jesus Christ, in which case it will flourish, or else it accepts the premise that one may be indifferent to the Crucifixion and seek another way to flourish, though this is impossible. For Christians to accept that Judaism is a just position to take is equivalent to asserting God's revelation is irrelevant to creation. We have no business hurting Jews, but a Christian society must either exclude Jews from power or else lose its Christianity. There is no neutral stand point, because one's position on this reveals the most fundamental orientation of a man to his neighbour. What society can possibly be built where the worst injustice is deemed acceptable?

It is not OK to crucify Jesus. Before we even consider His Divinity and Messiahship, it is not OK to condemn an innocent man. It is not OK to frame Him, to break the Law of Moses to do so, to accuse Him of crimes, sins and blasphemies which He never committed, yet which His prosecutors cease not to commit themselves. It is not OK to order torture. It is not OK to manipulate a crowd to secure a conviction, nor to intimidate the judge to preclude an acquittal. It is not OK to bribe the guards of His tomb to make out that He and His followers are liars.

Ecce, to be at home in one's humanity, one must have pity for the man — the innocent, unjustly accused, maliciously framed, cruelly tortured brother. If an adult refuses to admit that Jesus existed or was crucified, this is so insupportable that it reveals bad will. If one is more concerned with one's own suffering than His, then one is fatally self-centred or ignorant. We generally start out so but are not meant to die so.

Thanks be to God, Jews cannot eradicate from their being the great calling God has given them. But so long as this remains unanswered, so long as they refuse Christ, then Jews inevitably have divided loyalties when they reside in Christian countries, especially if they are Zionists. If ignored, these divided loyalties will end in Gentiles being exploited.

Who is to blame for the usury which fed the phenomenal rise of the Jews such that banks are now more powerful than governments? Certainly the money-lender is to blame for his unjust rates. But the borrower, the Christian, is to blame for putting himself under their yoke. For what? A loan? For what? Often enough, for greed — thus, Jewish greed exposes Gentile greed. Every monetary transaction involving over-charging or frivolous spending invariably feeds the beast. It empowers mammon. It is time we pulled back, personally at least, until debts are cancelled (cf. Lk 19:8) and usury is made illegal again.

This is critical because of the escalating destructivity of war. All wars are bankers' wars. How much longer will Gentiles be so imbecile as to allow financiers to provoke us into mutual slaughter? How easily we allow third parties to stir our bellicosity and pride. How stupid we are to be given the same lesson century after century and never learn from it.

Once we are ready to face the problem, the proven approach of *Sicut Judæis* safeguards against two errors. One is to unjustly hurt Jews. The second error is naively to lower the nation's guard against their perfidy; for to deny that Jews will betray the countries they live in is to deny that they will put their own people's interests first. But why should they not? To act unpatriotically is unnatural.

The solution is that they have no citizenship in nations where they reside without converting to the cult. And as it is doubtless too late to reverse the establishment of Israel, then it is needful to deny Israel a hand in international decision-making, because otherwise the opportunity will be misused to establish Israel as the nexus for global government.

The question of sharing power with Jews has moved up since 1948 from an internal, national matter to an international matter. Because Jews were emancipated, they garnered enough power to have Israel created. And now Israel has a voice among the nations as one among equals. The basis of that voice is that the Crucifixion is OK. Now it is proclaimed from the place that it happened. This is not natural or just, but a public despising of God. How we have been brow-beaten to say it is everyone's right to do this? No, it is not. It is true you cannot stop people rejecting God. But you can desist from pretending that such rejection does not have the most grievous spiritual effect on any society that tolerates it with equanimity, and cease ignoring that it must lead to disintegration on the political, social and personal levels. Or try building anything while insulting God!

There is nowhere to hide from this. Either a state is pleasing to God, publicly confessing Christ through all its institutions, in which case, Jews, like everyone, will have to wrestle with their conscience daily. Or else a state succumbs to those who hate the sight of the Crucifix, hides it, is silent about Jesus, endangering everyone to hell so that the Jews can have some peace of mind and prosperity on earth. Except, without converting, they will not find peace anywhere, just as Cain wandered tormented (Hos 9:17).

How realistic is it to hope for a political separation of Gentiles and Jews? Our parliaments and elected assemblies will never consent to it. That is because our democracies have long been fake. They work not for the people but for the banks. What is needful for a thousand reasons is the restoration of Christendom, of Christian monarchs in communion with Rome. This time round they should be constitutionally forbidden from falling into debt to usurers. If we reject this whole idea of a Christian order as absurdly medieval, then bring on the Antichrist instead.

We are trained to protest that we can all live alongside each other in harmony. But where has that ever been attempted without the Cross being gradually sidelined and degeneration the result? Rather, all can live in tranquility under the Cross, nobody can without it. Jesus said: *"He that is not with Me is against Me; and he that gathereth not with Me scattereth"* (Lk 11:23). This means if one is not a living member of the apostolic Church then one is a problem for everybody. This does not exclude Catholics also being problematic, nor does it justify any injustice or attempts at forced conversion. Rather it is to admit that life and history and creation have a single, awesome purpose: Jesus Christ.

It is a duty for Catholic nations to maintain their identity and culture in Christ and not to give way to Judaizing, to Protestantism, to worldly, materialistic philosophies which bring them to ruin. *Sicut Judæis* works. The salvation of Christians is endangered if they are made subject to Jews, as all too often this means the Cross will be removed from public life and few will find it. And it is best for the Jews by way of sparing them the consequences of acting out the mentality which pretends the Sacrifice of the Son of God should not receive public honour.

The Jewish search for a purely human messiah, which is descending further into the vapid messianism of a globalist order, which in turn sets the stage for the Antichrist, threatens mankind with the inverse of Jesus' loving Kingdom. Jesus Christ, King of Kings, knelt down and washed the feet of His Apostles. This is Truth. This gives life. The Antichrist will be pure deceit, pretending to care for people but devouring them — and most will worship him for it. They, like he, fail. But nobody is obliged to submit to this.

Undeniably, there is among some Christians an irrational hatred of Jews, whether we call it antisemitism or not. The hatred extends to disputing Jewish people exist and even denying that the Holy Family is Jewish!

Yet there is another antisemitism. It is among Jews themselves in rejecting their calling as the chosen people. This is seen in murdering the prophets and ultimately in the Crucifixion of Jesus Christ, the perfect Jew.

The devil stirs up both kinds of antisemitism, Gentile and Jewish, in order to postpone as long as he can a reconciliation of Christians and Jews, of Christ being All in All.[176]

---

[176] Cf. 1 Cor 15:28; St Ambrose, *De Fide*, Bk V, 181.

WEAPONISATION OF THE HOLOCAUST NARRATIVE

And it was night.

John 13:30

The Antichrist will inherit a totalitarian system and perfect it. Reality will be the opposite of what it is called. People will be so afraid to say what they think, that they will hardly be able to think, as their ideas atrophy. No one develops fruitful ideas alone. Unless we communicate, we cannot attain high truths. The devil is determined to hinder communication because it is essential to love, which is our God-given *telos*.[177] Today's cancel culture, which is thought control, is not accidental.

We can hardly speak openly about drag queen story hours, or the Covid-19 vaccination programme, without triggering a frenzied backlash which is facilitated by governments. Challenging the manufactured narrative frequently leads to ostracisation, loss of employment or even prosecution. How has so-called 'democracy' reached this point?

In the 1970s-80s, the usual lively disagreements in western political discourse became markedly vitriolic, notably with

---

[177] In the communion of the Blessed Trinity: the Father communicates the divine Nature to the Son, and these two communicate the same to the Holy Ghost. The communion of the angels and saints enjoys perfect communication with God.

opponents of socialism painted as inhumanely cold-hearted. A generation later, it became commonplace to see persons who rejected emerging dogmas have their reputations destroyed. If a public figure contradicted woke mania, he was swiftly persuaded to apologise. Soon everyone knew that expressing oneself independently risked sudden de-platforming.

Once enough exhibitions of crushing free speech had been staged that society acquiesced to persons being cancelled for 'abhorrent views', then the social machinery was in place to turn against influencers who effectively opposed the globalist agenda. The purpose is pervasive intimidation to prevent discussion and thereby to increase control through fear.

UN Secretary General, António Guterres, said in 2023: "We must confront bigotry by working to tackle the hate that spreads like wildfire across the internet." The UN Strategy and Plan of Action on Hate Speech defines hate speech as

> Any kind of communication in speech, writing or behaviour, that attacks or uses pejorative or discriminatory language with reference to a person or a group on the basis of who they are, in other words, based on their religion, ethnicity, nationality, race, colour, descent, gender or other identity factor.

This is a thin disguise for a worldwide war against truth.

The stages of degeneration toward this suffocating control are most obvious in questions concerning the Holocaust. Or rather, the abnormal absence of questions. It is not just conversations and careers which are shut down by hair-trigger accusations that the offender is a Nazi, but the pursuit of truth is shut down. This is the evil of those who make this accusation without basis: they are not chiefly interested in preventing genocide, but in eliminating people who think differently than they do. The hypocrisy is grotesque — using natural horror at tyranny to enforce tyranny themselves.

Prohibiting enquiry into the Holocaust is gestating a machinery that threatens to shut down free speech altogether. In several European countries, 'Holocaust denial' was, for decades, the only subject where a legal norm defined which opinions were permissible and which results of historical or scientific research were to be considered true. The declared motivation was honourable: to prevent the re-establishment of National Socialism;[178] and to ensure that relatives of Holocaust victims would not be humiliated by assertions that the mass murder and suffering were not real. But limiting discourse in this way is dangerously counter-productive.

We are told six million Jews perished under the Nazis, the majority of them gassed. Until 2020, I would not have questioned this — the mass murder was hellish enough however many died and by whatever method they were executed. But since Covid-19, it has become obvious that the public square is thoroughly infused with deception. The cruelty of lockdowns on children and the elderly, the brutality of law enforcement against the brave, the mass enforcement of injections against the Nuremberg Code, the summary closure of bank accounts and the pathetic compliance of politicians and bishops all reveal the reach of the globalists who hate us. In the institutions, their dominance is now close to total. It did not begin yesterday.

---

[178] The Austrian Chancellor Engelbert Dollfus was the first to issue an interdiction of the NSDAP (Nazis) as early as 1934.

The biggest lie in history is denial of the Crucifixion, the holocaust of the Son of God. Deliberate deception about it began when the Sanhedrin bribed Roman soldiers to say the Body of Jesus was stolen by His Apostles (Mt 28:12-15). The lies about God and man have multiplied ever since. By no means unconnected with this, it has occurred to many people, especially after 2020, that the predominant account we are given about the Holocaust is deliberately incomplete.

The four sub-sections of this chapter concern weighty matters which deserve open scrutiny. Have we been misled on the extent of the Holocaust? Was 'antisemitism' its only cause? How early was it realised that exaggerating the atrocities would grant Jews unprecedented political leverage? Has the Holocaust been weaponised against Catholicism because both the Holocaust and its weaponisation come from the same source, satan? If so, his machinations cannot succeed. Evil is futile.

No Questions on the Extent of the Holocaust

To question the figure of six million Jewish victims in WWII or the method of gassing is to be branded evil and can even lead to criminal charges, for, supposedly, one thereby risks atrocities recurring. But the opposite is true: preventing discussion creates suspicion, incredulity, distrust, resentment, tension and vicious violence. It is surely worth questioning how the figure of six million accords with what appears to be a pre-determined narrative.

The 1902 *Encyclopaedia Britannica* stated, "anti-Semitism… is not yet at an end" for "there are in Russia and Rumania six millions of Jews who are being systematically degraded".[179] Shortly after this, the *New York Times* reported that Constantine Pobiedonostzeff from "1890 to 1902… caused 6,000,000 Jewish families to be expelled from Russia."[180] A year later, in 1906, liquidation was the aim.

> Startling reports of the… future of Russia's 6,000,000 Jews were made… in Berlin… by Dr. Paul Nathan… that the Russian Government's studied policy for the 'solution' of the Jewish question is systematic and murderous extermination.[181]

In 1911, the American Jewish Yearbook stated, "Russia has since 1890 adopted a deliberate plan to expel or exterminate six million" Jews.[182] After WWI broke out, "The annihilation of the six million Jews… in the Russian domains goes on in a well defined and systematic manner."[183]

Once the Bolshevik Revolution prevailed, Germany became the enemy. The American Jewish Committee (AJC) campaigned for relief "to save from starvation six million Jews who are the helpless victims of the German terror."[184] Fundraising headlines announced: "Appeals to America to Act Quickly if Lives of some Six Million Jews are to be Saved"[185] and "127,000 Jews Have Been Killed and

---

[179] *The Encyclopaedia Britannica*, 10th Edition, Vol. 25 (London, 1902), p.482.

[180] *The New York Times* (1st Nov 1905).

[181] *The New York Times* (25th March 1906).

[182] *American Jewish Year Book* Vol. 13 (1911), p.308.

[183] *The Jewish Criterion* (PA, 25th June 1915), p.2.

[184] *The Galveston Daily News* (TX, 6th April, 1919), p.8.

[185] *The Daily Courier* (PA, 4th Aug 1919), section 2, p.1.

6,000,000 Are in Peril" with the report "that they are going to be completely exterminated".[186] The stated threat came not from natural misfortune but antisemitic lust for a holocaust.

> The Crucifixion of Jews Must Stop! From across the sea... six million human beings are being whirled toward the grave by a cruel and relentless fate... Six million men and women are dying from lack of the necessaries of life... through a bigoted lust for Jewish blood. In this threatened holocaust of human life...[187]

The message was that the pains of WWI had not ended for the Jews.[188] "Six million Jews... are facing annihilation through lack of food and disease."[189]

At a 1930 Zionist meeting in New York to bid farewell to emigrants to Palestine, Dr Shmarya Levin "expressed the opinion that six million Jews of Eastern Europe are doomed to perish."[190] Rabbi Stephen Wise, founder in 1897 of the New York Federation of Zionist Societies, underlined that the threat was unrelenting: "Six million Jews in Eastern Europe face starvation, and even worse, during the coming winter."[191] Chaim Weizmann, President of the World Zionist Organisation, testified that "almost six million Jews... are

---

186 *New York Times* (8th Sep 1919), p.6.

187 *The American Hebrew* (NY, 31st Oct 1919), p.582.

188 *Indiana Weekly Messenger* (9th Oct 1919), p.1 & 4, "Six million souls... in Poland, Lithuania, Russia, Palestine, Galicia, Turkey, Syria, Romania, Greece, and Bulgaria are in imminent danger of starving to death this winter."

189 *The Landmark* (NC, 26th March 1920), p.2.

190 Jewish Telegraphic Agency (20th Feb 1930).

191 *The Montreal Gazette* (28th Dec 1931), p.25.

doomed... They do not know today what is going to happen tomorrow".[192] WWII was looming.

> A depressing picture of 6,000,000 Jews in Central Europe... slowly dying of starvation... Now antiSemitism has spread to thirteen European nations, and threatens the very existence of millions of Jews.[193]

The President of the Board of Deputies of British Jews, Professor Selig Brodetsky, said, "Six million Jews... are trapped like rats in lands where democracy, freedom, and human decency are not understood".[194]

There is no question that those who were well informed could see calamity coming. (In November 1938, Pius XII programmatically began asking numerous countries to accept Jewish refugees.) But it is remarkable that the figure of six million featured so presciently. Already in 1939 was written:

> If Hitler gains control of Spain with the help of Franco, [will life in Spain] be any different than it is today in Germany, Austria and Czechoslovakia where 6,000,000 Jews have been murdered?[195]

In January 1940 it was reported:

> At the present time six million people of Hebrew blood are held in prisons or concentration camps in central

---

[192] Peel Commission on the future of the British Mandate for Palestine (Jerusalem, 25th Nov 1936). Chaim Weizmann became the first President of Israel.

[193] *The New York Times* (23rd Feb 1938).

[194] *The Guardian* (London, 4th April 1938), p.11.

[195] Jon Perez, Secretary, Rome Popular Front, *Daily Sentinel* (Rome, NY, 31st Jan 1939), page 11.

Europe and an additional three million in Russia are denied the living of normal lives and the right of religious freedom.[196]

"The lives of six million Jews have been uprooted by the psychopathic, political ambitions of totalitarian leaders";[197] "if the Nazis should achieve final victory, '6,000,000 Jews in Europe are doomed to destruction'."[198]

The [UK] Chief Rabbi [Joseph Hertz], who spoke on behalf of Empire Jewry and Jews of the United Nations, as well as of all six million Jews in Europe, said that the deliberate extinction of the whole house of Israel was being carried out by Hitler's sadists and quislings on a scale beyond compare even in the annals of Israel.[199]

In December 1942, the British Foreign Secretary, Anthony Eden, read in Parliament a joint statement from the Allied Powers, as reported in Australia:

Statements issued... in London, Washington and Moscow, told of German barbarity and of proof of the Nazi determination to exterminate Jews... It is estimated that there are between five and six million Jews in Occupied Europe... Hitler's oft-repeated intention to exterminate the Jewish people in Europe.[200]

---

[196] *The Jefferson Bee* (IA, 23rd Jan 1940), p.2.

[197] *Ohio Jewish Chronicle* (28th June 1940), p.1.

[198] Nahum Goldmann, Administrative Chairman of the World Jewish Congress, as quoted in the *Joplin News Herald* (MO, 25th June 1940).

[199] *The Palestine Post* (1st Nov 1942), p.1.

[200] *The Courier-Mail* (Brisbane, 19th Dec 1942).

That same month, a Jewish member of the UK Parliament, Samuel Sydney Silverman, urged Australia, Canada and South America, to absorb "five or six million Jews", with urgency, forecasting that

> Within the next 10 days the diabolical German objective of exterminating all Jews remaining in Nazi-dominated Europe may be achieved.[201]

The newspaper article reported that the Jewish Congress declared that 2,000,000 Jews had been exterminated so far. The same assessment was given on Christmas Day of 1942 by Jewish publisher Victor Gollancz.

> Of the six million Jews or so who were living at the outbreak of the war in what is at present Nazi-occupied Europe, a high proportion — between one and two million — have been deliberately murdered by the Nazis and their satellites... Unless something effective is done, within a very few months these six million Jews will all be dead.[202]

The Anglican leadership of England and Wales released a statement at the beginning of 1943, that they were "profoundly stirred" by Parliamentary declarations describing "Hitler's plans to exterminate six million Jews in occupied Europe".[203]

---

[201] *The Barrier Miner* (New South Wales, 23rd Dec 1942).

[202] Victor Gollancz, *Let My People Go* (pamphlet, 25th Dec 1942), appearing in: *The Massacre of a People: What the Democracies Can Do* (Jewish Frontier Association, NY, 1943), p.22.

[203] *The Canberra Times* (25th Jan 1943), p.2.

Toward the end of 1944, "a documentary record of the German massacre of approximately 6,000,000 European Jews" was prepared in Moscow by the Soviet revolutionary Jew, Ilya Ehrenburg, in collaboration with members of the American Jewish community. With the first of five volumes completed, US newspapers reported on the contents of Ehrenburg's *Black Book of Soviet Jewry*.

> Data available to the editors indicated that between 5,000,000 and 6,000,000 Russian Polish and western Europe Jews were killed and an additional half million Jews face probable death in Hungary now.[204]

At the beginning of 1945, the *New York Times* reported under the headline, "6,000,000 JEWS DEAD"

> The Jewish population in Europe has been reduced from 9,500,000 in 1939 to 3,500,000... Of the 6,000,000 European Jews who have died, 5,000,000 had lived in the countries under Hitler's occupation.[205]

The forecasts and reports cited above, of six million Jews being annihilated, span more than four decades, starting before WWI began. They are a fraction of hundreds of other similar examples.[206] Post-war estimates have not varied from the pre-war prediction. It is as if a pre-determined script were being fulfilled.

---

[204] *The Daily Register* (IL, 27th Nov 1944), p.4; *The Youngstown Vindicator* (OH, 27th Nov 1944); *The Leader Post* (Saskatchewan, 28th Nov 1944), p.2.

[205] *New York Times* (8th Jan 1945).

[206] S.A.R. Lynch, *Six Million Open Gates* (2012), with scans of original articles.

To obtain accurate statistics of the Jewish population during WWII was, understandably, enormously difficult. The *American Jewish Year Book*, compiled in New York under the auspices of the AJC, in their 1945 edition reported:

> Estimates as to the number who have perished in Nazi gas chambers and concentration camps and through disease and starvation vary, but the consensus seems to be that about half of [European Jewry] have been victims of Nazism.[207]

This was not calculated by tabulating known deaths, but by the overall difference between pre-war and post-war populations. These estimates were repeatedly revised, the former increasing and the latter decreasing, so that the differential grew from about 4.5 million to 6 million.[208]

The AJC informed the Nuremberg tribunal that six million Jews had died, though the Allied Powers were skeptical. Questionable testimony to substantiate the number was subsequently obtained by torturing SS officer Rudolf Höss (hanged in April 1947) and granting a life-saving plea deal to the notoriously dishonest SS officer Wilhelm Höttl (d.1999).

It did not require years of investigation for the extent of the atrocities to come out, as is to be expected from historical

---

[207] *American Jewish Year Book* Vol. 47 (1945), p.635.

[208] *American Jewish Year Book* Vol. 40 (1938), p.546, estimated that there were 9,137,051 Jews in Europe. Subsequent volumes printed an unrevised estimate of "nine million" Jews in Europe (including Russia): Vol 43 (1941), p.662; Vol 44 (1942), p.427; Vol 45 (1943), p.579; Vol 46, (1944), p.499. The 1945 Year Book revised the pre-war estimate of European Jews given in 1938 from 9.14 million to 9.75 million. In continuity with earlier editions, it put the pre-war worldwide Jewish population at 15.75 million. The 1947 edition (p.737) revised its pre-war estimate to 16.64 million (1939) and post-war world total of 11.27 million (1947).

analysis.[209] The opposite occurred — the death toll had been given by affiliates of the AJC several decades in advance, though with the culprit pivoting from Russia to Germany.

It does not change our heartbreak for Jews who suffered so unspeakably during that period and who died so cruelly. Whatever the actual number who died, what happened was horrific. But another layer of evil is added if it were part of a narrative set in advance. This figure is not a calculation based upon case data. It is a target. Beside the evil of mass murder, is a numbing suspicion that the killing is embedded within a diabolical manipulation. The narrative is told to bring itself about — annihilation — in reverse imitation of the Creator: *"For he spoke and they were... created"* (Ps 32:9).

After the staggering numbers, why is gassing so accentuated as the main method of execution, except because of its shocking inhumanity? There were many more victims who were shot, or worked to death, or who died from typhus or other illnesses, or from Allied bombing, or just as tragically, after liberation by suddenly eating too much. People were bulldozed alive into graves to save bullets. Others escaped from Europe but disappeared from the records

---

[209] Until as late as 1949, the *World Almanac*, also based in New York, showed little variation between pre-war and post-war figures of the Jewish population. Probably on the advice of the AJC, by 1950, the *World Almanac* brought its numbers into line with the *American Jewish Yearbook*.

Editions of the *World Almanac* from 1925 to 1948 record a stability of the world Jewish population of between fifteen and sixteen million. It is understandable that the *Almanac* would not update its statistics for every edition with thorough research, but would simply extrapolate from previous years. The 1950 *Almanac* revised its estimates to give a pre-war figure of 16.64 million (1938) and a post-war figure of 11.37 million (1948). The 1947 and 1949 *Almanacs* appear to be missing from the otherwise comprehensive Internet Archive. In their place is a link to a video about Nazi concentration camps.

after changing their name and denying their roots, calculating it was safest not to be known as a Jew. Furthermore, an unknown number vanished in Stalin's USSR.

All these deaths and disappearances are tragic, but precisely because industrial-scale gassing of people is so demonic, it is exaggerated by people with an agenda to fill Gentiles with shame, and also, it seems, to traumatise Jews. This way the two sides may forever be kept apart. We can consider three very different accounts of what happened.

We are told that the Nazis, with a sense of invincibility and obsession for efficiency, diligently kept prison records. These records, captured by the Soviets and released by President Gorbachev in 1989, tallied with Arolsen archives showing total deaths, of all nationalities and ages, from all causes, including old age and disease, in the fifteen major prison camps, as under 400,000.[210] This data, which seems egregiously under-counted, is raised by Gerard Menuhin. But instead of countering him with sober argument, his awkward points can be dealt with simply by saying that Menuhin is a self-hating Jew. Ignore everything he says or else you are a Holocaust denier, a Nazi who, given the chance, would co-operate in genocide. Do you still have questions?

Israel's official memorial to the Holocaust, Yad Vashem, recounts that Germany began gassing systematically in 1940, using carbon monoxide to euthanise mental patients and the chronically sick, the victims being mostly German and Polish. In late 1941, Poles and Soviet POWs were being gassed in the

---

[210] This figure is apparently corroborated by 1980 research findings of the International Red Cross. See Gerard Menuhin, *Tell the Truth and Shame the Devil* (2016), p.115-19. The figure does not include those killed without any registration.

back of crowded trucks, by pumping exhaust fumes in. In 1942, small gas chambers were built in three locations: Belzec, Sobibor, and Treblinka, using gas from diesel engines. Although other smaller sites existed, in 1943, gas chambers were expanded in Auschwitz, using Zyklon B, so that "more than one million people were gassed to death there".[211] The estimate has been steadily declining since the 1945 assessment that four million had died in Auschwitz.[212]

The Auschwitz-Birkenau State Museum now estimates that "around 1.1 million people perished in Auschwitz" during the five years of its existence, noting that of these, "around 1 million people were Jews."[213] Of those victims, many died in ways other than gassing. The museum reports that Auschwitz was the main liquidation centre, its five successive gas chambers being destroyed by the Germans in 1942, 1943, 1944 and 1945 respectively. The most solid evidence in Auschwitz for the gassing is the much visited Crema 1 chamber, a reconstruction built after the War.

After decades of contrary claims, it has been widely admitted that there never was a gas chamber in Dachau, where a delousing station and crematorium had been fallaciously identified. Likewise, it is no longer contested that there were no gas chambers in Germany, but only in occupied Poland. Some say these buildings, too, were not for killing but for hygiene or crematoria. Their arguments are not crass. What makes them more compelling is that many hundreds of

---

[211] https://www.yadvashem.org/odot_pdf/Microsoft Word - 6234.pdf

[212] Hermann Langbein, *People in Auschwitz* (2004), p.385.

[213] https://www.auschwitz.org/en/history/auschwitz-and-shoah/the-number-of-victims/

people have been charged, fined or imprisoned for 'Holocaust denial'. Is this how to defend the truth?

Given these accounts, why has the world been so ready to believe a more inflated version of history, a logistical and technological impossibility, that the majority of Jewish victims were gassed? An Auschwitz survivor wrote in 1945,

> Two weeks ago we had a mass meeting in Belsen under the slogan: 'Six million gassed Jews — World, where is your conscience?'[214]

This message went out to shape popular perception and endures. In 2016, a critic of Donald Trump accused him on his election campaign of sounding "exactly like... Hitler [who] had six million gassed to death".[215] When Diane Abbot, MP, lost the Labour Whip in 2023 for alleged antisemitism, an online forum carried the comment: "She appears to have let the circa six million gassed by the Nazis slip her mind".[216]

These tangential cases demonstrate what everyone knows — 'Hitler' and 'Nazi' are used arbitrarily to excoriate. If, on social media, someone actually questions particularities of the Holocaust narrative, then a barrage of abuse is fired on him. Depending on the circumstances, he could lose his livelihood. But why not allow debate? Cranks will be exposed, relegated organically to the fringe and ignored. Why, instead, do we witness a hair-trigger, fatally tense death-trap around the whole subject?

---

[214] Norbert Wollheim, translation of Letter to Hermann E. Simon (26th Aug 1945).

[215] *News Press*, Mailbag for 29th Oct 2016. Letter from [H S-L], Matlacha, FL.

[216] Posted 23rd Oct 2023 on the Sheffield Forum by [C].

While the popular perception of what happened in the Holocaust is distorted, the truth cannot be ascertained by criminalising those who question the dominant narrative, as is the case in Israel, Canada and more than a dozen European countries.[217] Such censorship inevitably perpetuates division. Not only do the numbers and causes of death matter, but also questions about how and why the Holocaust arose. If that cannot be openly discussed, it will happen again.

No Questions on the Causes of the Holocaust

After prohibiting discourse on the extent of the Holocaust, the prevailing perspective permits no explanation of it except antisemitism. It becomes antisemitic even to ask of causes or to believe Jews did anything to provoke murderous enmity.

However, after making a deep analysis of social, economic and theological causes, warnings of an impending calamity were issued in 1890 in the Jesuit periodical, *La Civiltà Cattolica*.[218] In 1892, Fr Georg Ratzinger (great uncle of Benedict XVI) wrote:

> A reaction against the jewification of our culture is now building momentum among the common man. That movement is hardly perceptible today, but it will grow like an avalanche. That movement would be irresistible at this very moment if it were not lacking a leader.[219]

[217] Michael Bazyler, Yad Vashem, *Holocaust Denial Laws and Other Legislation Criminalizing Promotion of Nazism.*

Auschwitz-Birkenau State Museum, *Deniers in Different Countries.*

[218] *La Civiltà Cattolica, The Jewish Question in Europe* (1890).

[219] Dr Georg Ratzinger, *Jüdisches Erwerbsleben* (1892), p.84.

Fr Ratzinger's sombre warning of a backlash against "jewification" was not heeded and a Führer ('leader') did come to Germany. To now hide the history behind Hitler's rise is to invite something similar to recur. Politically correct censorship is deadly.

In 1920, when varying opinions could still be offered, Winston Churchill compared harmful Jewish influence troubling post-WWI Europe to the Jewish role in the Bolshevik Revolution. Among the worst aspects is a sense of godlike superiority zealous to destroy lesser peoples.

> The same evil prominence was obtained by Jews in the brief period of terror during which Bela Kun ruled in Hungary. The same phenomenon has been presented in Germany (especially in Bavaria), so far as this madness has been allowed to prey upon the temporary prostration of the German people. Although in all these countries there are many non-Jews every whit as bad as the worst of the Jewish revolutionaries, the part played by the latter in proportion to their numbers in the population is astonishing.[220]

With revolutionary Jews determinedly destabilising Bavarian and German culture with an aim to replace them, it is dangerously superficial to reduce the cause of hostilities to irrational antisemitism.

Before Germany began systematically deporting Jews, a 1938 letter from G.M. Beerbower of Hollywood was

---

[220] Winston Churchill, *Illustrated Sunday Herald, Zionism versus Bolshevism* (London, Feb 1920), p.5.

published in Florida under the title *Kill Off the Germans*.[221] The author vents at Germany seeking world domination in WWI, causing 36 million deaths at a cost of 186 billion dollars to the world economy. Seeing that Hitler planned to do worse, Mr Beerbower wrote that Germans should be expelled from America (because they are fighters seeking to hurt Jews), unless a few could prove their pacifism. He called for massive spending on weapons, needful due to the German "monster which cannot be civilised". He concluded: "Nothing but almost complete extermination of the savage whites will insure peace on earth and good will toward men". Here, the Angel of the Nativity's blessing (Lk 2:14) is invoked for huge armament procurement, aimed at exterminating the Germans.

A Harvard Professor of Anthropology, Dr Earnest Hooton, who was Jewish, advocated from 1941 the "complete obliteration of the German state" and measures to *"Breed war strain out of Germans"*.[222] This eugenic idea involved expatriating German men to scattered locations and restricting them from marrying German women, while settling Allied forces in Germany specifically to marry German women. Fixation with race and bloodlines did not begin with Aryans, but has been a constant and needless obsession of Judaism, a carnal misreading of the OT.[223]

---

[221] Letters to the Editor, *Miami Daily News* (12th July 1938).

[222] Earnest Hooton, *Peabody Magazine* (Jan 1943), p.3. Also *The Harvard Crimson* (Nov 1941) and *The Western Socialist* (June 1943).

[223] Once it had been recorded that Jesus Christ, the Son of God, is the Son of David and Son of Abraham, then there was no further need of genealogies and concern for bloodlines (Mt 1:1; Tit 3:9). Apostolic succession is enough.

One of [Karl] Marx's early friends, Moses Hess, widely known and respected as one of the first socialists in Germany, subsequently revealed himself as an extreme Jewish racist, whose views about the 'pure Jewish race' published in 1858 were not unlike comparable bilge about the 'pure Aryan race'. But the German socialists, who struggled against German racism, remained silent about their Jewish racism.[224]

Nurtured in this artificial silence, Theodore N. Kaufman proposed in his 1941 brochure, *Germany Must Perish*, that,

'German extinction' [could] be achieved by sterilizing all Germans of procreation age (males under 60, females under 45) within a period of three years after the war's end, Germany to be sealed off during the process and its territory then to be shared among other people, so that it should disappear from the map together with its people…

The *New York Times* described the proposal as 'a plan for permanent *peace* among *civilized* nations'; the *Washington Post* called it 'a provocative theory, interestingly presented'.[225]

Heavyweight Jewish-American press nodding publicly at plans for the medical genocide of Germans in 1941 by no means justifies mass killings of Jews, but adds more insight

---

[224] Israel Shahak, *Jewish History, Jewish Religion: The Weight of Three Thousand Years* (1994), p.30.

[225] Douglas Reed, *The Controversy of Zion* (1978), p.481. The three-year timescale differs from the calculation shown above in the *Canadian Jewish Chronicle*.

than bare accusations of 'inexplicable antisemitism' as to why the Holocaust happened.[226]

It was commonly said (before February 2023), that Ukrainians showed the Nazis how to execute Jews *en masse*. The reason invariably given is that Ukrainians are savagely antisemitic. It is not so often said that these Ukrainians were taking revenge for the Holodomor, wherein some five million of their countrymen were starved to death in a deliberately engineered famine. This 1930s genocide was organised by Bolsheviks, a movement spearheaded by Jews. The Holodomor does not justify mass executions in reprisal. But it does overturn the claim that Ukrainians are mysteriously antisemitic, as if hostile to Jews without cause.

Searching deeper into the roots of Ukrainian and Jewish antagonism, one would be hard pressed to find an analysis more fair-minded or meticulously researched than that given by Alexander Solzhenitsyn in *Two Hundred Years Together: A History of the Russians and the Jews* (2001 in Russian). He details that pogroms against Jews broke out in Odessa in 1821, 1859 and 1871, the latter seeing hundreds of Jewish taverns, shops and homes destroyed during a three-day frenzy, albeit without human fatalities. Greek merchants harboured resentment toward Jews due to perceived unfair competition. When Jewish-owned businesses were ransacked, their wares were not so often stolen as deliberately destroyed, as if in an act of redress rather than theft. Solzhenitsyn recounts that decades later, these early incidents were recast,

---

[226] Contrast Greer Fay Cashman, *The Jerusalem Post, 'Inexplicable Antisemitism' Still a Worldwide Problem — Herzog in France* (21st March 2022).

by people whose emotion, imagination or agenda outstrips their historical competence, as bloodthirsty massacres.

In reality, pogroms were more widespread in 1881 and in these Jews were actually killed. Russian (Ukrainian) landowners rented massive tracts to Jewish capitalists, and these parcelled out the land with hiked up rents for peasants, often beyond their ability to pay.[227] This fostered a seething anger toward the Jews more than toward the landowner class. Pogroms were not motivated by antisemitism, but because the Jews so often served as bailiffs for an oppressive upper class.

Further, Jewish-owned distilleries and taverns made a fortune from the propensity of the Ukrainian or Russian peasant for drink. Excessive alcohol was the ruin of many men and thereby their families. The two parties were caught in a deathly embrace; Jewish love of business and aloofness from other races was ensnared with Slavic love of drink plus bureaucratic corruption which rendered the government unable to regulate the problem. The widespread ruination generated hatred.

Who is to blame here? Within an otherwise cohesive society, such exploitation is tolerated as the messiness of life. Some are weak, some are greedy; such is fallen man. But should another race exploit your own countrymen, this is borne with grumbling if the times are 'good'. When bad times hit, then it is all dry tinder ready to ignite. Something turned the hatred murderous.

Some say Ukrainians, or Russians, or Gentiles in general, are innately antisemitic. Other researchers say the Tsarist

---

[227] John Doyle Klier, *Russians, Jews, and the Pogroms of 1881–1882* (2011), p.4.

government targeted the Jews as a scapegoat to cover for their own failings. Solzhenitsyn gives evidence of socialists instigating pogroms as a way of heating up the revolution: violent disorder and killing Jewish landlords and traders was a step toward wider anarchy and killing Tsarist landowners and nobility. This last factor invites us to look into an abyss: have atheist Jews sacrificed Orthodox Jews, or peasants, for political purposes (Jn 11:50)? Were victims mere expendables in an anarchical campaign to impose a new order?

Solzhenitsyn demonstrates that the socialist revolutionaries were by no means mostly Jewish. Also, that most Jews were by no means socialist revolutionaries. But even so, there was an indisputable propensity for Jews to be involved in, and even to lead, the revolution.[228] These were atheists, fallen away from any belief in God. And they did not mind having the more religious Jews in the towns and rural areas hurt, or even murdered, as collateral damage for the higher cause of what would become Bolshevism.

The Bolshevik takeover of 1917 followed governmental failure to deal with the pogroms, though not for want of trying. Through much of the nineteenth century, a full assimilation of Russia's Jewish population had been widely advocated. Sympathetic to this approach, an Imperial Decree of Tsar Alexander II in 1859 accelerated the programme, which involved making the Jews almost equal in rights with the native inhabitants. The goal was not necessarily a sign of sympathy for the Jews, but a frustration with the grievous challenge of managing a population within a population. But

---

[228] Michael Galka-Giaquinto, *Bolshevik Extremism in Ukraine* in *Western Influence in the Cover-up of the Holodomor* (2019), p.10.

total assimilation is nothing other than soft annihilation — a loss of identity — and many Jews, understandably, were not going to accept that. Something different happened.

First, the Zionist movement grew much stronger. Influential Jews lamented that integration in Russia (or anywhere) was impossible. The Jews must move to Palestine and take it for themselves. They had nowhere else. In parallel, the Russian intelligentsia began demanding full emancipation of the Jews: equal rights but no cultural integration.

Before the 1881 pogroms, there was a widespread sense that Jews, even with limited rights, benefitted far more from Russia than they contributed. Each awarding of new rights resulted in Jews acquiring increased economic control over Russians. Shortfalls in Jewish conscripts for the military was another measurable indicator. The Jews did not feel a sense of patriotism for the Motherland. The failed attempt to solve this through assimilation, bringing up Jewish children to be culturally Russian, was gradually replaced with the notion that emancipation was the answer; award Jews full rights of citizenship. The need to protect Russians from Jews was forgotten with a powerful call to protect Jews from Russians. The Jewish victim became the hero of Russian progressives.

Prior to WWI, this philo-semitism reached an extreme pitch which we can easily recognise today.

> [N]ot only did Russian society firmly defend the Jews against the government, but it forbade itself and forbade anyone to show any trace of a shadow of criticism of the conduct of each Jew in particular.[229]

---

[229] Alexander Solzhenitsyn, *Two Hundred years Together* (trans. 2003), Vol I, 11.

In these circles, it was not enough to desist from criticising Jews. One had to praise them or one was suspect. Solzhenitsyn continues,

> Not only the opposition parties, but also the large midlevel bureaucracy, trembled at the thought of appearing 'unprogressive'. One had to be entirely independent financially or possess outstanding spiritual freedom to have the courage to withstand the pressure of the general current. In the legal, artistic and scholarly worlds, any deviation was immediately ostracised.

This is the woke culture we suffer today. Whoever refuses to signal being pro-pride, pro-BLM, pro-trans is not welcome in so-called open society. The intolerance flows from the most volatile subject of all: the Holocaust. Question that and you become an associate of genocide. Yet it is precisely this mindless conformity which paves the way to catastrophe.

The febrile climate enveloping the Russian political left was followed within a generation by the Bolshevik Revolution, then the Holodomor, then the hellscape of Stalin's Gulag. If today it is the global elite whose mindset is as controlled and controlling as was that of the elite in pre-revolutionary Russia — so intolerant of independent voices — what does that portend for what we are all about to experience at a worldwide level? Freedom is precious. Destroy it anywhere and it becomes vulnerable everywhere.

Before progressive Russia reached the stage of prohibiting criticism of the Jews, after the 1881 assassination of Tsar Alexander II, a painful lesson was articulated by the ninth

Commission for the Organisation of the Life of the Jews. Breaking cultural tradition means breaking a people.

> [T]he difficulty of resolving the complicated Jewish Question compels us to turn for instruction to the old times, when various novelties did not yet penetrate either our own or foreign legislation, and did not bring with them the regrettable consequences which usually appear upon adoption of new things that are contrary to the national spirit of the country.[230]

If that paragraph is too dense, Solzhenitsyn follows it with the conclusion: "From time immemorial the Jews were considered aliens, and should be considered as such."

Notwithstanding good personal relations, Jews cannot mix politically with Christians, for we differ diametrically on the murder of the Messiah, the Saviour of the World. Excusing the Crucifixion poisons the social and political wells in a spiritual assault against our greatest good. Jesus is at the heart of all human-divine reality. One's disposition toward Him, and the disposition of a society, is the difference between blessings and curses, order and chaos, life and death, in time and in eternity. If Jews believe crucifying Jesus was sinful, let them loudly say it. Otherwise, the only way they can manage to attain equal rights in Christian countries is by having this matter buried. This is to everybody's cost. One cannot serve the commonweal while holding hostility to Christ.

Russians through centuries, like other nations, severely limited the rights of the Jews, not with malice, but to protect both parties. Protection of Jews is demanded by God, Who

---

[230] Alexander Solzhenitsyn, *Two Hundred years Together* (trans. 2003), Vol I, 5.

marked Cain so that any who hurt him would suffer sevenfold. Gentiles must respect that. But Jews must admit that Cain's penance was to wander. When they attempt to settle, it does not work: if they assimilate, they lose their identity; if they achieve emancipation, they dethrone the Prince of Peace, inviting such disorder and resentment as erupts in violence. There is no escape from the penance God sets for us, because His desire is to purify us through it.

The notion that Zionism offers a way out, by providing the Jews with a nation of their own, only scales up the problem. Israel itself seeks emancipation among the nations. Its manner of pursuing its aspirations threatens to cause such ferocity as to put the Holocaust in the shade. I mean nuclear war. It will not go well for Israel. The way to avert it, I believe, is given in the next section of this book, *What Can Catholics Do?* But before coming to the resolution, there is more to say about the depths of the difficulties of Jewish and Gentile hostilities.

The complexity of the origin of pogroms is cut through to simplicity by a telling incident of 1473. A three-day riot against Jews erupted in Catholic Cordoba.[231] What caused it?

On Holy Thursday, while the city was venerating the Blessed Virgin Mary, a Jewish girl poured water, or more likely emptied a chamber pot, from her window onto a statue of the Virgin being carried through the streets in procession. It is obvious why this sparked savage violence in a city already tense. It is hard to think of a worse provocation. Imagine the reaction of a Spaniard, a young man or a family father, accustomed to carrying a sword and perhaps fighting for his

---

[231] Alonso de Palencia, *Cronica de Enrique IV*, Tomo III, Capitulo IX.

country during the *Reconquista,* in a period when justice and order were largely in the hands of engaged subjects (as they must be). It would have taken exceptional virtue to channel their rage into equanimity. Of course nobody hurt the converso girl. She was just a teenager. But for the rest, it got horrifically out of hand. That is wrong — even criminal — but antisemitism was not the cause. The Jewish community had brought this girl up to have contempt for the Virgin Mary, for nobody has a spontaneous hatred of Mary. Manifestly, the girl felt it would earn approval from her elders to commit such an act.

Undoubtedly, the web of causation was more complex. But I am trying to extract what is irreducible, definitive. The fact that we hear neither apologies nor justifications for such blasphemous affronts proves this is the depth of the matter. Theologically, the *mysterium iniquitatis* cannot be explained. To blame centuries of conflict on antisemitism is an unconvincing rationalisation used to avoid theological truth.

Do Christians sin in pogroms? Assuredly. Gravely. That has to be dealt with. But if we falsely identify the root as antisemitism, cycles of retaliation will continue. Centuries of violence escalated horrendously into the Holocaust. Given Israel's foreign policy, the next stage could be nuclear. St Paul saw a stupendous flash of light on his way to Damascus, and converted. Must it go so far to reach that end again?

Rounds of revenge are no solution. What might have worked would have been maintaining the Church's policy of *Sicut Judæis,* or Russia's *Pale of Settlement.* But these were overturned long ago by the enemies of Christendom, opening the way to the unspeakable sufferings under the Nazis. Now a barely checked narrative of "six million" "gassed" is used to take revenge on the world and shape geopolitics.[232]

Much worse than exploitation of the Holocaust *post factum,* and thus dishonouring the dead, is the apprehension that the horror might have been foreseen for this purpose.

No Questions on Leveraging the Holocaust Narrative

Honest Jews have admitted that the Holocaust narrative affords unheard of political leverage.[233] It is unsettling to appraise how early that exploitation may have begun.

The Federation of American Zionists were told in 1900, "There are 6,000,000 living, bleeding, suffering arguments in favor of Zionism".[234] The immense distress would likely move anyone who heard Rabbi Wise speak of it. At the Tenth Zionist Congress in Switzerland in 1911, Max Nordau gave notice of "the downfall of six million creatures... for no war has ever yet destroyed six million human lives".[235] Speaking at Carnegie Hall, Rabbi Wise alerted his audience that an attempt at genocide was underway.

---

[232] Invoking six million has not ceased. In 2018, Israeli Prime Minister Netanyahu told President Putin, "Iran is seeking to commit another Holocaust by exterminating six million more Jews". *Times of Israel* (9th May, 2018).

[233] Norman Finkelstein, *The Holocaust Industry: Reflections on the Exploitation of Jewish Suffering* (2003). Moshe Zuckermann, *'Antisemit!': Ein Vorwurf als Herrschaftsinstrument* (2014). Vera Sharav, *Never Again Is Now Global* (2023).

Gerald Kaufman, MP, Hansard, 407 (15th Jan 2009), "The current Israeli Government ruthlessly and cynically exploit the continuing guilt among gentiles over the slaughter of Jews in the holocaust as justification for their murder of Palestinians."

[234] Rabbi Stephen Wise, at Cooper Union, NY. *New York Times* (11th June, 1900).

[235] *The Jewish Criterion* (PA, 1st Sep, 1911), p.1. Max Nordau (aka Simon Südfeld) was co-founder of the World Zionist Organisation.

Russia is now asphyxiating the Jews. It does not dare to offend the nations by blood spilling, so it is slowly, but surely grinding out the lives of 6,000,000 Jews.[236]

Leading Zionist Jacob de Haas pointed out in 1915 that,

the only point that all warring elements are agreed upon is that at the end of the holocaust the Jews and Palestine will be more closely related than at present.[237]

In Vienna, 1918, Professor Carl Balod, assured that,

It is quite possible for Palestine to find room for five to six millions... 800,000 hectares will suffice to produce the food of six millions of people.[238]

The Zionist cause brought in enormous wealth through Jewish generosity, especially from the USA.[239] 1921 saw the launch of Zionist fundraisers for six million dollars, a target chosen more than once to represent suffering Jews.[240] The 1938 Vice-President of the Zionist Organisation of America warned it was urgent to help "as many Jews as possible out of the hell of Europe", urging American Jews to "swing moral

---

[236] *New York Tribune* (12th Sep, 1912), p.9.

[237] *The Boston Sunday Globe* (26th Sep, 1915), p.46.

[238] *The Columbus Jewish Chronicle* (OH, 28th June, 1918), p.1, address to the German Committee for the Promotion of the Jewish Palestine Settlement.

[239] *New York Times* (15th Sep 1919), "Jews Expect Drive to Pass $10,000,000: Industries and Professions Pledge $6,000,000 for Philanthropic Building Fund."

[240] *New York Times*, (19th June 1923), "BALTIMORE — Six million dollars has been raised [in] the past two years by Jewish organizations in the United States devoted to the rebuilding of Palestine."

and financial powers into the channels of evacuating some 6,000,000 Jews to Palestine".[241]

At a Mason City synagogue, Mr David Tannenbaum spoke in 1940 of a new Jerusalem, stressing that

> Palestine offered the only solution to the six million Jews who are homeless, starving and sick in central and eastern Europe today.[242]

A Workers Union, in 1944, blamed Britain for appeasing fascism and reneging on the Balfour Declaration by refusing to open Palestine to Jewish refugees in 1939, declaiming,

> History records no parallel to the bestial cruelties inflicted on the Jewish people of Europe by the Nazis and their satellites, whose coldly calculated program of extermination of all European Jews very nearly succeeded, almost six million Jews having been murdered in cold blood... the British Empire stands guilty as a murderer of tens of thousands of people who might have been alive.[243]

It would have been fairer for Britain to accept the refugees herself than send them to Palestine, or else one could blame Britain for the "tens of thousands" of Palestinian deaths caused by capitulating to Zionism. In any case, pressure on Britain mounted, even while she was mourning her own dead who had sacrificed themselves to end the war.

---

[241] *Rochester Democrat and Chronicle* (NY, 16th June 1938), p.18.

[242] *Mason City Globe Gazette* (IA, 20th Jan 1940), p.16.

[243] Resolution Palestine, United Electrical, Radio and Machine Workers of America Convention Proceedings (25th-29th Sep 1944), p.227.

> You [Prime Minister Clement Atlee] now propose to continue to keep these doors shut against our survivors, after six million of our people perished, for whose death your country (Britain) is not without blame.[244]

Rabbi Stephen Samuel Wise spelt out the consequences.

> The Christian world, and I include England, of course, in the Christian world, suffered six million of the people of Jesus of Nazareth to die in a most horrible manner. The Christian world owes the Jews some reparation.[245]

In 1948, half a century after being elected to the Zionist General Action Committee, Rabbi Wise saw the creation of the State of Israel. Reparations from Germany, ongoing today, are approaching $100 billion.[246]

Though the Holocaust has become an industry for some, ideology is more powerful than money, even than blood. Rudolf Kastner, Zionist leader in Hungary, negotiated a deal in summer 1944 with Adolf Eichmann. For allowing 1,700 hand-picked Zionists to go to Palestine, at $1,000 per head, Kastner, with approval from the World Zionist Organization, collaborated with the SS to sooth the fears of a vastly greater number of Hungarian Jews being sent to the camps.[247] Kastner is not faulted for helping some Jews escape, but for securing it through the betrayal of uncountably more.

---

[244] *The Canadian Jewish Chronicle* (5th Oct 1945), p.6.

[245] Rabbi Stephen Wise at a UN Peace Conference in San Francisco (May 1945).

[246] US Department of State, *The JUST Act Report: Germany* (2020).

[247] The macabre arrangement was exposed in a 1953-55 libel trial.

The interplay of Zionism and the Holocaust is not clean. There is an unspeakably sinister force behind both. We are required to accept that there are Germans, Austrians, Poles and Ukrainians capable of using war as a cover for industrial genocide. Are there Jews who are capable of exaggerating the atrocities in order to advance Zionism, or worse, of tolerating mass murder for the sake of a still larger goal?

Is the real horror made more horrifying in order to dehumanise Germans, then Gentiles, and finally Christians? Already in 1945, Zionists laid the charge:

> It was our very unhappy conviction all along that the responsibility for the extinction of six million Jews in Europe was not Hitler's alone. The Entire Christian world shares that responsibility.[248]

This antichrist accusation developed further. A Jew who was ordained as a Catholic priest, who drafted *Nostra ætate*, who worked in New Jersey and New York through the 1960s, who vociferously rejected *Humanæ vitæ*, who devoted himself to integrating the Marxism of the Frankfurt School with Liberation Theology, who left the priesthood in 1978 and married a former nun, who admitted in his 2016 autobiography that he hid his homosexuality for decades specifically to retain influence as a theologian, including promoting sexual perversion in the Church, wrote in 1977:

> After Auschwitz the Christian churches no longer wish to convert the Jews. While they may not be sure of the theological grounds that dispense them from this

---

[248] American Zionist Emergency Council advert, *New York Post* (27th Sep 1945).

mission, the churches have become aware that asking the Jews to become Christians is a spiritual way of blotting them out of existence and thus only reinforces the effects of the Holocaust. The churches, moreover, realize the deadly irony implicit in a Christian plea for the conversion of the Jews; for after Auschwitz and the participation of the nations, it is the Christian world that is in need of conversion.[249]

It is the author who is in need of true conversion. Are we meant to despise the whole German people, even today, for the horror of mass gassings, and then distrust ourselves too, as if murderous racism is inherent to the souls of Gentiles, and even Christianity is at fault? Is this an accusation against the God Who made us and Who gave Christianity to us? It comes from a *peritus* of Vatican II, appointed by Cardinal Bea, friend of the AJC. This is the dark spirit of Vatican II.

Louis Marshall, co-founder in 1906 of the AJC and later its President, was not a Zionist, but he wrote in 1918 that it was unstoppable, adding mysteriously: "Zionism is but an incident of a far-reaching plan. It is merely a convenient peg on which to hang a powerful weapon."[250] Ambivalent about Zionism itself, in the same letter Marshall clarified that while his interest in Jewish affairs was religious, he had "never favoured the creation of a sovereign Jewish State". Yet he was much enthused by this movement "replete with poetry" and its potential for something larger: "It is regarded by the

---

[249] Fr Gregory Baum, *Rethinking the Church's Mission after Auschwitz* in *Auschwitz: Beginning of a New Era?* edited by Eva Fleischner (1977), p.113.

[250] Letter to Max Senior (26th Sep 1918), *Louis Marshall: Champion of Liberty: Selected Papers and Addresses,* Vol 2 (Jewish Publication Society, 1957), p.722.

religious-minded of all creeds as tending to bring about the fulfilment of ancient prophecies."

Christians who believe that line have been utterly misled. But whoever manipulates religion is sure to fail, even as the one manipulating them, satan, is certain to fail. He, too, is "replete with poetry", of the darkest kind. The Zohar passage following, a medieval kabbalistic text, is typically obscure.

> The sacrificial offering… the smoke ascends [until] the soul of all comes… a supernatural light is stimulated and everything enters the holy of holies… Here is the mystery of mysteries. That which is not known and of which there can be no account, the Will that cannot be conceived… then everything is a single Will without limit… He who cleaves to His Master… inherits all the worlds.[251]

This is the spearhead of the rejection of Jesus. This "single Will" is totalitarianism. The promise is to inherit "all the worlds", echoing the temptation which the devil put to Jesus. The "supernatural light" is not Christ but is Lucifer himself. The "sacrificial offering" is preceded by mention of the role of Levitical priests, but as the Zohar was written only a few hundred years ago, its visions require the rebuilding of Jerusalem's Temple, satan's pet project since AD 70.

The voice of this poisonous poetry is of him who led the wild heresies of the Gnostics, promising secret knowledge that cannot be grasped. The cadence is of the Quran, a text whose entire value is in its Arabic poesy, for whenever it is

---

[251] *The Wisdom of the Zohar, An Anthology of Texts*, Vol 2 (translated from the Hebrew by David Goldstein, 2008), p.613-14.

translated nothing good is left, no food for the soul. The medieval kabbalists did offer their lord dark sacrifices, and he did reward them with deceptive advancements in science, in alchemy, in money, in power. The voice is the one which inhabited the mind of Teilhard de Chardin, who regurgitated it into the Jesuits, and who is the lodestar of Jorge Bergoglio, whom nobody can understand. But by his fruits we know Francis, he who has attacked the traditional Latin Mass with more destructive effect than any man alive (*Traditionis custodes*). This is satan's scheme.

The kabbalist texts refer repeatedly to the OT, but absent is the rationality and beauty of God. The Word of God, from Genesis to the Apocalypse, from Adam's *"deep sleep"* to the final awakening, tells that the Crucifixion is the crux of creation, the centre of history, the threshing floor where every soul is judged — wheat or chaff.

The chief crucifier, the devil, wants to overturn the Word, wants his own words to take shape. He cannot create matter so he hates it, especially the flesh, for he is filled with envy, as he can never become, like the true Word of God, incarnate. He hates Mary's motherhood as much as her virginity, hates all that God ordained for procreation, where man shares in God's work, opening the gates to new life.

A few pages after the esoteric passage quoted above, the kabbalistic insanity continues, promising the revealing of mysteries by stages, where is stated, "There are six million open gates, and Anael is the chief guardian of them." Anael is said to be an 'archangel', that is a demon, of sexuality. Those "gates" are not gates of life (Ps 23:7-10), but represent ways into a dark temple. After this comes a closing climax, "Then with awe, trembling, fear, and terror, songs and praises ascend to the Lord of all".[252] That "lord" is not God.

Kabbalah is an unfathomably perverse abyss. What interest do its numerologists have in the number six million, a six with six zeros?[253] It is ten times the number of warrior Hebrews who escaped from the power of Egypt (Num 1:46). Only two of them entered into the Promised Land, this time with a different six hundred thousand men *"that are able to go forth to war"* (Num 26:2,51,65).

What merit is there now in holocausts, in whole burnt offerings, in sacrifices? Catholics and kabbalists have diametrically opposed understandings of the Scriptures: *"Introibo in domum tuam in holocaustis; reddam tibi vota mea"* — *"I will go into thy house with burnt offerings: I will pay thee my vows"* (Ps 65:13). Pay your vows to God, and this holocaust means Holy Mass. Pay your vows to satan, and it is something unthinkable.

Woefully, mankind is capable of anything. This question I scarcely dare to ask: have Jews made victims of Jews? I do not mean at the level of the *Kapo*, the low-level functionaries of prison self-administration. I do not mean in the manner of Rudolf Kastner, taking advantage for his Zionist cause by betraying vast numbers of Jews with deadly lies. Rather, at an elite level, very distant, and much more brutal. Was the Holocaust the worst betrayal since the *"night"* that the devil

---

[252] *The Wisdom of the Zohar, An Anthology of Texts*, Vol 2 (translated from the Hebrew by David Goldstein, 2008), p.620 (purportedly from *Zohar Hadash Yitro*, 38d, but I have been unable to verify this from the original text).

[253] A rabbi of Ohr Somayach reports "*Mosad Hayesod* [p.204-205] cites [Elijah ben Solomon Zalma (d.1797)] the Vilna Gaon's commentary on the Zohar that 'the number 666 contains hidden within it exalted and lofty messianic potential'."

entered in, and Iscariot went out, and returned to Jesus with a kiss (Jn 13:30)? The voice of the Zohar is satanic, the same as ruled Caiaphas. There is no one it demurs to kill.

Such evil backfires, defeated by its victims, even as the programme rolls on. A five-hour documentary directed by Vera Sharav, entitled *Never Again Is Now Global* (2023), challenged and exposed the Covid-19 lockdowns and vaccination programme. The premise of the series was that as the Holocaust was engineered by calculated use of fear and propaganda, and involved eugenics and the total perversion of medicine, so also did the worldwide Covid regime. A number of the interviewees were Holocaust survivors. Also featured prominently was the courageous but kabbalist Dr Vladimir Zelenko, now sadly passed away.

The series did not shy from criticising powerful Jews advancing the Covid regime. Parallels were drawn between profiteering from the Holocaust by big business (including IBM, pharma and oil), and profiteering from the Covid tyranny. The documentary lamented that of all the peoples in the world, it was Israelis who suffered some of the most relentless pressure to be injected with a democidal gene-therapy. And it was the Israeli government which did this.

Vera Sharav, who as a child escaped the Holocaust, mentioned in the documentary that her father taught her, as an essential survival strategy, to question everything, and accept nothing at face value. Question everything. The filmmakers were willing to question whether, through Covid, Jews were profiteering financially and politically from inflicting grievous harm on Israel's population. But I do not know if the viewer was meant to question whether the same had happened in the Holocaust, which became one of the key arguments for the 1948 establishment of the State of Israel.

But who can scrutinise these matters? Today, the International Holocaust Remembrance Alliance is working worldwide to criminalise "antisemitism", including,

> Making mendacious, dehumanizing, demonizing, or stereotypical allegations about Jews as such or the power of Jews as collective — such as, especially but not exclusively, the myth about a world Jewish conspiracy or of Jews controlling the media, economy, government or other societal institutions. Accusing the Jews as a people, or Israel as a state, of inventing or exaggerating the Holocaust. Accusing Jewish citizens of being more loyal to Israel, or to the alleged priorities of Jews worldwide, than to the interests of their own nations.[254]

The power to persecute whoever dares raise questions does not guard us from totalitarianism but requires *building* totalitarianism. Why? Because this level of control is totalitarian. In order to silence whichever handful might resist the narrative, one needs to govern all with fear. This tool of control is then used to silence opponents on everything. Minority rule becomes absolute rule, all knowing their supine place, realising that they are hapless subjects of invisible powers and that they must not step out of line. Pervasive cancel culture, big tech censorship, invented threats about white supremacists have all developed from the total taboo called Holocaust denial.

---

[254] www.holocaustremembrance.com

The answer is what it has always been: freedom of enquiry, of expression, of association, of debate. The truth will come out because the world is simply not antisemitic. We want the truth. Where Jews have suffered, we will commiserate. The notion that people who deny the Holocaust must be prosecuted is a conclusion drawn from the premise that Gentiles fundamentally hate Jews and therefore need to be kept down. It is a false premise and a deeply corrosive conclusion. In a free discussion, truth wins.

The Futility of Evil

As satan inspired the Holocaust, he has also inspired the exaggerations around it. The first because he hates Jews, the second because he hates Catholics. He is terrified by the approaching reconciliation in Christ of these two groups, that is, by the conversion of the Jews.

But satan is ready to bring false Catholics and Jews together if he can have them conspire against Christ. This collaboration explains the shameless entrapment in 2008 of Bishop Richard Williamson, used for the purpose of holding traditional Catholicism in abeyance. The perpetrators, from inside and outside the Church, instrumentalised the Holocaust to pursue an antichrist agenda.

The lie that runs through all history is countered by the Truth that precedes and outlives it: the traditional Mass.[255] In 2007, Pope Benedict XVI greatly served Catholicism by officially recognising that the traditional Latin Mass had never been abrogated and that priests did not require

---

[255] Fr James Mawdsley, *Crucifixion to Creation: Roots of the Traditional Mass Traced Back to Paradise* (2023).

permission from a bishop to offer it. In parallel, talks were progressing between the Vatican and the SSPX, a traditional priestly society, which promised to give an enormous boost to faithful Catholics. Happily, on 21st January 2009, the Vatican revoked excommunications from four bishops of the SSPX (penalties, one could argue, which were unjustly or invalidly imposed in the first place). But within the Vatican, ideological enemies of tradition, who knew this move was coming, had a plan to sabotage this profound healing in the Catholic Church.

Many months previously, Bishop Williamson, then of the SSPX, was interviewed by Sveriges Television (of Sweden). After the interview, but with the cameras secretly running, the journalist threw in what seemed like a spontaneous question, to which the Bishop answered that the "historical evidence is strongly against six million Jews having been deliberately gassed". The bishop went on to question how could it have been even logistically possible to gas millions of people. He expressed disbelief that gas chambers existed, raising pertinent factors, such as the absence of large airtight chambers, the operational complications introduced by the toxicity of the corpses, and that chimneys suitably tall for lethal chemicals did not show on reconnaissance photographs.

In a normal world, these matters would be discussed by historians, by experts and academics, and careful journalism would draw more voices into the conversation. In a free media, outrageous ideas struggle to maintain traction, while difficult questions cannot be sidelined. This is part of the process for how historical truth can be established. But this is not at all what happened. The truth about the Holocaust was not the purpose of the question. Rather, a mine with a delayed detonation was being deliberately assembled to explode in Benedict XVI's face.

The TV station sat on the interview footage for months. It was only broadcast after the Vatican announced the lifting of the excommunications of the four bishops. Immediately after, in fact. Predictably, a media frenzy followed. With Benedict publicly savaged and scarcely supported, and with absurdly ignorant calls for Bishop Williamson to be excommunicated anew, the much hoped for open reconciliation of the papacy with tradition was indefinitely postponed.

The public discussion which ensued was nothing to do with the Holocaust or history. Rather, sensitivities on this subject were exploited for another purpose. The Holocaust was used as a weapon. Countless cardinals, bishops, journalists, NGOs, activists, ideologues and commentators piled in against Tradition, against Benedict, all the while exhibiting their credentials as 'more mainstream than thou'. Bishop Williamson, who thanks to his deep faith offers up his current suffering, was never the primary target. Not even Benedict. It was the reconciliation with the SSPX that the enemies sought to hinder. God, for His own higher purpose, permitted them success. For now.

Men inside and outside the Church planned this ambush, long in advance, in order to serve an anti-Catholic goal. It was calculated evil. Our worst enemies on earth are members of the Roman Curia, which seems unthinkable, except for the warnings from Christ Himself (Mt 7:15; 13:24-30).

satan wants to stop the conversion of the Jews. Therefore he uses anyone he can to attack both the Church (*terminus ad quem*) and the Jews (*terminus a quo*), desperate that these two distrust each other. Certainly, the devil will lose to Jesus, Who makes *"the two in Himself into one new man, making peace... killing the enmities in Himself"* (read Eph 2:11-22).

All nations become one in Christ. Jews and Gentiles are one in Christ. Jews do not lose their Jewish identity in becoming Catholic. The reason the theme of the conversion of the Jews is so powerful in the writings of St Paul is undoubtedly because of the abounding graces of his own conversion. By birth a Benjaminite, he never ceased being a Jew (even though the root of that word is from 'Judah').

> *Are they Hebrews? So am I. Are they Israelites? So am I. Are they descendants of Abraham? So am I. Are they servants of Christ? I am a better one.* (2 Cor 11:22-23 RSVCE)

Taking hope from Saul-Paul's example for other Jews, relying on the power of the Holy Ghost, St Augustine writes:

> The Lord Jesus, in that discourse which He addressed to His disciples after the Last Supper... exhorted them to bear patiently the persecution of wicked men, of whom He speaks as *'the world'... 'If they have persecuted Me, they will also persecute you'* (Jn 15:20). Here He clearly points to the Jews, the persecutors both of Himself and of His disciples... *'They hated Me without a cause'...* Yea, indeed, some there were who had seen and still hated, whom the testimony of the Comforter converted to the faith which works by love.[256]

The last line means St Paul. God can convert anyone.

---

[256] St Augustine, *Tract 92 on St John's Gospel* (Jn 15:20). Feast of the Conversion of St Paul (25th Jan), Matins, *Lectiones* VII-IX.

Must Jews, meanwhile, languish without land, without a home? Every other nation has a patch of land on earth, which serves its people to find their eternal inheritance in Heaven. Only Israel is different. They were a people without land; yet a people promised land before they were born, as they waited in the loins of Abraham. Finally, they took their land by conquest, fighting against evil they cleared Canaan to inherit it, as God had promised. But the blessings did not stop there.

With Christ's Apostles, the Israelites had the chance to inherit the whole world; to give up fields and stones in order to win the spiritual sphere for souls of all nations. Some Jews took this path; others delayed and then took it; others refuse it until today. They will not find peace under any earthly fig tree or keep any olive grove secure, except they convert and find life everlasting in the Church. It is their calling. God *"appointed a ruler for every nation, but Israel is the Lord's own portion"* (Sir 17:17 RSVCE). Israel is not meant to remain a geographical confinement, for the whole *"earth is the Lord's and the fulness thereof: the world, and all they that dwell therein"* (Ps 23:1). Bishop Williamson's view is that Jews are made by God for leadership in the Church.

Isaiah suggests that the blindness of heart will continue without conversion until *"the cities be wasted without inhabitant, and the houses without man, and the land shall be left desolate"* (Is 6:9-13). This could mean a spiritual devastation of the Church, or else of the social order, or both. It may look like the end, but it will not quite be the end. As such a spiritual state heralded the first Advent of Jesus, the prophetic passage (ending Isaiah 6) leaves room to hope for a final conversion of the Jews prior to Jesus' second Advent.

Until then, attempts to silence Bishop Williamson or to marginalise Catholic Tradition undermine the best protector that the Jews have, for if Jews reduce the Church's role in society, they will be exposed once again to become victims of pagan fury, as under the Nazis. It is better for the Jews to let Catholics speak, not to hinder the Church's flourishing.

The Holocaust was an antichrist work born of antichrist ideologies. To blame God (as did Elie Wiesel); to denounce Pius XII for inaction (as did Yad Vashem); to hold "the Entire Christian world" responsible for it (as did Rabbi Wise); to suggest that the conversion of Jews to Christianity is itself a Holocaust, a way of spiritually "blotting them out of existence" (as did Fr Gregory Baum); are all examples of profound spiritual blindness. Jews searching for their enemy might ask who is behind Kabbalah — as the spirit it is serving is not Holy, then what will the fruits of it be (Gal 5:18-25)?

Until 1940-41, the Nazi's stated policy was to deport Jews from Germany. This was not bare antisemitism but self-defence, of a type which many nations have taken, and which calls Jews to an examination of conscience. After this, the Nazis took advantage of war to effect slave labour and mass murder. These are pure wickedness for which the perpetrators must answer. Jewish victims cannot be to blame for this evil.

Christians (whom I have met) do not hate Jews, but many of us hate the emerging vision of a world without Jesus. The next section asks *What Can Catholics Do?* There is no attempt here to offer political answers. These are bound to fail unless a spiritual foundation is first laid in men's hearts. For this, God has given us all the means we need — in Scripture and Tradition.

PART III: WHAT
CAN CATHOLICS DO?

Jesus to Jerusalem — *If thou also hadst known, and that in this thy day, the things that are to thy peace; but now they are hidden from thy eyes.*

Luke 19:42

Truth is the cure for chaos. Truth matters because it serves the growth of the Church, the defence of her members and, in God's time, the conversion of the Jews, *"so all Israel should be saved"* (Rom 11:26).

Truth matters because failure to manage the Jewish Question apart from the salvific work of Christ (combining judicious segregation with charity), results in the ruin of all concerned. It matters, lest cowardice and infidelity blind us to

St John's apocalyptic warnings. His vision foretells the attempt to enslave us through a collaboration of the dragon (Apoc 13:2), which is satan; with the first beast (Apoc 13:1), representing a secular, globalised power; and the second beast (Apoc 13:11), a religious deception from the 'Holy Land', or Israel, a one-world religion, likely claiming to be Abrahamic, or Noahide.

The Jewish Question matters because our political and spiritual freedom are tied up in it. To discern who actually has power, observe whom men fear to criticise. Nowadays, few venture to raise the subject of the Jews, or their relation to the nations in which they live, or their refusal to admit the Crucifixion of Jesus was a cruelty devoid of justice, besides being totally against the Law of Moses. Who dares to talk about these things in the Church? Who can begin to talk about these themes in the public square or at a social setting, unless they are practiced and willing to break free?

We are programmed on what we can say about Jews: preferably nothing. From here a more invasive control develops, for if we give way on one issue, voluntarily surrendering the search for truth on one point, then we forfeit freedom on all points. Everything becomes someone else's decision, his choice to permit or veto our voices.

While spiritual enmity to Christ undermines civilisation, each must be aware of his own sins. It will avail no one on Judgement Day to point the finger at heretics (Gnostics, Arians, Protestants); or curators of debt (usurers, bankers); or provokers of impurity (pornographers; transgender theorists); or warmongers capitalising on endless carnage for 'patriotism', 'humanitarianism', 'security' (why do we keep falling for these lies?). They will all answer to God. So will we. There is a whole world of struggle within us, enough for a lifetime. But by God's grace, gain control of your soul, and you will share in the victory over totalitarianism. The defeat of sin, whether personal or global, is found in Christ alone.

We live in an upside-down world, accepting the opposite of reality on a number of themes. Scripture shows how Jews tried to wipe out Christians. Yet somehow there is a general acceptance of the opposite, as if the Church has persecuted Jews. This inversion of truth is achieved through a stream of lies so relentless, that it seems only those who believe their own inventions are capable of producing it.

How can worldviews be so contradictory? Some say God chose the holiest of people for His own, and there are Jewish saints to support this. Others opine God chose the most hard-hearted people, thus proving His efficacy, and there are episodes enough to support this. But regarding the election of the Chosen People, the Scriptures say that it is because of Abraham's faith that God keeps his descendants as the apple of His eye. Yet it avails nothing to be after Abraham in the flesh if one is not also of his Christ-loving spirit (Mt 3:9-10). This marks the division of two camps.

For the desires of the flesh are against the Spirit, and the desires of the Spirit are against the flesh; for these are opposed to each other. (Gal 5:17)

There are Orthodox Jews who understand that in the fight between good and evil, the fate of every soul is at stake. These decry the atheistic materialism which is plunging the world toward a totalitarian doom. The Temple Institute warns:

The future scenarios described by Zechariah and Ezekiel seem very real today. A vortex of hubris and wanton abandon is sucking entire societies into a black hole of meaninglessness.[257]

These Jews know that behind the world's troubles is a failure to attribute everything good to God and to thank Him for it. But they see every attack on Israel as an assault on goodness, an assailment on the life and hope of mankind. I agree completely, with one obvious change: where the Temple Institute writes 'Israel' (in the continuing message below), we should understand not a natural entity, but supernatural — the Church:

> The all-out war currently being waged against Israel by the nations of the east, west, north and south, is nothing less than a war against the G-d of Israel. *'Jews, Zionists, the people of Israel, the nation of Israel,'* are all a pretext. The war being waged is a war against the inconvenient presence of HaShem in the world. Eliminate G-d and mankind can run amok, uninhibited and unbridled. What some might call freedom and pursuit of happiness is the exact opposite.

These Orthodox Jews have a profound analysis of the totalitarian threat facing the world. Now that the Church hierarchy is abandoning the Truth, could it be time for Jews to complete what their forbears began — the earthly task of the Church in overcoming evil? Three massive trends suggest the conversion of the Jews might be in bud:

---

[257] The Temple Institute, Subscriber email (14th Oct 2022).

• The rise of the Antichrist is presaged in the attempted take-over of nations by globalists. Plans for global digital IDs and currency show their ambition. Lockdowns and worldwide warmongering show their ruthlessness.

• Apostasy is apparent at the highest levels of the Church. The senseless Synod on Synodality seeks to relativise the sacrificial priesthood with empty alternatives. Blessings of sodomy are simulated while sanctuaries are polluted with pride flags and blasphemous sermons. *Traditionis custodes* is lawless evil, an hysterical aversion to God.

• There is an exponential increase in the number of Messianic Jews, growing by tens of thousands in Israel. Though they have major shortcomings theologically, they fervently present Jesus as the promised Christ to other Jews.

If the conversion of the Jews is close, what will provoke it? Spiritually, the Holy Ghost; materially, the Apostolic liturgy. Therefore, we have much more than a duty to uphold Catholic Tradition. In this Jews may recognise their full heritage: the life of the Temple and Tabernacle; their Holy of Holies; their altar and sacrifice; their priesthood and high priesthood; the eternal delight of Abel, Abraham and Melchisedech; the rectification of Eden — and in the midst, the Real Presence of God. By assisting at the traditional liturgy, Gentiles serve their own salvation as well as the salvation of Jews.

Meanwhile, we Gentiles do well to remember we were grafted in, a wild branch accepted into God's olive tree, while the Jews are the natural branches. If they do not persist in unbelief, they will take to the tree very well (Rom 11:23).

Jesus repeatedly diagnosed the blindness of Jews hostile to Him (Mt 23:16-26; Lk 6:39; Jn 12:40). His own disciples began blind too. After Jesus explained His Eucharistic doctrine, He asked His disciples: *"Do you not yet know nor understand? Have you still your heart blinded?"* (Mk 8:17). These men became the founding generation of the Church. Can the Lord not also lift the veil from the hearts of more Jews so that they become the crowning generation? Like God, the Hebrew idiom makes a big deal of the "first and last", the "things before and things after". Can we expect the last generation of Christians to be awesome like the Apostles?

The Jews have their part. For our part, in the following three chapters, we will look at the Good Friday Prayer for the Conversion of the Jews, the traditional liturgy more broadly, and the measureless reward for loving OT saints. The recommendations accompanying these three themes concern our spiritual life because this is where battles are lost or won.

GOOD FRIDAY PRAYER FOR THE JEWS

But even until this day, when Moses is read, the veil is upon their heart. But when they shall be converted to the Lord, the veil shall be taken away.

2 Corinthians 3:15-16

Catholics have a one hundred per cent certain way of bringing about the conversion of the Jews: namely, to pray for it on Good Friday in the traditional manner. We cannot control when this conversion will happen, but it is in our hands that it will happen.

There is no prayer so perfectly formulated for the purpose as the traditional one. It minces no words; it forms deep understanding; it demands our hearts be filled with charity. Most importantly, praying it integrally requires a restoration of the entire traditional liturgy, for the whole liturgy has one spirit. The good consequences of that will be immense.

Precisely because this prayer is so vital, it has long been targeted for change. Ever since the Church's resistance to the spirit of this world began crumbling in the 1950s, this prayer has been changed and diluted by the Vatican more times than any other public prayer, eviscerating it to appease enemies of mankind, powers who do not want the Jews to convert. It was in order to utterly bury the old prayer, and more importantly to exclude its spirit, that the secularisation of the entire liturgy got underway and continues today.

For Catholics seeking to withstand this disintegration, to pray the prayer properly requires profound fidelity and understanding, considerable courage, plus a reverence for the venerable liturgy, combined with a loving awe at former generations of saints. The constellation of these virtues in a soul is highly pleasing to God, disposing Him to hear and answer the prayer. This is why it is guaranteed to work. In translation the pre-1955 prayer reads:[258]

> Let us pray also for the perfidious Jews: that our God and Lord would remove the veil from their hearts; that they also may acknowledge our Lord Jesus Christ.

> Almighty and everlasting God, who drives not away from Thy mercy even the perfidious Jews: hear our prayers, which we offer for the blindness of that people: that, acknowledging the light of Thy truth, which is Christ, they may be delivered from their darkness. Through the same Jesus Christ, Thy Son, Our Lord, Who lives and reigns with Thee in the unity of the Holy Ghost, God: for ever and ever.

> R. Amen.

---

[258] *Oremus et pro perfidis Judæis: ut Deus et Dominus noster auferat velamen de cordibus eorum; ut et ipsi agnoscant Jesum Christum, Dominum nostrum.*

Omnipotens sempiterne Deus, qui etiam judaicam perfidiam a tua misericordia non repellis: exaudi preces nostras, quas pro illius populi obcæcatione deferimus; ut, agnita veritatis tuæ luce, quæ Christus est, a suis tenebris eruantur. Per eundem Dominum nostrum Jesum Christum Filium tuum, qui tecum vivit et regnat in unitate Spiritus Sancti, Deus: per omnia sæcula sæculorum. R. Amen.

Our understanding and devotion are further deepened by appreciation of the setting of the prayer within the Sacred Triduum, the most powerful liturgy of the Church year.

Liturgical Setting of the Good Friday Prayer

God wants us to love the ancient liturgy, receiving it as the creation of the Holy Ghost to continue the work of Calvary for the salvation of the world. God wants us to love our enemies and pray for them even though we will be insulted, marginalised and perhaps penalised for it. God wants us to withstand arrogant hierarchs who think they are greater than Tradition (bullies attempting to impose a man-centred liturgy) and that we utterly reject the demonic forces behind them.

While the personal dispositions of hearts bear on the efficacy of prayers, there is no prayer so powerful in itself as the public prayer of the Church, that is, her liturgy. God cannot ignore these prayers because He formulated them Himself (with man). Given that God hears *"two or three gathered"* in His Name, then the public prayer of the Church cannot fail (Mt 18:19-20). Our Lord told us at the Last Supper: *"Whatsoever you shall ask the Father in My Name, that will I do"* (Jn 14:14; 15:16).

Jesus gave this assurance the evening before He died, that is, on the same liturgical day as His death. There is no day more important to the redemption of man than Good Friday, which stands at the heart of the Sacred Triduum. Our Lord promises: *"Ask, and you shall receive; that your joy may be full"* (Jn 16:23-24). One thing remaining on earth to fill our joy is the conversion of the Jews. We ask for it on Good Friday using a prayer that is 1,700 years old, extant in the earliest sources. The themes in it go back to the Apostles. Therefore, to lovingly maintain this prayer is to honour the saints of all generations.

Thus Good Friday stands through the Church's long lifetime at the apex of her annual calendar. What happens that day? The chief services are the Divine Office, the Mass of the Presanctified and, typically, the Stations of the Cross. All three are continuously concerned with the Crucifixion.

Leaving the Office (*Tenebrae*) and Stations for the reader's own reflection, the Mass of the Presanctified consists in four elements, each one manifestly about the Cross. First, is the long reading of the Passion from St John's Gospel; second, the Great Intercessions, modelled as Jesus' prayers from the Cross for our salvation; third, the veneration of the Cross, bowing to and kissing the instrument of our redemption; and fourth, the Mass of the Presanctified itself, a unique arrangement fitted to the day of the actual Crucifixion (rather than its usual memorial, Holy Mass).

The Prayer for the Jews comes in the second element, the Great Intercessions. Examining these nine Intercessions, we find they are faultlessly ordered.

The first Intercession is for the Church. The second is for the pope. The third for all orders and grades of the faithful. With these three prayers Jesus takes care of His Bride.

The fourth intercession is for governors of state. By now the Lord has cared for Church and State, in that order.

The fifth is for catechumens and the sixth for the necessities of the world (against disease, famine, dangers). God wants our good in everything, including that we turn to Him to ask for it.

The final three cover three species of infidelity by praying for the return of schismatics and heretics, for the conversion of the Jews and for the conversion of pagans. This threefold division acknowledges those who have fallen away from the promises of baptism (Christians), those who once had the Old Covenant but now refuse the New (Jews) and those who have rejected all revelation or not yet heard the Gospel (heathen).

On Good Friday, literally every human alive is prayed for, offering them graces which they may freely accept.[259]

Each of these Great Intercessions, between its bidding and its Collect, involves a genuflection by everybody present, except the prayer for the Jews.[260] Omitting a genuflection at this point is an ancient practice,

> explained in the *Ordo Lateranensis* (c.1120) and the *Ordo Romanus* XII (c.1190), by reference to the fact that the Jews bent their knees in mockery of Christ during the Passion.[261]

The Church did not wish her children to genuflect where genuflections had been associated with the ridicule of the Lord. The Jews mocked Jesus day and night (Mt 27:42,44; Mk 14:65; 15:32; Lk 22:63; 23:39; Ps 21:7-8; Is 53:3),

---

[259] Don Pietro Leone, *The Council and the Eclipse of God* (Feb 2023), XI, 4, "Ministers of the Church [exercise the *munera*] for the benefit, that is to say for the sanctification and salvation, of all men: not only of the members of the Church, but also of the whole World. God transmits through the Church not only the entire Faith and the Sacraments, but also… 'Actual Graces', being those individual graces which enlighten the mind and strengthen the will, such as the inspiration to conversion and the strength to follow it, graces which are bestowed not only upon the members of the Church, but also upon the whole World."

[260] If a deacon and sub-deacon are ministering, then the celebrant omits all these genuflections during the Great Intercessions.

[261] International Una Voce Federation, *Position Paper 28*, Appendix C (Feb 2016).

including His Kingship, whereby the Herodians mocked His nobility too (Lk 23:11). The Roman soldiers were not accustomed to bowing down to any prisoner, but having seen the *Rex Judæorum* parodied by the Jews, contemptuously the soldiers knelt down to Him, doubtless imitating His accusers (Mt 27:29; Mk 15:19; Jn 19:2-3). Enthused, the Romans dressed Jesus in purple, crowned Him with thorns and nailed *"The King of the Jews"* on top of the Cross (Jn 19:2,19).

With all this context, to protest that the Gospels do not explicitly mention "genuflections" by Jews, as if that invalidates the traditional rubric of not kneeling during this Good Friday prayer, is to hurl another insult at Jesus.[262] The point that should strike us is that by handing their King over for execution, the Jews committed treason. Hence in the traditional prayer, they are twice described as being perfidious (*"perfidis"*, *"perfidiam"*). The word can mean faithless, unfaithful, incredulous. In the extreme case, it means treacherous, treasonous — which is what happened on Good Friday. Realising the reality of this informs the prayer with meaning more than do arguments over semantics. And that is why we do not genuflect, so as not to imitate mockery of Our Lord. Never again.

Perfidy is distinguished in the Great Intercessions from the *fidelity* of the Church, the *infidelity* of schismatics and heretics, and the being *without faith* of the heathen who have not heard the Gospel (elsewhere called *infidels*). As *per*-jury

---

[262] International Una Voce Federation, *Position Paper 28*, Appendix C (Feb 2016), concludes, "There is a parallel in the Mass of Holy Thursday, when from the earliest times the Pax (Kiss of Peace) is omitted. Medieval liturgical commentators explain that it would not be fitting to use the kiss, since on this day we remember Judas Iscariot's betrayal of Our Lord with a kiss."

is to culpably go against one's oath in court, so *per*-fidy is to go against good faith.[263] The Jews are *unfaithful* because they have not kept the obligations of the Old Covenant, which obligations include embracing the New, receiving the Messiah, recognising Him as the Seed promised to Abraham, the Prophet announced by Moses, the Son of David sent to inherit an eternal throne. Perfidy, said on Good Friday, refers to the Jews rejecting Christ and having Him crucified.

> *[Pilate] saith to the Jews: Behold your king. But they cried out: Away with Him: Away with Him: Crucify Him. Pilate saith to them: shall I crucify your king? The chief priests answered: We have no king but Caesar.* (Jn 19:14-15)

This is treason. The prayer calls us to face that reality. And the prayer requires us to pray for those who deny it happened, or deny it was unjust, or who blithely do not care. Any attempt to maintain the Old Covenant today, while actively rejecting the New, participates in the same perfidy.

Instead of suitably praying for these souls, Catholics have been sliding for decades into the same treachery, that of preferring Caesar to Christ. The descent has been publicly led by clerics drawing their flocks into the new treason.[264]

---

[263] In the first intercession, members of the Church are described as *"stabili fide"*, with "steadfast faith". In the third prayer, these serve *"fideliter"*, "faithfully". The fifth prayer asks that Catechumens grow in *"fidem"*, "faith". The seventh prayer is for heretics who by the devil have been led astray from the Faith. The eighth is for the Jews, *per-fidis*, who have gone against the faith. The last prayer is for the pagans, or infidels, which word comes from *in-fidelis*, meaning without faith.

[264] Once in Jerusalem, agents manipulated the crowd to shout *"Crucify Him!"* Now the same satanic forces have Catholics at the *novus ordo* crying the same words during Holy Week: *"Crucify Him!"*. It is symbolic. *"Father, forgive them, for they know not what they do"* (Lk 23:34).

Escalating Assault on the Prayer

The first attempt to change the Good Friday Prayer which achieved an official response from the Vatican, was made by the *Opus Sacerdotale Amici Israel* (Clerical Friends of Israel). This association of Catholic clerics was established in 1926 by two Dutch priests, Fr Anton van Asseldonk and Fr Laetus Himmelreich, in close collaboration with a convert from Judaism, Francesca van Leer. Within a year, the association counted among its members almost twenty cardinals, two hundred bishops and two thousand priests.

Whatever their goodwill, the founders promoted the heresy of chiliasm, imagining a thousand-year reign of peace on earth with a leading role for the Jews. Francesca's background traversed being an anarchist, a communist, a Zionist, then a 'nun', but evidently not Catholic, as she married and was mother of a child. Fr Himmelreich baptised her two days after he met her, although she had virtually no Catholic catechism.[265] She was searching for meaning but was in no condition to feed theological ideas up the Catholic hierarchy.

Fr Himmelreich was captivated by her. He wrote a book, *The Kingdom of Israel (Das Reich Israels)*, which delighted Francesca. She believed that if it had received an *Imprimatur*, it would have brought a 'revolution' to the Catholic Church, which is the constant aim of Judaism. The three hundred (arch)bishops and three thousand priests who finally joined the *Amici*, even if with good intentions, were misguided. When the blind follow the blind, all fall into a pit.

---

[265] Marcel Poorthuis und Theo Salemink, *Laetus Himmelreich OFM (1886–1957), Zwischen München, Jerusalem und Dachau* (May 2017), p.4.

Thanks be to God, the Vatican resisted the lobbying of the *Amici Israel* to change the Good Friday prayer. Rafael Cardinal Merry del Val, Secretary of the Holy Office, wrote in 1928 to Pope Pius XI:

> This report put forward by the so-called *Amici Israel* strikes me as completely unacceptable, indeed even rash. We are dealing with ancient prayers and rites of the liturgy of the Church, a liturgy inspired and consecrated for centuries that includes condemnation of the rebellion and betrayal perpetrated by the chosen people who were at once unfaithful and deicide... I would hope that these *Amici Israel* would not fall into a trap laid by the Jews themselves, who insinuate themselves throughout modern society and seek with whatever means to minimise the memory of their history and take advantage of the good will of Christians.[266]

Pius XI was thereby convinced, that despite enormous pressure, it was unacceptable to change ancient prayers and rites for the sake of pleasing the world. The most venerable traditions may only be adjusted if it is certainly for the glory of God and the salvation of souls. Cardinal Merry del Val, by his solid mindset and forthright appraisal, saved the Church in his day, as he warned Pius XI not to overstep his power. The *Amici Israel* were disbanded by a papal decree in 1928.

Predictably, the lobby did not give up. Jews bridled at being called "perfidious" in Catholic prayers. A former Chief Rabbi of Rome, Eugenio Zolli, who converted to the Catholic

---

[266] Rafael Cardinal Merry del Val, note to Pope Pius XI (7th March 1928).

faith, petitioned his friend Pius XII to remove the accusatory adjective. Still reluctant to do this, the Pope authorised an allocution in 1948 explaining that, in this context, perfidious does not mean treacherous but incredulous.

The pressure continued. In 1951 and 1955, Pius XII decreed radical changes to the Easter Triduum.[267] These included instructions for all to genuflect during the prayer for the Jews, as with the other Great Intercessions. He was not motivated by the good of the Church but under duress to please the Jews, who did not want our liturgy to single out their spiritual condition. Therefore it is an invalid instruction, as the pope has no authority to oppose the mission of the Church and he cannot require anyone to quail from it.

The open door in the current situation is, that although the faithful cannot force priests to restore the pre-1955 rites, still everyone who is motivated by charity can refuse to genuflect at this point in the Good Friday ceremonies. Thereby they uphold tradition. God sees and hears them. It is so simple.

If anyone were to accuse the faithful of disobedience or disunity for not genuflecting or for using old missals, this is false. It is clerics, the hierarchy, who are being unfaithful, who are breaking unity with Tradition, departing from the wisdom of previous generations. It is the innovators who need to get back on course, not those who maintain Tradition.[268]

---

[267] Pope Pius XII, for all his qualities, revealed his sometimes failing judgement in that he approved the Bea Psalter in 1945 (Cardinal Bea's modernist translation of the Psalms, totally out of harmony with the spirit of the Divine Office).

[268] One might argue that by accommodating Jewish sensitiveness through liturgical alterations, God will now bring about the conversion of the Jews. But this explanation is contradicted by the slew of disastrous changes which have accompanied and followed the unwonted 1955 directives, which cannot be of God.

With Pius XII being succeeded by a more amenable pope, the lobbying by Jews intensified.[269] In 1959, John XXIII removed both mentions of perfidious from the prayer. This deletion had the unintended consequence that, without this adjectival qualification, the prayer then read, "Let us all pray for the Jews". This indiscriminate version ungraciously implies that those Jews who have already converted are no longer counted as Jews.

In 1961, the AJC sent a memorandum to the Vatican on *Anti-Jewish Elements in Catholic Liturgy*, acknowledging "with appreciation" the 1955 addition of a genuflection. They wrote that its omission until then "was greatly offensive to Jews who were aware of it and knew its intention was to humiliate them".[270] If the intention of the Church had ever been to humiliate Jews, then it would have been proper to change it. But for Catholics who believe that the Church is animated by divine Love, and who understand that the liturgy is all to give glory to God, then the reason offered for making the changes is untenable. The Church's failure of fidelity here has seen the whole liturgical tapestry suffer an unending unpicking, resulting in the abysmal chaos of today.

---

[269] In 1949, Pope Pius XII granted an audience to Professor Jules Isaac, a French scholar of Catholic-Jewish relations. Isaac presented the pope with a list of eighteen points to reshape Catholic thinking about Jews. Some of the points were misdirection, including that "the trial of Jesus was a Roman trial, not a Jewish trial", which overlooks the prior nighttime trial. Other points were pernicious error, such as "Judaism is not a degenerate faith. Christianity was born of it." In truth, Christianity was born of the Old Covenant, not Judaism. Isaac assessed that he made much more impact with his June 1960 visit to John XXIII. See Judith Rice of the American Zionist Historical Society, *Jules Isaac & Pope Benedict XVI*.

[270] AJC, *Anti-Jewish Elements in Catholic Liturgy* (1961), I. This followed the memorandum, *The Image of the Jews in Catholic Teaching* (1961).

In the same 1961 memorandum, the AJC gratefully acknowledged,

> the specification by the Sacred Congregation of Rites, in 1948, that the expressions *perfidis Judaeis* and *Judaica perfidia* may be translated as signifying simply a lack of faith in the Christian revelation; and finally, the elimination of the words *perfidia* and *perfidis* by Pope John in 1959, and the subsequent authorization of this change by the Sacred Congregation of Rites.

These changes would never have been enough. The memo continued, "Nevertheless, anti-Jewish passages remain within Catholic liturgy. These are found in…" It then listed

> liturgical books of the Church, such as *Missale*, *Graduale*, *Vesperale*, *Antiphonale*, *etc.* which serve the public worship in parish churches and cathedrals.

These traditional books and services barely exist now. Also listed for change are "homilies and officially approved commentaries upon the public liturgy", for within

> the public worship of the Church, there are a number of passages and statements expressing hostility to the Jewish people. For the most part, these are found in the New Testament lectionaries.

Singled out as problematic is Jesus' prophecy: *"Tradent enim vos in conciliis, et in synagogis suis flagellabunt vos"* (Mt 10:17). This divine warning is still sung in the traditional Office (Magnificat Antiphon, First Vespers, Common of Apostles), but is absent from the new Liturgy of the Hours.

The conclusion of the memorandum is a clear preparation for Vatican II's *Nostra ætate*.

In the interest of better relations between the adherents of the historical monotheistic religions, we request the Church to seek ways of mitigating the impact of the liturgy of the triduum. Were the Church to select passages which would accurately convey its true attitude toward the Jewish people, or to produce or stimulate authoritative interpretation or commentary which would, for once and for all, lift the charge or implication of deicide from the Jewish people, it would make a great contribution to increased understanding between Catholics and Jews.[271]

Now the "better relations between the adherents of the historical monotheistic religions" has progressed far beyond 1965's *Nostra ætate*. If the Church is willing to "once and for all, lift the charge or implication of deicide from the Jewish people", which means to deny Jesus is God, then what is to prevent a man-made, global religion being established? The interfaith complex built on Saadiyat Island in Abu Dhabi makes concrete the "vision for the Abrahamic Family House" which "originated after the signing of the Document on Human Fraternity by Pope Francis" in 2019.[272]

To reach this level of vacuity, the Catholic liturgy had to undergo further dismantling. The Good Friday Prayer for the Conversion of the Jews was savaged in 1965 by Paul VI,

---

[271] AJC, *Anti-Jewish Elements in Catholic Liturgy* (1961), IV.

[272] Website of the Higher Committee of Human Fraternity [for World Peace and Living Together].

notably by deleting the petition that "our God and Lord would remove the veil from their hearts" and omitting all mention of their "blindness" and of "the light of Thy truth, which is Christ, [that] they may be delivered from their darkness". Do these erasures not represent a cowardly abandonment of those most in need, leaving them in the dark, leaving them cut off from salvation, abandoning them to satan, because we do not want to have stones hurled at us?

Making the prayer unrecognisable, Paul VI reworded it again in 1970 so as to ask God in the bidding to "grant them to advance in love of His name and in faithfulness to His covenant", an ambivalence which can be interpreted to imply that it is pleasing (faithful) to God to keep the Old Covenant without the New. The altered Collect also implied the OT without the NT offers a partial redemption.[273] These are woeful errors. The prayer is deliberately ambiguous. A retranslation in 2011 achieved cosmetic improvements.

One might object that the majority of changes to the Catholic liturgy were not carried out to placate the Jews, but rather to please Protestants or to help the Church fit in with the age of modernity. This objection overlooks that both Protestantism and modernity have resulted from the clash of the Jewish revolutionary spirit against the Christian order. Protestantism is a judaized form of Catholicism and modernity is a judaized form of Protestantism.

---

[273] The 1973 ICEL translation of the prayer reads: Let us pray for the Jewish people, the first to hear the word of God, that they may continue to grow in the love of his name and in faithfulness to his covenant. (*Collect:*) Almighty and eternal God, long ago you gave your promise to Abraham and his posterity. Listen to your Church as we pray that the people you first made your own may arrive at the fullness of redemption. We ask this through Christ our Lord. Amen.

While the new liturgy appeased the modern world, the traditional Mass still testified to unchanging truths. Pope Benedict XVI was pressured to rewrite the prayer for the 1962 Missal still used by traditional priests. This was the only text targeted for change in the entire 1962 Missal, which speaks volumes about its unique significance. Benedict's composition is vastly better than the *novus ordo* versions but it is fatally weak in comparison with the pre-1955 prayer. It says nothing about blindness nor removing the veil from their hearts. Fatally, an accompanying genuflection was stipulated. Once again, these changes were made ostensibly to please "our Jewish friends".[274] In reality, they were to please our Jewish enemies, though they will never be pleased.

If one understands that there really is a veil on the hearts of the Jews and this is why they are blind to the light of Jesus Christ, then how can one bear a diluted version of the prayer? Men's spiritual blindness to Christ is the human analogue of what satan suffers superlatively — he cannot see God, he never did, he is excluded from the beatific vision forever. It is deplorable that the Church turn her back on these souls in their extreme spiritual need.

It has been suggested that the changes to the prayer do not matter because it is not the form of a Sacrament. The effect of the prayer is not *ex opere operato*, and therefore it can still be effective. But this argument, relying on the inner disposition of hearts, raises the question of why change the prayer at all?

---

[274] Peter Seewald, *Light of the World* (2010), p.107. Pope Benedict XVI explained, "The formula was such as to truly wound the Jews, and it certainly did not express in a positive way the great, profound unity between Old and New Testament. For this reason, I thought that a modification was necessary in the ancient liturgy, in particular in reference to our relationship with our Jewish friends."

It is only licit to modify the liturgy to achieve an undoubted benefit for the Church. But the new variants are inferior. This is disastrous, revealing the hearts and minds of Catholics have grown cold. The changes suggest we fear the world more than we fear the Lord; love the applause of men more than love to please God (Mt 10:28; Jn 12:43). It is anti-Christ. How shall we know the Truth if the liturgy is deliberately diluted?

This is my problem with the changes: they are not born from love of God. They claim to be from love of neighbour, a wish not to wound. But they ignore the wounds of Christ. The hierarchy thinks these can be glossed over for the sake of not upsetting Jews. This is a hellish deception which abandons Jews to damnation and draws us down there too. Or what else is the significance of the changes?

We must face what the Jews did on Good Friday and realise that God still offers His Mercy to their followers, calling them to conversion. We must admit what they did and realise we do it with our sins too. Therefore we must repent and put God first. God's openness is cause for our rejoicing. If we cannot bear the divine extent of His forgiveness, souls will be lost. If we pretend there is no veil, souls will be lost. If we weaken our liturgy to please humans, souls will be lost. If we do not cleave to Tradition, souls will be lost.

Spread of Cancer Corroding the Liturgy

If Francesca van Leer (unofficial founder of the *Amici Israel*) was not herself a saboteur, an agent of deliberate revolution, it is obvious that other such infiltrators have been at work. After the Prayer for the Jews was crippled, other Good Friday Intercessions were enfeebled in 1965 under Paul VI.

From the first intercession, the petition was removed that the "principalities and powers" be subject to the Church, pointlessly granting free reign to satanists and globalists (cf. Eph 6:11-12; Col 2:11-15). Look around.

The prayer for all grades of the Church had most of those grades ripped out. Deleted were the "Subdeacons, Acolytes, Exorcists, Lectors, Porters, Confessors, Virgins, Widows". Paul VI actually sought to have the minor orders abolished, a spiritual onslaught against the priesthood and Holy Eucharist. The deletion also looks like a demonic aversion to Virgins and Widows, of whom the moderns have so little to say.

The Prayer for the Holy Roman Emperor had long been made optional, albeit Rome had allowed priests in Austria to continue to use it. For 1955, a new prayer was composed, "For those in public office", but by 1970 this was moved from its place immediately after the Church to become the penultimate intercession. No wonder, then, that our governments, neglected in prayer, are reverting to barbarism — clamouring for abortion and war.

The prayer for Catechumens was dumbed down. And whereas the traditional ordering gave priority to the sick, hungry and prisoners over followers of false religions, the 1965 order reverses this, signalling appeasement of the more powerful rather than care for the afflicted.

Paul VI's prayer for heretics indicates we share faith in Christ with them and asks that we all be made one in it. But if we already share it, how can we be made one in it? To deny any article of Faith is to have no faith whatsoever.[275] Whoever

---

[275] St Thomas, *S.Th.* II-II, Q.5, a.3.

rejects the Real Presence or Immaculate Conception has zero faith, only personal opinions of what seems good rather than receiving what God has revealed to be true. The pre-1955 prayer is explicit on the "Catholic and Apostolic Church" while the modern text vaguely mentions the "one church".

Pius XII's 1951-55 changes to Holy Week, followed by the wider devastation under Paul VI in the 1960s-70s, have taken the Church off a precipice. On Holy Thursday 2022, *America Magazine* ran an article titled: *"The Gospel of John has been used to justify antisemitism — so we should stop reading it on Good Friday"*. The author, a Jesuit priest, believes that the celebration of Holy Week has caused antisemitic attacks for one thousand years. "Reading John's Passion on Good Friday causes real harm" he writes, lightly dismissing it as "far more a matter of tradition than any theological necessity", not understanding it comes last for a reason (the last word being just like the first). He suggests St John's Passion was originally chosen for its drama and theatre, but faults this with inflaming anti-Jewish violence and argues we need to read a different Passion instead.

These anti-Christian notions can be traced back to Catholic clerics pleasing to the AJC. Among these was an Augustinian whom they quoted at length:

> The main lessons of Holy Week are taken from the Fourth Gospel, which, as is commonly recognized, is the gospel most frequently used as the basis for the vilification of the Jews and as justification for anti-Jewish measures… and even for the injustices and violence with which they were treated. The hostile

passages which we find in the Church fathers likening synagogues to temples of the devil... evil spirits in the fight against Christ's kingdom, have their literary origin in the Gospel of John... When the whole history of Christian hatred of the Jews is told and the account given of the pretended motives for it drawn from the New Testament, an impressive case could be made for the author of the Fourth Gospel being the father of Christian anti-Semitism.[276]

This conclusion is wild, for there is no writing in all the world so holy and productive of goodness as St John's Gospel; and there is no ceremony in all creation so powerful at evoking our own repentance and reluctance to judge others as the traditional Good Friday liturgy. The Augustinian author of this 1961 screed, a Jewish convert, prioritises man over God. Like him, the Jesuit author of the 2022 piece in *America Magazine* is so attentive to today's Jews that they have (de-)formed his mind on Scripture, on the Covenant(s), on history, and finally, on the Church. He has himself become like an enemy of the Gospel, thinking it harmful.

Having deferred to Jewish perspectives, the author then writes something solid for Christians, that on Good Friday,

> we are meant to confront the murder and self-giving sacrifice of the Son of God. Most homilists I know will tell you it is not a day where you really want to say much at all; the service itself speaks so eloquently.

---

[276] AJC, *Anti-Jewish Elements in Catholic Liturgy* (1961), II The Triduum, quotes Fr Gregory Baum, *The Jews and the Gospel: A Reexamination of the New Testament* (1961), p.98-99.

The article goes on to quote another priest referring to Benedict XVI's 2008 Prayer for the Jews as "quite beautiful… We pray for those who share the ancient faith with us." This priest has been throughly Judaized, totally indoctrinated. He says Catholics and Jews share the same ancient faith. No, we do not. The faith of Abraham, Moses and David is in Jesus Christ. This faith is shared by the Apostles and everyone in the One Church. And there are those to whom Jesus says, *"You are of your father the devil"* who claim to have Abraham for a father but who fail to *"do the works of Abraham"* (Jn 8:39,44). We do not share faith with these. Our Faith is in Christ or it is not Faith.

The Jesuit concludes that "the fact that we have changed other elements in the Good Friday liturgy does not solve the problem" of reading St John's Passion. He writes that no new translation can help. It has to be swapped out, perhaps with that of St Luke. He does not realise that this lamentable act of violence against Tradition will solve nothing.

The Jesuit author's goodness and his corruption are shown together in the last paragraph of the piece:

> The Gospel of John certainly has its place in the church and in our liturgical life. But on Good Friday, the point is not to wonder who should be blamed for the crucifixion, but how far Jesus was willing to go for us, the depth of his love. The Passion we choose to read on this most holy and solemn of days should reflect that.

The author thinks he knows better than St John, a witness of the Crucifixion. He imagines St John's Gospel provokes injustice. Consider the insanity of that. Though he recognises his suggestion is problematic, the fact that such an idea could come into a priest's head is frightening. The liturgy is built by God (with man) to be indestructible, to be efficacious, to win redemption. It succeeds. To toy with it is to raise oneself above God.

If one is persistently unwilling to do one thing God requires, then all falls away. If we are not willing to pray properly for the conversion of the Jews, we lose everything, just as if we were to abandon any other souls. It is unchristian. This is now demonstrated. The whole liturgy is ravaged, the teachings of the Church are confused and the moral life of many of her hierarchy involves unchecked evil.

Mindful that the liturgical descent got underway in decisions made to accommodate Jewish aspirations once articulated by the *Amici Israel*, if we would now get the prayer for the Conversion of the Jews right during the solemn services of Good Friday, then we have a chance to get the whole liturgy right, for this is the hardest prayer to recover. It is hardest in the sense that the world will oppose it the most, and even recent popes must be loyally resisted. But it is easiest in that the faithful do not even have to move to succeed: with abundant charity and grace in their hearts, desiring the conversion of the Jews, they need only refrain from genuflecting during this prayer.

In one of its last acts before being abolished by Francis, the *Pontifical Commission Ecclesia Dei* (PCED) granted in 2018 an indult for fifty traditional communities around the world to offer the Holy Week ceremonies according to the pre-1955 rites. This was to be *ad experimentum* for three years. After 2020, the approved communities were to report to Rome what kind of benefits or difficulties this return to Tradition brought to the faithful. It sounded very promising.

However, instead of reporting back and a decision being made for the wider Church, the project alerted the enemies of God that true worship was making a comeback. The PCED was abolished in 2019. When lockdowns were imposed in 2020, the experiment was tacitly extended for one year. Partial lockdowns persisted in 2021, but by then most involved thought it inopportune to raise the matter with Francis for fear of a mercurial and dishonest response. This was prescient. In 2020, the Vatican had sent out an extraordinary survey to the bishops of the world to ask their assessment of Latin Mass communities in their dioceses. Like Francis' Synods, it was a premeditated charade. The results were egregiously misrepresented and used as a pretext for *Traditionis custodes* in July 2021. The enemies of God want Tradition finished off. So the experiment with the pre-1955 Holy Week was derailed.

My point here is not to complain of evil, but to identify a way through the Red Sea. For there is a fatal misconception surrounding the experiment and a dangerous sting built in.

The misconception lies in the attempt to limit access to Tradition. To keep the immemorial rites of Holy Week does not require special ecclesiastical permission for priests in good standing or for the faithful who wish to attend. Measures to restrict the venerable liturgies ought to be roundly ignored and the consequences born manfully.

The dangerous sting came in the second of two conditions which free-falling Rome laid upon the places to be granted permission. The first condition, to which the fifty apostolates had to agree in advance, was to offer the three main services of the Triduum at the modern times — respectively the evening (Maundy Thursday), afternoon (Good Friday) and sundown (Holy Saturday).[277] The false assumption at work is that the liturgy is a dramatic reenactment rather than a mystical union with Heaven which transcends day and night.

If it seems bizarre to have imposed that petty condition, perhaps it was meant as a cover so the second condition did not stand out on its own? Nevertheless, it does stand out. It was instructed that the 2008 Benedictine version of the Prayer for the Jews must be used *with a genuflection.* This reveals that for modernists in Rome (who were frightened by the work of the PCED), pleasing the Jews, even at the cost of salvation, holds a veto on optimum worship of God. That is what it boils down to. They think unless we genuflect for the Jews (of course not *to* them), they can forbid the ancient ceremonies altogether. It was as if to say: you can have everything you want, all the ancient liturgy (minus one crucial prayer), provided you kneel to Zion.

satan said: *"All these will I give Thee, if falling down Thou wilt adore me"* (Mt 4:9). Jesus refused. So should we.

---

[277] Over centuries, celebration of the main Triduum services had crept to rather early in the day, even beginning before noon. Moderns mocked the practice of singing of "this night" during the day of Holy Saturday, insisting on moving the Vigil ceremony until after sundown. They overlook that the "night" is this world, and the "day" is Heaven. Moreover, as the liturgy somehow makes present the mystery being celebrated, then when the Vigil takes place in the morning it is just as effective in overcoming that spiritual "night".

MAINTAIN THE TRADITIONAL LITURGY

For I would not have you ignorant, brethren, of this mystery… that blindness in part has happened in Israel, until the fulness of the Gentiles should come in. And so all Israel should be saved.

Romans 11:25-26

Our Catholic duty, our life, our sweetness and our hope, involves preserving the apostolic liturgy, chiefly by ministering, serving or assisting (being attentively present) as faithfully as one can. We have nothing better on earth. Of itself, upholding Tradition holds open the widest bridge for the final conversion of multitudes of Jews. The old Mass is best for us and for them.

When we hear 'Old Testament' and 'New Testament', we might first think of Sacred Scripture. However, these Testaments, or Covenants, are primarily rituals, the first in the blood of lambs, the second in the Blood of the God-Man. The Sacrifice of the Mass is the spiritual translation of the OT. Just as we can find Jesus in the Old and New Testament Scriptures, He can also be found in the Old and New ceremonies: the Temple rites and Holy Mass. This is a major reason to preserve Tradition: to keep the connection apparent.

Throughout the Traditional Mass, the OT shadow can be discerned. When Jews see that in Mass are fulfilled the various sacrifices of Abel, Abraham and Melchisedech, whose lives Moses recorded in the Torah, then they have a greater chance to see that the whole life of Moses, too, points prophetically to Jesus (Dt 18:18). This is key: to follow Moses faithfully means to come to Christ.

Today there are advanced efforts by Jews to revive the Temple worship, requiring detailed research into the ancient rites and their meaning. In parallel, Catholics are striving to restore the traditional liturgy. Both endeavours require a deep understanding of worship. Having an eye on the progress of the 'other side' may help provide answers to vital questions: Why a lamb? Must it be killed? Why blood? What is an altar? Why do we need priests? Why must the sacrifice be offered in the holy place? Where is the holy place? Searching for answers, Christ will be found.

The Church inherited the foundation and structure of her liturgy from Jews. Christ instituted the Mass and gave the Church authority to develop it. It was Jews, the Apostles, who began this. There is vast Jewish heritage behind Catholic liturgy, notably the Roman Rite. The many Jewish successors of St Peter include Pope St Evaristus (✝107), who

> was by birth a Greek Jew... It was he who divided among the Priests the titles of the Churches in the city of Rome, and commanded that seven Deacons should attend the Bishop when he was executing his office of preaching the Gospel. He commanded, in accordance with the tradition of the Apostles, that marriages should be celebrated openly, and that a Priest should be asked

to invoke a blessing thereon. He ruled the Church for nine years and three months. He held four Ordinations in the month of December, wherein he ordained seventeen Priests, two Deacons, and fifteen Bishops.[278]

The tremendous continuity in the life of the Temple and the Church is because they have the same DNA. The transition between them is analogous to birth: suddenly one starts seeing, breathing, moving freely. Such continuity offers the fullest way to understand what the Prophet Zechariah said of *"the seed"* and *"the vine"* and the *"dew"*:

But now I will not deal with the remnant of this people according to the former days, saith the Lord of hosts. But there shall be the seed of peace: the vine shall yield her fruit, and the earth shall give her increase, and the heavens shall give their dew: and I will cause the remnant of this people to possess all these things. And it shall come to pass, that as you were a curse among the Gentiles, O house of Juda, and house of Israel: so will I save you, and you shall be a blessing: fear not, let your hands be strengthened. For thus saith the Lord of hosts: As I purposed to afflict you, when your fathers had provoked me to wrath, saith the Lord, and I had no mercy: so turning again I have thought in these days to do good to the house of Juda, and Jerusalem: fear not. (Zech 8:11-15)

How might Jews see this is a call to Holy Mass? For two thousand years, few Orthodox Jews (those who care about the

---

278 Feast of St Evaristus (26th Oct), Matins, *Lectio* III.

minutiae of Temple worship), have witnessed a traditional, apostolic liturgy. Now the Internet is bringing new possibilities. As Orthodox Jews seek to resurrect Levitical 'wave offerings' with lambs, grain and wine in Jerusalem, they might be intrigued to learn that when a priest offers the *oblata* in Holy Mass (bread and wine which become the Lamb of God), he, too, 'waves' them, that is to say, he makes a sign of the Cross with them in a manner gestated of old. There is no need to restore the Levitical priesthood. It lives now in the Church. There is no need to kill any more lambs. Holy Mass entails not only the Mosaic and Temple sacrifices, but more fundamentally, the sacrifices of the patriarchs, including Abraham, to whom the irrevocable promises were made. Everything is fulfilled in Jesus' Sacrifice.

The new Mass devastates these connections between Catholicism and Moses. Hence satan prefers the new Mass, because he does not want the Jews to recognise their ancient heritage alive today in the Church. He trembles over the conversion of the Jews because after that it is all over for him.

Conversion of the Jews in Each Traditional Mass

The traditional rubrics depict both the blindness of the Jews and their conversion. In a Solemn High Mass, the harmonious movements and similar vestments of priest, deacon and subdeacon hint at the Blessed Trinity, three persons with united purpose. But for ages the Church has seen a still richer symbolism in the three sacred ministers. Fr Barthe explains:

> The subdeacon represents the Old Testament, Jesus
> Christ yesterday, who was proclaimed partly in the

sayings of the prophets, and partly in figures by the saintly individuals who preceded his coming. As is appropriate, the subdeacon always occupies the lowest rank, that of incompleteness.[279]

The deacon, meanwhile, represents Jesus Christ Incarnate, coming to proclaim the Gospel in its fullness. And the celebrant represents Jesus Christ in eternity, glorified in Heaven and among us.

As to the Jews' blindness, the subdeacon stands during the Canon at the bottom of the altar steps, wearing a humeral veil and with the ends of it holding the paten in front of his face so that he cannot see the action at the altar save for the major elevations. In former times, the paten could be a huge plate so it was practical for it to be taken away from the altar for the consecration. This pragmatic reason did not prevent the Church investing the rite with spiritual meaning: the blindness of the OT to the mysteries of the Passion. Note that the veil is removed from the subdeacon at the "forgive us our sins" of the *Our Father*.

This illustrates that Catholics do well to maintain their traditions even when they do not understand them. The understanding of particular rites ebbs and flows within the community over generations, nothing essential being lost.

As to the final conversion of the Jews, there is a very ancient rite and another very venerable custom, long preserved, whose meaning is perhaps now ready to blossom. The first — the moving of the Missal during Mass — and the

---

[279] Abbé Claude Barthe, *A Forest of Symbols: The Traditional Mass and Its Meaning* (2023), p.25.

second — the lighting and extinguishing of candles — each speak of coming conversion. How so?

The Catholic altar has an epistle-side (south) representing the OT and a gospel-side (north) representing the NT. For Mass, the Missal begins on the OT side. Before the Gospel is read, the Missal is transferred in procession over to the NT side. This represents the coming of Jesus Christ, sending His Apostles to preach the Gospel to the nations (to the north). The Missal remains here with the nations until after Holy Communion. Once all have received, the Missal is transferred back to the 'Jewish' side, standing there for the closing Propers and the end of Mass. So we see the Word of God, which is Jesus Christ, begins with the Jews, then goes over to the Gentiles, but in the end returns to the Jews.[280]

This symbolism is not accidental. The meaning of the procession of the Missal over to the north-side for the Gospel originally and always signifies the Covenant passing from the Jews to the Gentiles. The return of the Missal can then be interpreted, as it long has been, as a token of our confidence that in the end the Word will be received by the Jews, that is, in their final conversion to Christ.

Reinforcing this pattern, the distribution of Holy Communion may not proceed backwards (from gospel-side toward epistle-side). In detail, to receive Holy Communion the faithful kneel in a row at the altar rail. The priest begins distributing at the epistle-side and moves from person to person toward the gospel-side. Once he reaches the end of the

---

[280] The Last Gospel, which is technically after the Mass is ended, is said on the gospel-side. This may represent the Word persisting when history is over. Feasts with a proper Last Gospel have the Missal itself carried over again for this.

row, it is forbidden for him to continue by distributing in the other direction, but he walks directly over to the epistle-side to begin again. This direction and movement shows a progression from Jews (epistle) to Gentiles (gospel), then a leap back to the beginning, a sudden return to the Jews.

For this same reason, it is also an immemorial custom that whoever lights the candles before Mass should begin with those on the epistle-side and then light those on the gospel-side. (If more than two candles are to be lit, then he begins by lighting the candle closer to the tabernacle and then moving outwards.) This order is not trivial but follows the course prescribed for incensing the altar (epistle-side, gospel-side, again epistle-side). After Mass when the minister has returned to the sacristy, the candles are put out in reverse order, first those on the gospel-side and finally those on the epistle-side. All of this signifies Jesus Christ, the Light of the World — Who promulgates Himself from the tabernacle — begins with the Jews, then goes over to the Gentiles, then goes out from the Gentiles and is last seen still lit with the Jews. A related pattern is followed in extinguishing the candles at *Tenebræ*.

How important is all this? The rubrics allow no other course for the Missal than that which promises the final conversion of the Jews. It is similar for the distribution of Holy Communion. As for the candles, some might say it is not the end of the world if the server lights or extinguishes them in the wrong order. I disagree. It is disastrous for the Church to casually abandon her customs, for they instruct us. Some things might be lost without harm, however if they are lost by negligence or by the arrogance of innovation, then this lack of reverence will carry a cost to someone's salvation.

In the *novus ordo,* the altar is often reversed and the missal does not move, so it is not meaningful to speak of epistle-side and gospel-side. Holy Communion is usually distributed to a queue, again forfeiting the south-north-south movement. Some altars have candles at one end only. The consequences of heedless changes include a great loss of meaning.

Every priest should care about these things and take responsibility for correcting lacunæ in the formation of his servers. A ten-year-old can easily handle such details, though he might not grasp their importance. Decades later he will remember that *details matter.* That is a good lesson for the liturgy. There is nothing superfluous in Heaven.

The Close of the Liturgical Year

The liturgical calendar contains deeply woven heralds of the final conversion of the Jews. One of these occurs on the penultimate Sunday of the liturgical year. At Matins of *Dominica IV* in November, we hear the Prophet Hosea foretelling that God's own people will be cut off (*Lectiones* I-III, Hos 1:1-11). This happened, but it does not end there. In the second nocturn, St Augustine interprets Hosea as predicting the conversion of the Jews. After expounding on the incoming of the Gentiles, he writes:

> Concerning them that are now Israelites according to the flesh, that will not now believe in Christ, but shall believe hereafter (that is, their children shall believe, for these shall die, and go to their own place), this same Prophet giveth witness, where he saith: *The children of Israel shall abide many days without a King, and*

without a Prince, and without a sacrifice, and without an Altar, and without a Priest... (Hos 3:4). To whom is it not manifest that such is the state of the Jews now.[281]

St Augustine writes confidently of the children of unbelieving Jews hereafter believing, which passage has been carefully selected for the liturgy just before Advent.

When this Sunday coincides with the XXIII Sunday after Pentecost, then the third nocturn gives St Jerome's genius interpretation of the raising of Jairus' daughter as signifying the conversion of the Jews toward the end of time:

> A certain ruler, desiring not to be kept out of the mystery of the true circumcision, besought Christ to recall his daughter to life. [But her resurrection is postponed because] a woman, diseased with an issue of blood, thrust herself in... even as it is written... *Blindness in part is happened to Israel, until the fullness of the Gentiles is come in and so all Israel shall be saved* (Rom 11:25-26). Behold, a woman, diseased twelve years with an issue of blood, came behind Him, and *touched the hem of His garment.* In St Luke's Gospel it is written that the ruler's daughter was about twelve years of age (Lk 8:42). Note therefore that this woman, who typifies the Gentiles, had been diseased for the same time that the Jewish nation, typified by the ruler's daughter, had been living in faith.[282]

---

[281] *Dominica IV in November*, Matins, *Lectiones* IV-VI. St Augustine, *City of God*, XVIII, 28.

[282] *Dominica XXIII Post Pentecosten*, Matins, *Lectiones* VII-IX. St Jerome, *Commentary on St Matthew's Gospel*, II (Mt 9:18-26).

The Jews having faith under the OT are symbolised by the girl who lived healthy and grew, while the Gentiles, that is the old woman, were sick and could find no cure. When Jesus came, the ruler of the synagogue (Jairus) declared his daughter was dead. That is, the faith of the Jews ended. Going therefore to heal them, along the way Jesus cures the bleeding woman — or the Gentiles whose life is pouring out, who are made well by their faith in Jesus. At the end of the pericope, Jesus raises Jairus' daughter from the dead. He always knew He was going to do this! It is the final conversion of the Jews, from being dead in faith to regaining their spirit and tasting the banquet: *"Her spirit returned, and she arose immediately. And [Jesus] bid them give her to eat"* (Lk 8:55).[283]

The Church consciously chose the XXIII Sunday after Pentecost for this exposition, because the approaching end of the liturgical year signifies the end of time. In the traditional calendar, the Feast of Christ the King comes on the last Sunday of October, or more pertinently, the Sunday prior to All Saints. It means that once the world recognises Christ as King, then a saintly order will be enjoyed in this world. Shortly after this comes the Sunday whose texts resonate with the conversion of the Jews, and all that remains is the Last Sunday after Pentecost, which is a warning of the Last Judgement, because then comes Advent — Jesus coming not finally as a babe in a crib, but as Pantocrator radiating glory.

---

[283] St Jerome continues his commentary: *"And when the crowd had been put out, He entered and took her hand and the girl arose* (Mt 9:25). For they were not worthy to see the mystery of one who was to rise again, since they were deriding with unworthy insults the One who was going to raise her. Unless the hands of the Jews, which are full of blood, should first be cleansed [by Jesus touching her hand], their dead synagogue does not rise."

The new calendar has distorted this signification of feasts and has eviscerated the readings of Matins. It is as if satan wants to obscure the revealed truth by dismantling tradition.

Not everyone can go to the relevant books to learn these things, but all can share in upholding the traditions so they are never lost. Even infants have their role. A two-year old does not know that in regard to the XXIII Sunday after Pentecost, Dom Prosper Guéranger wrote about Jer 23:5-8:

> This passage is equally applicable to the conversion of the Jews, and the restoration of Israel, which are to take place at the end of the world. This was the view taken by the chief liturgists of the Middle Ages, in order to explain thoroughly the Mass of the twenty-third Sunday after Pentecost.[284]

A two-year old does not know that here Dom Prosper quotes Abbot Rupert of Salzburg (✝1130), showing how the Church has long understood the intertwining of Scripture and Tradition to foretell the conversion of the Jews:

> Holy Church is so intent on paying her debt of supplication, and prayer, and thanksgiving, for all men, as the Apostle demands, that we find her giving thanks also for the salvation of the children of Israel, who, she knows, are one day to be united with her. And, as their remnants are to be saved at the end of the world, so, on this last Sunday of the Year, she delights at having them, just as though they were already her members! In the Introit, calling to mind the prophecies concerning

---

[284] Dom Prosper Guéranger, *The Liturgical Year*, Vol. XI, *Time After Pentecost,* II, *Twenty Third Sunday after Pentecost.* [Jer 23 is no longer the Epistle of that day.]

them, she thus sings every Year: *My thoughts are thoughts of peace, and not of affliction.* Verily, His thoughts are those of peace, for He promises to admit to the banquet of His grace, the Jews, who are His brethren, according to the flesh; thus realising what had been prefigured in the history of the patriarch Joseph. The brethren of Joseph, having sold him, came to him, when they were tormented by hunger; for then he ruled over the whole land of Egypt; he recognised them, he received them, and made, together with them, a great feast; so, too, our Lord Who is now reigning over the whole earth, and is giving the bread of life, in abundance, to the Egyptians (that is, to the Gentiles), will see coming to Him the remnants of the children of Israel. He, Whom they had denied and put to death, will admit them to His favour, will give them a place at His table, and the true Joseph will feast delightedly with His brethren.

The benefit of this divine Table is signified, in the Office of this Sunday, by the Gospel, which tells us of our Lord's feeding the multitude with five loaves. For, it will be then, that Jesus will open to the Jews the five books of Moses, which are now being carried whole, and not yet broken — yea, carried by a child, that is to say, this people itself, who, up to that time, will have been cramped up in the narrowness of a childish spirit.

Then will be fulfilled the prophecy of Jeremias, which is so aptly placed before this Gospel: *They shall say no more: The Lord liveth, who brought up the children of*

Israel out of the land of Egypt! But, the Lord liveth, who hath brought out of the seed of Israel from the land of the north, and from all the lands into which they had been cast. (Jer 23:7-8)

A two-year old does not know that a twelfth century liturgical scholar from Salzburg was cited by a nineteenth century liturgical scholar from France, and this work was uploaded onto the Internet by a twenty-first century Catholic in the USA. But a two-year old does not have to know these things. Instead, he can assist at the XXIII Sunday after Pentecost and his presence, even if he is noisy, is a sign of hope to everybody present that the Church is not dead, that there is a new generation to inherit the traditions so that they will reach unto the end, when they will doubtless contribute to the conversion of the Jews who recognise that everything was foretold and maintained by the Church. Then, fully satisfied with His children, the Lord Jesus will come again.

Another subtle sign of the conversion comes by 30th June's Commemoration of St Paul. Nobody knew more about the Jews' conversion, wrote about it more authoritatively and desired it more strongly, than St Paul. He once held enmity to Christ for the sake of his brother Jews but after his conversion he was ready to postpone entering Heaven if he could use the extra time to persuade his blind brothers (now his persecutors) of the Faith (Rom 9:3). We keep the Feast of the Conversion of St Paul on 25th January. This date, toward the end of the Christmas cycle, can stand for the coming to Christ of many Jews soon after Jesus was born. Then we remember St Paul's life again on his Commemoration at the end of June. This can stand for a similar conversion yet to come.

In Matins of the Feast of St Paul's Conversion we hear from his letter to the Galatians:

The gospel which was preached by me is not according to man. For neither did I receive it of man, nor did I learn it; but by the revelation of Jesus Christ. For you have heard of my conversation in time past in the Jews' religion: how that, beyond measure, I persecuted the church of God, and wasted it. And I made progress in the Jews' religion above many of my equals in my own nation, being more abundantly zealous for the traditions of my fathers. But when it pleased Him, Who separated me from my mother's womb, and called me by His grace, to reveal His Son in me... (Gal 1:11-16)

In the most dramatic and famous conversion in history, this most zealous Jew, who persecuted the Church, became her greatest Apostle to the Gentiles. It was an act of God, *"when it pleased Him... by His grace, to reveal His Son"*.

When God is pleased He will do it. Traditional Catholics are reminded of all this on 30th June, the Commemoration of St Paul. The readings and antiphons of Matins are about finishing the course, the final victory. For St Paul, that must include the conversion of his beloved brethren. And this should be a burning desire for us too.

The Three Most Sung Canticles on Earth

Further hints of enduring hope in the eschatological role of the Jews are nested in the key canticles of the Divine Office: the *Benedictus*, the *Magnificat*, the *Nunc dimittis*. The first is sung at Lauds, summing up the beginning of everything. The last is sung at Compline, summing up the end of everything. The *Magnificat* is sung at Vespers, which is a deeper beginning and end, not of the solar day but of the liturgical day. All three carry an almost inaudible whisper about the conversion of the Jews. And Mary has the best part.

Just before sleep, when darkness has descended, the Church sings the *Nunc dimittis*, the inspired prophecy of Simeon in the Temple. Gazing upon the infant Jesus, taking the babe in his arms, he sang by the Spirit:

> *My eyes have seen Thy salvation, which Thou hast prepared before the face of all peoples: a light to the revelation of the Gentiles and the glory of Thy people Israel.* (Lk 2:30-32)

He beholds God's Promised One newborn, and knows that the entire unfolding of God's Plan is certain. God's paths are straight, so for Simeon having the beginning before his eyes is equivalent to seeing the ending. In two phrases Simeon tells us how all history must run from that moment on: *"revelation to the Gentiles"* followed by *"glory of Thy people Israel"*. After the Light of the World has gone out to the ends of the earth, then there will be a *"glory"* for Israel as few have ever seen on earth (think of the Transfiguration). It must surely be the conversion of the Jews. How did Simeon see the end of history? Because holding the little One in his arms and adoring is *the same* as being held forever in the arms of God.

With this in mind, one can hear in the *Benedictus* each morning at Lauds a reminder that God never forgets His promises. The following words of the Levitical priest, Zachary, whose son John introduced Jesus to multitudes of

Jews, evidently applies to the early Church. But a more glorious uproar will be caused by seeing it further fulfilled in the last generation of Jews, too.

> *To perform mercy to our fathers and to remember His holy testament. The oath, which He swore to Abraham our father, that He would grant to us.* (Lk 1:72-73)

I might well be wrong. But I cannot see Abraham's name without thinking God will move mountains for him. God has given him billions of spiritual descendants already. Why not add at the end many who are thought to be lost?

At Vespers, around sundown, the traditional rubrics (pre-1960) require not infrequently that the Psalms of the day's feast be united with the chapter, hymn and antiphon of the approaching day, with orations for both. Thus, Vespers serves as a hinge seamlessly joining the successive feasts of an unceasing banquet. It is the highpoint of the Divine Office. And the Magnificat is the high point of Vespers: structurally and experientially, with its beauty and incense, chants and silences, movements and stillness, familiarity and mystery. With the Magnificat being close to the close, that is near to the end, one has become fully immersed, aware that the end is near but not yet having the sense it is over. And what do we sing at the end of the Magnificat?

> *He hath received Israel His servant, being mindful of His mercy. As He spoke to our fathers: to Abraham and to his seed for ever.* (Lk 1:54-55)

This song made perfect sense when Mary first sang it. It was fulfilled then and has been fulfilled every day ever since.

The visible fullness of what God accomplishes grows and grows through Church history. Mary saw all the potential, all the implications of the Incarnation, knowing everything was won through it. History repeatedly demonstrates that God *"hath put down the mighty from their seat, and hath exalted the humble"* (Lk 1:52). So Annas, and Elymas, and Arius, and Mohammed, and Luther, and Lenin have been brought down, as will happen most definitively with the Antichrist.

After all the good things promised and attained line by line in the Magnificat, who can read its close — about *Israel, mercy, Abraham, his seed for ever* — without looking forward to the conversion of the Jews?

With Vespers usually marking the beginning and end of each liturgical day, Mary's words may prompt us to think of those many Jews who converted at the beginning of the Church's day as well as those who will convert at the end. The Mother of God closes her canticle with these words suggesting hope for conversion, knowing always that *"no word shall be impossible with God"* (Lk 1:37).

LOVE ABRAHAM, MOSES AND DAVID

As touching the election, they are most dear for the sake of the fathers.

Romans 11:28

Catholics can prepare for the conversion of the Jews by assisting faithfully at the traditional liturgy. We can increase the effectiveness of our prayers through ardour, that is, by increasing our love for the Jews. If this seems challenging, it is made easier by admirable Hebrews we encounter in the Scriptures, who help us to hold the Church's doors open continually for their descendants, until the final conversion is accomplished.

Fostering this love is not difficult. We find Jesus alive in Jacob, Joseph, Joshua, Job and Jeremiah, in their mysteries, visions, conquests, sufferings and sorrows. If we love God, we will venerate these vessels of Christ, just as the Apostles and Church Fathers did, and as the Church esteems them in her liturgical calendar (for example, Habakkuk, 15th January; Isaiah, 6th July; Elijah, 20th July).

Seeking to name the greatest figure in the OT, it is not difficult to settle on the last three candidates but it seems impossible to pick between them. Who can rank the holiness of Abraham, Moses and David? There is enough drama in the life of each to be engrossed by them. They are resplendent with virtue, drawing us by their tenderness and care for the lowly. It would be perverse not to love them. But what shall we think when we discern that they were created and guided by God, through their holiness, character and experiences, to paint us a picture, punctuated by centuries, of the Three Divine Persons?

Abraham, the Great Patriarch, saith Holy Writ, *"is the father of us all"* (Rom 4:16). His God-given name means *"father of many nations"* (Gen 17:5). He withheld not his beloved son for God's sacrifice. In Abraham we see from afar the Father.

Moses, who as an infant escaped the king's murderous decree (Ex 1:16; Mt 1:16), is more Christlike than any, for his meekness, for his speaking to God *"face-to-face"* (Ex 33:11), for his leading God's people through death (the Red Sea). Moses is the greatest of the OT prophets. He illustrates the Incarnation of the Second Person of the Blessed Trinity in coming down from the royal court to his people, but they thrust him away, not understanding that *"God by his hand would save them"* (Acts 7:25). Moses went away but never forgot his people, he prayed for them and in God's time returned to them. All this anticipates Jesus Christ, the Son.

David, the third of the three, was so uniquely filled with the Spirit (1 Kgs 16:13; Mk 12:36; Acts 4:25), that there is no one in all the world whose words are sung so often and to such fruitful effect as his — the ceaseless, worldwide chanting of the Psalms in the Divine Office. What transparency of soul is required to compose songs which elevate the whole world forever? The voice heard in the chant brings peace through strength. Evidently, the spiritual strings of David's musical heart make him a singular instrument of the Holy Ghost.

In multifarious ways, Abraham, Moses and David depict the Father, Son and Spirit. Each is lovable in himself, yet combined as a personal sign of the Blessed Trinity, the goodness of these men is stratospheric. This is only discernible through the revelation of Jesus Christ.

Moreover, while the Three Persons of the Holy Trinity, identical in their Divine Nature, are all made known in Jesus Christ (the Son shows us the Father and breathes into us His Spirit), so the greatest men of God in the OT all closely prefigure Jesus Himself: all of them are good shepherds; all warriors who rescued their captive kin; all suffered and were ever ready to give their life for God. Their stories, like the whole OT, are about Jesus.

Jesus was sent to succeed totally in His care for the sheep, as Abraham, Moses and David were each sent to succeed in their full measure. Jesus loses none who are given to Him but will resurrect them on the Last Day (Jn 6:39), saying to the Father that He has guarded all those souls entrusted to Him and *"none of them is lost, but the son of perdition: that the scripture may be fulfilled"* (Jn 17:12; Ps 40:10). Even in Gethsemane, Jesus' thoughts were to save others, even the least, fulfilling His word, *"Of them whom Thou hast given Me, I have not lost any one"* (Jn 18:9).

This great shepherding we see prefigured in Abraham, who went on a dangerous mission to rescue the lost. Succeeding in battle, *"he brought back all the substance, and Lot his brother, with his substance, the women also, and the people"* (Gen 14:16). The significance of Abraham saving Lot is immense. It is the whole of history! Lot was the son of Abraham's deceased elder brother. Therefore, Abraham was fulfilling the duty to make sure that his elder brother's name and memory should not die out — which signifies securing eternal life for the elder brother. In this act, Abraham represents the Christian nation (the younger brother) rescuing the last generation of Jews (the son of the elder brother).

Moses, who spent his middle forty years as a shepherd, lost none of his people at the Exodus. He accepted no compromise with Pharaoh, insisting on the liberation of even the weakest, *"Our young and old, with our sons and daughters"* (Ex 10:9) and all *"the flocks shall go with us: there shall not a hoof remain of them"* (Ex 10:26). This prefigures Jesus' saving the whole Church. Central to the action of the Exodus is the strength of Moses' heart, for without it the weak would have been left behind. It is a clue for us of the omnipotent love in Jesus' Most Sacred Heart.

David, in battle,

> *recovered all that the Amalecites had taken, and he rescued his two wives. And there was nothing missing small or great, neither of their sons or their daughters, nor of the spoils, and whatsoever they had taken, David recovered all. And he took all the flocks and the herds, and made them go before him: and they said: This is the prey of David.* (1 Kgs 30:18-20)

From Israel's ancient enemy, David won back everything: all persons, small and great, sons and daughters. He even won an increase, *"prey"*, which might stand for the extra graces and virtues which Christ's people gain by enduring evil, by patient suffering, which renders souls holier than if they had lived an easy life in paradise.

God shows in advance what is coming, for men's minds needed millennia of preparation to be able to see the scope of the Messiah. Jesus the Redeemer fulfils all the rescue work of Abraham, Moses and David. In their successively defeating the Mesopotamian (northern) kings, the Egyptians and the Amalekites, we ultimately glimpse Jesus redeeming us from satan, sin and death. None could share in any of these ultimate victories — defeating hell — without Jesus, the Son of God.

Is this hard to see? Over many centuries, God spoke through the Law, the Prophets and the Writings of the coming Passion and Resurrection of His Son, yet none until the Blessed Virgin Mary could understand. Now we all need Our Lady to dawn in us.

Condensing the long timescale of the OT into the lifetime of Jesus, in Whom all history and prophecy is capitulated, when the Lord told His Apostles of His approaching Passion, they were unable to take in what He was telling them:

Then Jesus took unto Him the twelve, and said to them: Behold, we go up to Jerusalem, and all things shall be accomplished which were written by the prophets concerning the Son of man. For He shall be delivered to the Gentiles, and shall be mocked, and scourged, and spit upon: And after they have scourged Him, they will put Him to death; and the third day He shall rise again. And they understood none of these things, and this word was hid from them, and they understood not the things that were said. (Lk 18:31-34 cf. Mt 16:21-23; 17:22-23; 20:17-23; 26:2; Mk 10:32-40; Lk 9:22,44-45; 17:25; 24:25-27,44-45)

Like all who until then had been attentive to the Tanakh (the OT), the Apostles heard God's Word but its full meaning was hidden from them. St Luke explains *"this word... was hid from them, so that they perceived it not. And they were afraid to ask Him concerning this word"* (Lk 9:45).

The death of the Son of God at the hands of man was something too terrible for us to face, so our loving Father hid the worst of it until the last moment. When it did hit, God gave joyful relief on the third day by His Resurrection. The hearts of the Apostles were opened, as have been the hearts of all those who have believed through their preaching.

Jews cannot find Jesus Christ in the OT unless He opens their hearts. He desires to. Meanwhile, if we Christians do not find Him in the OT, then we have yet to learn how to listen. Saints Peter and Paul show Jesus is the OT (Acts 2:22-36; 3:18-26; 26:22-23; 28:23-24), as for their parts do St Philip, St Stephen, St James, St Jude and the four evangelists. In fine, all the NT authors understood that the OT is about Jesus Christ. The OT is fully Christian. The New is Old, the Old is New.

Jews today who love Abraham, Moses and David are thereby approaching Jesus Christ. Orthodox Jews stand out for the first steps. We may help serve their realising the end of the journey if we find a common basis in our sincere love of Hebrew patriarchs, prophets and kings. If we live as true sons of Abraham, if we hold Moses in affectionate awe, if the

Church ceaselessly sings the Psalms of David, will it not serve that the Jews finally confess the Blessed Trinity?

Welcoming the Conversion of the Jews

Some Christians succumb to Marcion's heretical prejudice against the OT Scriptures, protesting that the OT belongs only to Judaism. Rejecting this false wall of separation, Christ's vessel of election, St Paul, leaves no doubt that everything good about the Jews is at home in the Church. He emphasises his Jewishness to the Jews precisely to arouse them: *"If, by any means, I may provoke to emulation them who are my flesh, and may save some of them"* (Rom 11:14). Commenting on this, St Thomas finds multiple ways in which Jewish jealousy of Catholics and Catholic jealousy of Jews can serve as a motor for salvation.[285] If we find we are jealous of Jews, this can be purified for a very good end.

Being moved by 'holy envy' (a right desire to imitate the saints), removes the risk of being injured by its opposite, unholy envy. Among the baptised, some reject out of hand the coming conversion of the Jews, resenting that grace be given to one-time enemies. But against such sentiments, Scripture warns sternly. Through *"the envy of the devil, death entered the world"* (Wis 2:24). Cain envied Abel. The sons of Jacob through *"envy"* sold Joseph into slavery (Acts 7:9). Aaron was *"envied... in the wilderness [by] Dathan and Abiram and their men and the synagogue of Korah, in wrath and anger"* (Sir 45:18 RSVCE). Scripture tells us these outsiders conspired against the High Priest specifically because God

---

[285] St Thomas Aquinas, *Commentary on Romans* 11:19.

chose him out of all the living to offer sacrifice to the Lord, incense and a pleasing odour as a memorial portion, to make atonement for the people. (Sir 45:16)

This is the perpetual story! Those who offer the inferior worship murder those who offer the greater. Those who know their offerings are inadequate hate to be reminded of it by seeing true worship. This is why Francis issued *Traditionis custodes*. But should a claimant to the papacy be prone to murderous envy?

Even Aaron and Miriam envied their brother Moses because he

> erected… the tabernacle, delivered… the laws, and established the priesthood in keeping with the teaching given to him by God… As he arranged everything in [the tabernacle] in the required manner, among his family he aroused against himself envy, that congenital malady in the nature of man.[286]

St Gregory calls envy "that congenital malady in the nature of man". Saul envied David even while the latter served and saved him. Pilate knew that the chief priests delivered Jesus up *"out of envy"* (Mk 15:10). After this the high priests and Sadducees, *"filled with envy"*, had the Apostles imprisoned (Acts 5:17-18).

---

[286] St Gregory of Nyssa, *Life of Moses*, I, 61. He continues: "Even Aaron, who was endowed with the honours of the priesthood, and his sister Miriam, driven by a most female-like jealousy against the honour given to Moses by God, so railed against him that deity was provoked to punish their trespass. Here Moses showed patience most worthy of admiration, because, when God punished the irrational envy of the woman, he made his nature prevail over anger and appeased God on behalf of his sister."

May God preserve us from envy when those He chooses finally come through by choosing God themselves. Jesus' parable of *The Two Brothers* (Lk 15:11-32) tells of the Gentiles departing from their father's house to fornicate in idolatry and eat pig swill in their spiritual misery. Meanwhile the elder brother, the Jews, kept close to their father and served in his house. When the prodigal son returned, he was embraced by his father and kissed, dressed, honoured and feted. This is the life of the Church. Jesus challenged the listening Jews, signified by the resentful elder brother standing outside, not to be envious but to look forward to their reward. Can it be that over two thousand years the brothers are changing places? Now Christians are the elder brother, and what will we think if we see the Jews returning from the outer darkness? Will we scorn them, protest their infidelity? Will we refuse to join the feast, refuse to rejoice? If we refuse, then we have only hell. Let us desire our estranged brother come in.

Is the massive growth of Messianic Jews a sign of a coming conversion? Perhaps. Many of them do not believe in the Divinity of Christ or in the Blessed Trinity and many do not receive sacramental baptism, so they are not Christians. But it is a movement, a recognition of the historicity of the Gospels, the goodness of Jesus, the truth from His lips and the anointment of God upon Him, His Christ, the Messiah.

Perhaps this movement of Messianic Jews is hinted at in the NT by Apollos of Alexandria, so gifted in refuting and convincing the Jews from the Scriptures, yet who needed a fuller teaching and to be brought into the Church before he could reach his God-given potential (Acts 18:24-28).

God has written His Christ into the OT. We can find Him there and show the Jews. If they will not listen to us, God will find a way to move them when He chooses.

For God speaks in one way, and in two, though man does not perceive it. In a dream, in a vision of the night, when deep sleep (תַּרְדֵּמָה) falls upon men, while they slumber on their beds, then he opens the ears of men, and terrifies them with warnings. (Job 33:14-16 RSVCE)

It is as if God speaks in one way, and in case He is not heard, then gives the same message through a *"deep sleep"*. If Christians understand the meaning of Adam's *"deep sleep"* (תַּרְדֵּמָה Gen 2:21), we may provoke the Jews to jealousy, and they may be slowly consumed by the question of the Passion laid down in the OT. In God's time, they will recognise it and will hunger to return to the household of the Father.

There is plenty of help from Heaven. St Gregory of Nazianzus (✝390), extolled the Machabees for heroically giving their lives for Christ before Jesus had even given them the example of His own Passion:

There is a mystic and subtle idea, which seems very likely to me and to all lovers of God, that none of those who were crowned with martyrdom before Christ came, could have been so, unless they had had faith in Christ.[287]

The Machabean Martyrs are commemorated on the first day of August, which is the Feast of St Peter in Chains. The

---

[287] Machabean Martyrs (1st Aug), Matins, *Lectio* IX. St Gregory of Nazianzus, *Sermon XX on the Machabees.*

Office of the day relates that the chain by which St Peter was once bound by King Herod in Jerusalem was brought to Rome in AD 439. The reigning pope displayed this with another chain by which St Peter was bound, this one by Emperor Nero in Rome. It "came to pass that they became so fastened together, the one with the other, that they seemed no longer two but one chain".[288]

Is this a mystical image of Jews and Gentiles becoming one in Christ? Under a sign of the Fisherman's sufferings, of persecutions suffered in Jerusalem and then in Rome, faithful souls of the OT and NT are bound together. These holy chains, encrusted in jewels, becoming joined were venerated as never before. Such should be our love for faithful souls we encounter in the OT, who precede us to Heaven, who intercede for us now. They love us. We should love them.[289]

This ardour inflames our prayers, including on Good Friday, that the light of Christ rescue the Jews from their darkness. If they have their hearts opened to see Christ is the truth throughout the OT, then it behooves us to see that too. The Fathers and Scholastics knew it well. It is a truth which modernity — globalism — seeks to eradicate.

---

[288] St Peter in Chains (1st Aug), Matins, *Lectiones* IV-VI.

[289] Day VII in the Octave of All Saints, Matins, *Lectio* V; St John Chrysostom, *De Martyribus, quod aut imitandi sunt, aut non laudandi* (*Operum, Tomus* III), "It ought not to be hard for us to copy others, when we see what they of old time did without any examples before them, so that in them who copied not others, but set example for others to copy, and in us who copy them, and in them which take example by us, Christ may be glorified in His holy Church. Thus from the very beginning of the world there have been the harmless Abel who was slain, Enoch who walked with God, and was seen no more, for God took him, Noah who was found righteous, Abraham who was tried and found faithful, Moses who was the meekest of men, Joshua who was chaste, David who was gentle, Elijah who was accepted, Daniel who was holy, and the three Children who were victorious."

Moses permitted divorce, because of the hardness of men's hearts. But God, Who is utterly monogamous, detests divorce (Mal 2:16). He does not cast off His betrothed in order to marry another. Rather He casts out in order to recall, to allure back into His embrace.

Christ's Bride is one. The saints before Abraham are one with those through to St John the Baptist, and with the Blessed Virgin Mary, these are one with the saints from the Apostles until our own day, and these are one with all the saints yet to come, including all the Jews who will convert at the close of history. This chain of faith, this unity of charity, is an eternal reality. We are called to live it now.

THE END

Abraham, your father, rejoiced that he might see My day: he saw it, and was glad.

John 8:56

To summarise this book: Part I calls Catholics to have faith in the Messiah, Jesus, the Son of God, and thereby to *"overcome the world"* (1 Jn 5:4). Part II requires us to have hope in heavenly help and reward, for if we are focussed on this fallen world alone we will go under. Part III is simplest and more excellent: have charity.

Unfazed by complexity, faith, hope and charity provide the spiritual perspective to avoid falling for two exaggerations about Jewish conspiracies — either over-estimating their extent or dismissing them as non-existent.

Anyone cognisant of the difficulties humans face when attempting to execute any plans will have a properly guarded view about the efficacy of conspiracies. If the organisation is secret, it is all the more difficult, indeed impossible, to avoid confusion, rivalries, leaks and betrayals. The more long-term the goal, the more vulnerable a conspiracy is to exposure or being disrupted by unforeseen events. A detailed strategy toward world domination, mapped out over centuries, seems a total absurdity. Humans are not intelligent enough to plot this, nor stable enough to carry it through. But satan is.

Assuredly, the devil cannot communicate a long-term plan to his devotees, for like humans, he does not know the future. He can only guess what will happen tomorrow. But as the Church grows, his target gets bigger. Unable to destroy her, he seeks to infiltrate her, to turn her to him so as to reach all men. His tool is temptation, advancing his agenda each time anyone sins without repenting. Spiritual corruption is an effective strategy. Parasitising the good, he is able to spread his darkness worldwide.

The Prophet Isaiah gives an intriguing warning to both Jews and Gentiles: *"Say ye not: A conspiracy: for all that this people speaketh is a conspiracy"* (Is 8:12). The conspiracy is so pervasive, so normalised, that it no longer appears to be a classic conspiracy. Much of it is out in the open. Given that the Prophet says the antidote to it is fear of the Lord (Is 8:13), it follows that its motor is disregard for God. Jeremiah adds:

A conspiracy is found among the men of Juda, and among the inhabitants of Jerusalem. They are returned to the former iniquities of their fathers, who refused to hear my words: so these likewise have gone after strange gods, to serve them: the house of Israel, and the house of Juda have made void my covenant, which I made with their fathers. (Jer 11:9-10; cf. Ezek 22:25)

The New Testament, too, is crystal clear about baneful *"conspiracies of the Jews"* (Acts 20:19; cf. 23:13). But in what do they consist? How are they held together?

Is there anything that all Jews share, given the virulent disagreements between atheist, Reformed and Orthodox Jews? Between Sephardic and Ashkenazi Jews? Between Zionists and non-Zionists? Who is supposed to coordinate these opposing parties?

The ultimate conspiracy is real but far more diffused than any number of secret societies or public associations could contain. It is more opportunistic than strategic. *"The Jews"* (those unconverted) have one thing in common: denial of Jesus as the Son of God. It is that which affords leverage for the devil (1 Jn 2:22). To be sure, he involves men of all nations. But the spiritual basis of the movement — active opposition to the true Messiah, the only One Who can bring order and peace to this world — gives the Jews a leading role.

Three elements of the satanic conspiracy stand out, each sustained by rejection of Jesus: its localised aspiration (land; a Temple); its fuel (Mammon); and its global goal (*tikkun olam*, 'repairing the world', or more darkly, 'returning the divine sparks'). These constitute something much more enduring than a collusion of personal interests.

The concrete aspiration which has burned in the hearts of countless Jews for two thousand years is to regain the land of Israel, or more specifically, to rebuild the Temple in Jerusalem. Not every Jew has cared about this, but it has never been forgotten. The community has carried it forward. It cannot be by accident that the Temple rebuilding stage is so closely approached. It has required incredible determination.

Will power is not enough. Advancing Jewish interests has required incalculable amounts of money. It has taken millennia of moneylending to gain dominance in global finance. Such a long-standing development can hardly be held together by human coordination. Rather, it is love of money that has achieved it, devotion to mammon. Gentiles can be avaricious, too. But Talmudic contempt of Gentiles has given a competitive edge to Jews accumulating and deploying wealth unjustly. Not all Jews have this contempt, but there can be few Jews who have not encountered the reality of it.

The third element holding the conspiracy together is its mystical aspiration: *tikkun olam* (תִּיקוּן עוֹלָם), 'repairing the world'. Variants on this are alive across the Jewish spectrum of beliefs. Humanist Jews may seek to serve it through social justice, including climate alarmism and wokism. Mainstream Judaism holds it to be foremost a matter of prayer and redemptive suffering. Maniacs yearn to achieve it by imposing Noahide Laws on all Gentiles. Kabbalists think it can be achieved through esoteric rituals. The worst turn the Torah on its head, insanely imagining that the very violation of the Torah is its ultimate fulfilment. This antinomian madness despises order, claiming the emancipated man is the one who can break every law, especially the laws of God.

The various strains of *tikkun olam* all share a rejection of Jesus, thereby reinforcing each other despite their differences. The tip of the spear is hardened by the most dedicated kabbalists, for whom power is in teaching that truth is a lie and lies are truth, that good is evil and evil good. They seduce Gentile elites so the nations will follow. The case of William Blake (d.1827) and European nobility is illustrative.

Blake went on to proclaim the necessity of overturning the Ten Commandments, of achieving divine vision through 'an improvement of sensual enjoyment,' and of believing that 'the road of excess leads to the palace of wisdom.' ...Advocating the breaking of Jewish law and using sexuality as a vehicle for spiritual vision, find their closest parallels in... Frankist- and Sabbatian-influenced contemporaries of Blake... Recent archival discoveries [uncover] the long-suppressed esoteric underground in London, which received Jewish and Masonic emissaries from Poland and other Eastern European nations, who infused their antinomian and esoteric beliefs into the spiritual questings of various heterodox Christians, including two who were especially relevant to Blake — Count Nicolaus Ludwig von Zinzendorf and Baron Emanuel Swedenborg.[290]

Zinzendorf was a 'bishop' of the heretical Moravian Brethren. Swedenborg was a demon-inspired pluralist theologian. Blake's most famous lines are about building Jerusalem in England (his "dark satanic mills" might refer to churches). The three men were social justice warriors, seeking heaven on earth while at enmity with Holy Mass. When Catholics adapt themselves to Protestantism, most obviously since Vatican II, they are imbibing Kabbalah, spiritual poison.

An objective scholar of Kabbalah, Gershom Scholem, identifies revolution as the way to redemption, catastrophe as the necessary path to messianic utopia.

---

[290] Marsha Schuchard, *From Poland to London: Sabatian Influences on the Mystical Underworld of Zinzendorf, Swedenborg and Blake* (2008), I. Swedenborg was the son of a Lutheran 'bishop', ennobled in 1719 by the Queen of Sweden.

[T]he two aspects which the Messianic idea henceforth takes on and keeps in Jewish consciousness… concern the catastrophic and destructive nature of the redemption on the one hand and the utopianism of the content of realized Messianism on the other. Jewish Messianism is in its origins and by its nature — this cannot be sufficiently emphasized — a theory of catastrophe. This theory stresses the revolutionary, cataclysmic element in the transition from every historical present to the Messianic future…

This catastrophic character of the redemption, which is essential to the apocalyptic conception… finds manifold expression: in world wars and revolutions, in epidemics, famine, and economic catastrophe; but to an equal degree in apostasy and the desecration of God's name, in forgetting of the Torah and the upsetting of all moral order to the point of dissolving the laws of nature. Such apocalyptic paradoxes regarding the final catastrophe were accepted even into as sober a text as the Mishnah [the 'oral Torah'].[291]

The most corrupt of kabbalists make the connection backwards, believing that by causing disorder they can advance the redemption and that by violating nature on earth they can bring about order in heaven. This inversion of spiritual truth includes a misconception of redemption through suffering, as if *inflicting* suffering, even on innocent victims, can repair anything. It is a religious delusion born of

---

[291] Gershom Scholem, *Toward an Understanding of the Messianic Idea in Judaism* (1971), II & III.

centuries of resentment.[292] The truth told by the Crucifixion is that it is willingly *enduring* suffering, and offering this up for God's sake, that builds the Kingdom of God.

A conspiracy of *"the Jews"* is real in the sense of a con-spiration (shared-spirit) toward a joint goal: messianic utopia, directly contradicting God's Plan for redemption of the world through the Blood of His Son.

Gentile conspiracies do not endure. The natural diversity of sovereign nations means we can collaborate in nothing eschatological but Christ; the takings of our greed dissipate over time, not so assiduously kept in the family; dreams of world domination by Gentile megalomaniacs die out with failed empires. Gentile satanists tear each other to pieces.

In contrast, the aspiration of *tikkun olam* perdures in a people who desire a worldly messiah. It keeps the conspiracy alive: not human organisation, but spiritual alignment. Yet much stronger is the truth, the Christian nation, the Church. We do not need Solomon's Temple, for Jesus is the true Temple. We do not live for earthly riches, not moth-eaten or rusting trinkets, for Jesus tells us to store spiritual treasure in Heaven. We do not follow pseudo-messiahs, especially not the final charming, thieving deceiver, perfectly possessed by the devil, for we are disciples of Jesus the Christ, the Chosen One, Anointed by God with the Holy Ghost.

---

[292] Ariel Toaff, *Blood Passover* (2008), p.12 [translation] cites Israel Jacob Yuval on "mass suicides and child murders among the German Jewish communities during the First Crusade. The picture which emerges is one of Ashkenazi Jewry's hostile and virulent reaction against surrounding Christian society, a reaction finding expression, not only in liturgical invective, but above all, in the conviction that the Jews themselves were capable of compelling God to wreak bloody revenge against their Christian persecutors, thus bringing redemption closer."

Will men trade blessed eternity for hubristic modernity? It is unthinkable that the Covid regime could have been imposed worldwide if it did not suit the programme of Jewish elites. And it is unthinkable that it could have been sustained if the princes of the Church had stood with Christ. But Judas went to Caiaphas. So Bergoglio, Rome's bishop in white, serving the globalist elites, led the worldwide restrictions on churchgoing, to keep the faithful away from celebration of the Easter mysteries. And the hierarchy largely consented.

In conclusion, man cannot plumb the abyss, cannot understand evil. We can scarcely identify who conceived the Covid lockdowns or the *novus ordo* or other disasters which conspiracies might explain. But if we note what they target we can know thereby where the greatest good is: the Sacred Mysteries. The enemy attacks what is holy — the traditional Mass, the Sacred Triduum, the Good Friday Prayers. That these are so maligned by souls who love not Christ, reveals that they are among the greatest goods in the world.

Pray the old prayers on Good Friday; no one can stop you. Move heaven and earth to attend the pre-1955 Triduum. Whole-heartedly seek to assist at the traditional Mass each Sunday. And you do not need to worry who is concealed in the dark, hidden forces whose web of deceit we are not made to penetrate. But get to Mass and we can deal with the rest.

Why was Tradition ever abandoned? Because Catholics are being seduced away from Calvary by the enemies of the Cross, by globalists and satanists who dominate the world. The sign of their temporal success is Zionism. This is preparing the seat for the Antichrist by aspiring to rebuild Jerusalem's Temple.

The tremendous alternative to fill our horizon, as we hold hope in the return of Christ, is for Jews to inherit a far better land than Israel, and to join us in building a Temple made of living stones, souls sanctified in Christ. This is the glorious call of the Prophets, laid out by the Fathers and preserved in the traditional Office:

> What was foretold by Haggai the prophet, saying, *The glory of this latter house shall be greater than that of the former* (Hag 2:10). Now, that this is said of the New Testament, he showed a little above, where he says, evidently promising Christ, *And I will move all nations, and the desired One shall come to all nations* (Hag 2:8). For by such chosen ones of the nations there is built, through the New Testament, with living stones, a house of God far more glorious than that temple was which was constructed by King Solomon, and rebuilt after the [Babylonian] captivity.[293]

Jews are called to enter the land that they were promised: the One, Holy, Catholic and Apostolic Church — ultimately, Heaven. This will be the perfection of history. Hence the Jews are hated by satan almost as much as he hates Catholics. He knows what eternal shame they will bring on him, when, please God, they convert at the close of history.

---

[293] *Dominica XIX Post Pentecosten*, Matins, *Lectiones* IV-V. St Augustine, *City of God*, XVIII, 45.

ABOUT THE AUTHOR

Born in 1973, Fr James Mawdsley holds dual English-Australian citizenship. He was ordained a Catholic priest in July 2016, after seminary formation in Bavaria.

Fr Mawdsley was removed from ministry in 2020, and again in 2021, for refusing to comply with Covid restrictions and refusing to impose them on the faithful. After months without public ministry, he learned that his expected reassignment would not happen due to the local bishop's eagerness to implement *Traditionis custodes*.

Trying to understand who desired worldwide lockdowns, why the Church would succumb to them, and who sought to eradicate the traditional Mass, Fr Mawdsley concluded that it all comes down to a rejection of Jesus Christ Crucified. The global architecture required for subjecting the world has been built by centuries of false messianism; the Church hierarchy's self-subjection to this vision follows from decades of unfaithful infatuation with the spirit of this world; and the war against the Mass is a satanic agenda advanced by Kabbalah. All these currents are bound up with Judaism.

With Vatican policy blocking his ministry, Fr Mawdsley saw no option other than to raise publicly the issues covered in this book. In order to protect others from the potential fallout, Fr Mawdsley left his assignment without permission, thereby incurring a canonical suspension in 2022. He now lives where he grew up, in Lancashire, England, offering the pre-1955 Mass privately, praying for the day when the Church hierarchy will not obstruct priests from publicly offering the ancient and Sacred Triduum in all its integrity.